Directors'
Dilemmas

Also by Patrick Dunne, published by Kogan Page

Running Board Meetings

'An entertaining introduction to the game for the neophyte board director.'
Katherine Campbell, *Financial Times*

'Anecdotes, tips and observations for current and aspiring board members.'
The Sunday Times

'Not only on target, it's also amusing. A rare combination.'
Professor Jay Lorsh, Harvard Business School

'Lively, thought-provoking and relevant to directors of enterprises large and small.'
Tim Melville-Ross, director-general, Institute of Directors

When first published in 1997, the enthusiastic response to *Running Board Meetings* highlighted a glaring need for guidance on the subject.

Now revised and updated, Patrick Dunne's practical guide continues to provide step-by-step advice on every aspect of running board meetings. Packed with useful tips and techniques, he shows how to ensure that:

- you're always well prepared;
- every board meeting runs smoothly;
- necessary procedures are followed;
- the board's decisions are always acted on.

You'll also find out how to deal with those troublesome types such as the 'silent seether', the 'young pretender' and the 'really useless dead hand'.

Written in a lively and easy-to-read style, *Running Board Meetings* is essential reading for anyone who has to run or attend a board meeting.

£12.99   ISBN 0 7494 3014 1

Directors'
Dilemmas

Tales from the frontline

Patrick Dunne

KOGAN
PAGE

First published 2000

Apart from any fair dealing for the purposes of research or private study, or criticism or review, as permitted under the Copyright, Designs and Patents Act 1988, this publication may only be reproduced, stored or transmitted, in any form or by any means, with the prior permission in writing of the publishers, or in the case of reprographic reproduction in accordance with the terms and licences issued by the CLA. Enquiries concerning reproduction outside these terms should be sent to the publishers at the undermentioned addresses:

Kogan Page Limited
120 Pentonville Road
London
N1 9JN
UK

Kogan Page Limited
163 Central Avenue, Suite 4
Dover
NH 03820
USA

British Library Cataloguing in Publication Data

A CIP record for this book is available from the British Library.

ISBN 0 7494 3043 5

Typeset by Jean Cussons Typesetting, Diss, Norfolk
Printed and bound by Creative Print and Design, Wales

DEDICATION

To my Mother

Whose passionate belief in education made it possible and whose strong conviction that you should help anybody with a problem has always made me interested in adversity.

Thanks Mum

Contents

Foreword

Experienced directors are bound to recognize many of the situations described in this book. Those setting out to be directors will encounter more than just a few of them if they are successful in their ambition. I am particularly delighted to see much of use to another and frequently forgotten group of people who share the angst, the frustration, and the whole range of other emotions these situations cause. These, of course, are the friends or partners of directors.

The idea of *'a go in the boardroom simulator'* has considerable appeal. It is always easier to experiment when the consequences of getting it wrong won't threaten your livelihood or reputation. Hopefully you won't get airsick as you fly through the boardroom snowstorms with your engines on fire or try to make that perfect landing without the aid of an undercarriage. I agree with Patrick's view that when we face a dilemma ourselves it will usually feel different from the ones we have experienced or observed before. Yet he is also right that there are patterns and approaches that can be applied to take the stress out of situations and create the space for a better solution. As an ardent football fan the idea that creating space will generally lead to a smoother route to the goal has a familiar ring.

At 3i we are privileged to see so many of these dilemmas as part of helping entrepreneurs succeed in the extraordinary range of things they try to do. Watching them grow as individuals as well as businessmen and women as they chart their way through the many triumphs and disasters involved in building successful enterprises is deeply instructive.

What I like about this work is not just that it was written by someone from 3i, although it is nice for any chairman to see extracurricular creativity flourish in today's 'full steam ahead' corporate world. It is that I think it really does seem to relate to reality and it deals with those all-important human aspects in a no-nonsense and lively fashion. Humility and wit are vital attributes to have when trying to solve dilemmas. They are very much in evidence throughout the book. The cases are well chosen and thought-provoking. Thankfully I haven't observed or experienced them all. I hope you don't have to either.

I was delighted when Patrick popped in a couple of months ago to tell me that he'd written another book on boards. His first on board meetings hit the mark and I'm sure this will do likewise.

Sir George Russell CBE
Chairman 3i Group plc
Europe's leading venture capital company

Acknowledgements

The first person I must thank is my wife Rebecca. This book was started just after our tenth wedding anniversary. Such an occasion is of course a real dilemma for those who possess no judgement at all in buying anniversary presents. I shall always be grateful for her patience and tolerance. A present for life.

Our three boys, Patrick, Nicholas and Rory have all played a little part. Patrick, our 9-year-old, asks superb questions which go right to the heart of an issue. Nicholas's great sense of fun and energy are a constant message that life should be enjoyed and that difficulties are only temporary. Rory, our 3-year-old 'terminator', has the ability to destroy any item carelessly left in his path. A permanent reminder of the need to keep things out of harm's way and that you can still love people who break your favourite toys!

At 3i I have had much support from our chief executive Brian Larcombe, from my boss Rod Perry and the whole of the Marketing and Management Buy In and Independent Director teams. Tony Brierley our company secretary and his assistant Sabina Dawson have also been very helpful.

Sir George Russell, 3i's chairman, needs a particularly big acknowledgement not just for being prepared to write the Foreword but for his unstinting moral support for the project and his canny tips. As a former chairman of the Independent Television Corporation and current chairman of Camelot, he has seen his fair share of dilemmas.

My mentor, first boss at 3i and good friend David Wilkinson also deserves a special mention. David has always been an extremely good teacher of how to get yourself out of bother in business. His fine sense of humour and judgement make him one of the first people to turn to in a tricky moment. David has also kindly provided a couple of the dilemmas contained in this book and some wise words on the thorny matter of removing directors.

Karen Wolstenholme, my secretary, also deserves an acknowledgement. Her tremendous work rate and organization have kept me in the right place at the right time and made the day job so smooth.

At INSEAD I would like to thank Professor Manfred Kets De Vries for the trailblazing work he has done in researching successful people who go off the rails. He has also written a book about dilemmas in family concerns, which is well worth a read. My friend Professor Dan Muzyka also provided considerable encouragement.

From Cranfield, Leo Murray, Ruth Bender and Andrew Kakabadse and particularly Murray Steele who runs an excellent course for non-executive directors; thank you.

One group who have chosen to remain anonymous are the FTSE100 company secretaries who gave me some interesting tales from their AGMs. Thank you.

Finally I would like to thank all of those members of 3i's Independent Directors Programme who attended the 'Dilemma' events, for their wisdom, for their experience and for giving me the encouragement to write this book.

Introduction

What prompted the idea to write a book on dilemmas? Rather bizarrely it is probably the fact that as a boy I was fascinated by aeroplanes. How did they get up in the air? How did they navigate? How did they land so precisely? Who was on board? An endless source of amazement.

Then one morning at school the teacher told us about a terrible crash the night before:

‹The pilot had made his approach a little on the low side and as a result crashed on a factory close by. A lot of people were killed on the plane and in the factory. We should pray for the dead, for the relatives and especially the pilot.›

This accident left a deep impression on me. The overwhelming thought that occurred to me then and reoccurs to me now every time I hear of a crash was how horrendous it must have been for the pilot. What must have been going through his mind just before impact? One little mistake and suddenly he was facing not just his own imminent death but the horrible responsibility for the deaths of so many others. Imagine the awful horror of those last few moments when he knew what was going to happen but was powerless to do anything about it.

Clearly pilots have to possess skills, nerves and judgement to match their responsibility. They are also critically dependent upon the skills of many other professionals. Who knows where it really came from, but one day I started to think about the comparison between pilots and directors.

The analogy has only partial relevance. The nature of the passengers and the equipment is different. It is livelihoods rather than lives that are at stake for the director. Temporary loss of control or poor navigation is rarely as catastrophic. The comparison was simply intriguing.

This musing then stimulated the thought that it might be worthwhile to go and revisit some of the dilemmas I'd seen or been involved in. Perhaps looking at them in more detail and maybe finding some new ones to explore might come in handy one day. After all, who knows what new dilemma might be just around the corner? A little go in the boardroom simulator beforehand might be helpful.

Directors, and particularly independent directors or chairmen, often make their most significant contribution when the board or individual directors face a dilemma. Maybe venture capital is a particularly dilemma-prone occupation. Perhaps I'm getting more aware. Whatever the reason, those what might be referred to as 'defining moments', seem to come along more regularly these days. Yet it always seems difficult to find much written to relate to these situations. This is despite the list of over a thousand book titles containing the word 'dilemma' that can be found on the Internet.

Helping people through those magical moments of ownership, strategic, human or moral dilemma can be very rewarding. On the other hand watching a minor dilemma lead to a series of more damaging ones or seeing a successful enterprise destroyed by the wrong judgement at a pivotal moment can be a painful experience. Especially so if it means that the reputations and wealth of people you rate or hold dear are destroyed as a consequence.

Another facet of dilemmas that is intriguing is the role of friends and colleagues. What is it that stops many of us from providing that vital nudge or that timely little warning signal to a friend? Why is it that we prefer to watch them crash? Most likely it's the fear of 'getting it wrong'. It may not be that clear what the right thing to do is. Rarely are we in possession of all the facts. Moreover, we may not be that knowledgeable in the specific area concerned. It can sometimes look a hell of a lot easier to get it wrong than to get it right. Anyone with any common sense is instinctively wary of interfering where one doesn't have the expertise or knowledge.

Watching more seasoned campaigners tackle some of these seemingly intractable circumstances with calm, confident ease has been a tremendous learning experience for me. That basic question, that experienced probing of the facts, or that ability to help someone under pressure assess the issues, is far more valuable than any forensic accounting or legal skill in spotting mistakes in the board papers. The ability to help people to follow their convictions despite considerable discomfort is an invaluable mentoring skill. A fine sense of judgement is at the core of success in helping resolve dilemmas. Bringing that judgement to bear, though, will depend much upon the empathy and the relationship they have with those they are trying to help. The 'irritatingly right' are still irritating and while they may be accurate, if they can't get heard they end up being only as much use as the sycophantically wrong.

The idea of turning the 'dilemmas theme' into a book was really born out of a series of events we ran with members of the 3i Independent Directors programme. About 250 came to our six 'Directors Dilemma' events around the UK. These people are all experienced directors who chair or sit on the boards of companies 3i has backed, or other companies. They cover a wide range of sectors and size of business. They also cover the span of ownership situation – everything from the fledgling start-up team to the mature multinational public corporation. Having run a successful business, often as an independent start-up, buy-out or buy-in, they have that ultimate influencing advantage: they've been there.

At each of these 'Dilemma' events we chose three or four of the situations described later in the book. Before starting any discussion on the particular case we all wrote down immediately what our initial gut reactions were. We were keen to see if considered discussions led to different views. Then through a mix of role-playing and discussion we searched for some principles and approaches to apply to dilemmas in general as well as to the specific dilemma under consideration.

It turned out that the most important aspect of dealing with these dilemmas was how to communicate our judgement to achieve the desired result. All too often an inspired decision or course of action is undermined by poor, or ill-judged, communication.

The book is split into three sections. First there is a tour through dilemmas in general, then a look at basic principles for resolving them. This is followed by a series of over 20 dilemmas, each of which is described and discussed.

The dilemmas are based on real situations but I have taken the usual poetic licence in disguising the names and rolling some of them together. Some are brief, others much longer. Some have a full solution, others don't. Please remember that the descriptions of what actually happened in each case are simply that. You may well come up with a better solution. If you do, please drop me a note at 3i.

My intention in writing this book is to provide something that is thought-provoking, fun and helpful. I make no pretence that it covers all of the dilemmas a director may face, but I do hope you enjoy it.

Part 1

THE NATURE OF DILEMMAS

What's a dilemma?

'OK honesty is the best policy. Let's call that option A.'

'What's a dilemma, Daddy?' This was my son Patrick's timely interruption to the conversation Rebecca, my wife, and I were having about the wisdom of attempting to write a book about directors' dilemmas. Answering his question seemed like an excellent place to start.

Asking friends and colleagues for the meaning of the word revealed a wide variety of definitions. Like so many other things, how people were doing influenced their perspective. So there was the positive: *'It's about which opportunity to take to maximize the return for your effort'* roughly translated as, *'What to do with all the money?'* Then the slightly less rosy: *'It's about taking the least damaging alternative'* or: *'How do I get out of this mess?'*

'Dilemma' appears to be frequently confused with 'disaster'. There are lots of business books written about disasters. After all, a full-blown bloody mess usually makes for a rattling good read. Business disasters also have that additional feature in common with car crashes and other human disasters, namely that we are all compelled to become ghouls. We stare deeply at the tangled wreckage. Why? Is it to see what we can learn so as to avoid the same fate? Doubtful. The way we accelerate off afterwards suggests it has more to do with instinct. Observing someone else's misfortune is fascinating. Sadly, we seldom learn anything from it.

It is hard now to try and remember what I thought a dilemma was before starting this project. It was probably that a dilemma wasn't a disaster, merely a situation that might lead to or follow one. I'm sure that, as now, I would have thought that dilemmas were not necessarily bad things despite the considerable discomfort and pain that may surround them. Dilemmas can be tremendously catalytic. They frequently have the power to re-energize a situation or a group of people. Getting commitment on what to do and finding a new purpose in the process can be galvanizing even if not everyone emerges a winner. In fact it is usually likely that not everyone will emerge a winner.

'Shall we look in the dictionary, Daddy?'

This, or *'Shall we look on the Internet?'* is the normal response of a 9-year-old to a waffling father. A search on the Internet reveals a wonderful array of life's dilemmas, from what to serve for tea to what to serve in bed. But sadly nothing terribly helpful in defining dilemmas in a business context. So what does it say in the dictionary? Well, my trusty but rather old *Concise Oxford Dictionary* defines a dilemma as follows:

> *Argument forcing opponent to choose one of two alternatives both unfavourable to him; position that leaves only a choice between unwelcome possibilities.*

Not exactly what I think most directors mean by a dilemma. We seldom confine ourselves to just two options. What most of us really mean when we use the word dilemma is:

> *A tricky spot with no immediately obvious conclusion and where the alternative solutions all involve some degree of pain.*

WHY DO DILEMMAS OCCUR?

For me there are four fundamental drivers which cause dilemmas for directors and these are:

■ confusion over the role of the board;
■ the fact that there are humans involved;
■ situations change; and
■ money.

Before we get into the dilemmas themselves let's take a look at each of these drivers in turn. Real entrepreneurs of course will want to do this the other way around.

The role of the board

Lack of clarity over the purpose of the board will produce a regular flow of dilemmas for its members. Lack of unity over what the board is for will produce even more. If there isn't a lot of overlap between the views of your colleagues, the board will inevitably find it hard to deal with the most important issues. Moreover, it may not have even spotted what they are.

The role of the board will also evolve. Consequently, composing a board to fit the strategy for the business and for the ownership is a challenge.

So what is the role of the board? For me, there are three generic things that a board needs to do. These are to:

■ Ensure the right strategy is in place and that it is being followed.
■ Ensure there are the right resources in place to fit with the agreed strategy. The most important of these are human and financial resources.
■ Keep out of jail. By this I mean that the board needs to ensure that the company complies with all the appropriate regulations relating to its industry and the countries within which it operates.

These are fundamental and won't change. What changes is their nature. As the company enters new phases of development in scale, breadth and ownership the nature of the role of the board will need to change. The obvious examples are going public or entering new countries, but there are many more. More often than not it is when to change rather than what to change that presents the dilemma.

There are humans involved

'My wife told me countercyclical diversification wouldn't work, but I didn't listen to her.'

Get some therapy

The dangers of amateur psychology are obvious. Like most people who've been in large organizations, the sometimes even greater dangers of professional psychology are even more apparent. So what follows are merely personal observations from a voyeur, victim and occasional victor of dilemmas. If you want to read some good professional work on business psychology, Professor Manfred Kets De Vries at INSEAD has written several excellent books.

Whenever you feel the need to call in a professional to help, whethe in the form of a trained psychologist or highly regarded organizational consultant, remember Sam Goldwyn's cruel quip. When asked about the wisdom of visiting psychiatrists he responded:

‹ You'd have to be mad to go to one.›

This is worth remembering. Not so that we fail to seek good professional advice when needed but that so we know why we are seeking it and what we want the professional to do for us.

Of course it's bloody personal

'Didn't you explain to these outside consultants handling the restructure who I was?'

Naturally directors will think and act both as individuals and as a group. If they are a functional or business unit head they also have to remember to act as a board member. When the board's interests and those of the individuals on the board are perfectly aligned, and more importantly when they believe this to be the case, then there is seldom a problem. Yet frequently they are not. So when and why do we think and act as a group? In what circumstances are our thoughts and actions overwhelmingly personally motivated?

There probably aren't any easy answers to this question. One of the first rules of solving dilemmas is to try and figure out which of the participants is likely to do this. It's also true that once threatened, the most committed team player thinks personally. The threats that matter most to directors are likely to be those to their position, pride or purse.

When everyone else is acting for the team it's harder to put a selfish interest over that of the group. This applies as much to teams in the boardroom as to anywhere else. We've all seen what can be achieved by the high performing board supporting each other's performance and making considerable personal sacrifice for the good of the business. However, occasionally these personal sacrifices are made in the name of the good of the company when the real reason we make them is because we enjoy the challenge and can't stop ourselves. Similar, I suppose, to workaholics telling their partner, *'I'm only doing this for you.'* We may also have seen teams of stars unable to work together and sadly disintegrate into chaos.

Anyone who has been involved in family companies will also realize that most family company chairmen are parents first and chairmen second. It is extremely difficult to be objective about the true capabilities and potential of your offspring. You may also feel, if your child isn't up to the challenge of taking over from you, like the great coaches who have failed with their most important player. The feeling of failure as a parent, whether justified or not, causes considerable stress and pain.

Thinking about our own personal priorities can be quite revealing. If we really are under pressure, where will our first loyalty lie? Sometimes this is harder to answer for ourselves than for others. Uncomfortable though it might be it is nevertheless a very worthwhile exercise.

Are you the cause?

'Dear God, give Mr Perfect a tiny flaw.'

Ironically it was Richard Nixon who was quoted as saying:

❮ Don't let yourself become the issue. ❯

It is easy to be critical about someone else, much harder to recognize or do something about our own limitations. So how might we determine whether we ourselves are the cause of the dilemma?

The most obvious situation is where we have made a judgement in the past that has led to today's dilemma. It may or may not have been perfectly correct at the time but the consequences of our decision have led to today's issue. But what if it isn't a past judgement but current behaviour that's the problem. How do we know?

One phenomenon that I have frequently observed is the *'Entrepreneur's ear'*. This amazingly effective selective hearing device, implanted at birth, gives entrepreneurs the ability to ignore the advice that would stop them doing the tremendously successful things they do. As Ross Perot put it:

❮ The things I've done best are the things people told me couldn't be done. ❯

To realize how truly wonderful this piece of equipment is one only has to think of some of the most successful technological breakthroughs.

However, the *'Entrepreneur's ear'* is only useful if combined with consistently good judgement and a number of other characteristics. Even for the successful entrepreneur the feelings of invincibility that emerge during or after periods of great success tend to be the wax that clogs up the finer qualities of the *'Entrepreneur's ear'*. This loss of hearing can lead to a loss of contact with reality.

How do we spot whether a finely tuned *'Entrepreneur's ear'* is waxing up? There are usually a few clues and an increasing number of contradictions. Namely:

- You love people trying to pick your ideas to bits and proving that you are right. However, you find fewer and fewer people willing to challenge your views.
- While enjoying the increased speed of reaching agreement for your ideas, you worry about the whispering behind your back.
- You really do want some help and advice. The fact that no one seems prepared to come off the fence and give it to you is a source of considerable irritation.
- Some of the advice you have been getting has been poor, with the result that recent judgements have been questioned.
- Your top colleagues seem to keep disappointing you.
- When you play back the imaginary video of that last meeting you find a lot of silent seethers. (For more on the silent seether see page 30.)
- You wonder whether you are taking on too much. Are you out of your depth?
- You talk to yourself more than you used to.
- You have a partner who is a great leveller. He or she seems to be giving you that *'My, aren't you clever'* look more than usual.
- You find yourself less tolerant of criticism.

It is hard to keep a grip on reality if you don't have what I call a *'calibrator'* around. A *'calibrator'* is that person who is able to tell you what you don't want to hear in a way that makes you take the cloudy or rose-tinted specs off, or gain the conviction to sort the problem out. You seldom feel threatened or insulted or hurt by what they say.

Another device that comes in handy if you are trying to figure out whether you are the cause of the dilemma or whether you can help, is the *'respectometer'*. I've always felt that it must be a hell of a lot easier to influence someone who respects you. Pretty tricky to get anywhere if they don't. We are also much more likely to want to help someone if we respect them than if we don't. If you have no respect for any of your colleagues then it is fairly likely that you're the problem. Arrogance will always undermine respect and good judgement. So working out how influential you are may be a way of figuring out whether it's something that you are doing that is the cause of the dilemma.

You may be the root cause of a dilemma if you suffer from *'ideaitis'*. Some people have a natural talent for coming up with hundreds of great ideas. However, if we want to capitalize on this talent then our previous ideas will need to fund an increase in resources to implement the new ones. If they don't, they inevitably end up over-stressing the business. To be more precise, over-stressing those who are trying to implement the ideas and your boardroom colleagues who may be fighting for limited resources and talent. The only way of avoiding this position, apart from securing a limitless supply of cash and talent, is to stop doing things at the same rate you are starting others. This is fiendishly hard to achieve in practice but well worth the effort.

A related dilemma for a director is information overload. The fear of missing a key detail amongst the boring stuff motivates us to continue the ritual of reading as much as we can. Yet antennae can easily be damaged by the numbing of the senses that goes with too much reading and not enough listening. Getting the balance is as important as it is difficult. The discipline imposed by someone else believing you will read every word is something we do not discard lightly.

Do you want to be the solution?

Whenever you do want to be the principal resolver of a dilemma it is well worth asking yourself why before you get resolving. For some it may be the basic survival instinct kicking in. For others it may be just another conquest, a lucky break in which you feel very confident you can improve a situation and your own position in the process. What you are currently doing may be boring as hell and sorting something out may be a pleasant interlude in a career cul de sac. On the other hand you may feel a duty. Perhaps people always look to you to sort things out. *'Big brother or sister syndrome'* is perfectly natural. Guilt may be another reason, even if it is guilt about something else. Perhaps it is your chance to restore the balance. Whatever the reason it is worth knowing in case you're trying to solve the wrong problem or your motives are questioned later.

If you do decide you want to be the one to resolve a dilemma there are a number of things to think about before committing yourself:

- Your judgement. How good is it in situations like the one being faced?
- How strong are your influencing skills?
- What levers do you have to help?
- Watch out for *'saviour syndrome'*. Compulsive volunteers, however well intentioned, are not always helpful.
- How are you going to get a mandate to be the resolver?
- You may get hurt in the process. People may misunderstand your motives, especially if they are embarrassed by the situation or you stand to benefit personally.
- Sometimes people want to solve their own problems.
- Those most likely to get damaged may be natural and willing victims.
- Will you need to be recognized as the one who resolved it or are you quite happy to be a silent sorter?
- Will you be quite happy to resolve a situation even if there is no gain or perhaps even some pain for yourself?

Deciding that you want to be the one to resolve a dilemma doesn't mean you have to do it all on your own. The extra resilience and independence that many high performers have gained through difficult early years is a great strength in times of trouble. However, it can make them reluctant to ask for help.

The real dilemma stars for me are those who help others to help themselves. They manage to be the principal resolver while expending minimum effort and making least noise. These people are often comfortable with an imperfect solution but one that is long-lasting. They are probably superb at teaching their kids to ride a bike.

Growing at different rates

How much can people grow? Why is it that some people want to while others tell you to *'Bugger off, go and empower somebody else'*. It is probably a bit tricky to get to be a board member, particularly in an entrepreneurial business, if you don't like taking charge. Some of us regard a senior director coasting towards the finish line as lacking in ability or energy, or as a living example of the well-known Peter Principle that *'everyone will rise to their level of incompetence'*. However, sometimes they are coasting because they know others will supply the energy. They may be wisely saving their energy for something else that has more value to them.

What is an individual's capacity to develop once he or she is already a director? Why do some embrace change and others suffocate it? It obviously has to do with their intellect, their personality and their abilities. Confidence also has a lot to do with it. Experiences will shape, rekindle, neuter or sometimes shatter confidence. Vision and energy may outstrip ability. You are much more likely to feel better about a

. different role when you are confident about the last step you
..warked upon. Independent directors can do so much to help not just
young entrepreneurs but those much older or settled in their roles by
giving them the confidence to go further. Despite appearances, directors will frequently suffer loss of confidence about key aspects of their
role.

Can you avoid the Peter Principle? Life's experimenters obviously
can, but I think anyone can if they have the brains, personality and
ability to adapt. However, these will not be enough. The desire and
determination to develop must be there as well.

Watching a team of three in a successful start-up five years out is
fascinating. It is rare for them all to want to grow at the same rate even
if they are all capable of it. Some may well want to cash in their chips
and quit while they are ahead. Others may feel they have only just
begun, while many have simply been exhausted by the first stage of
their entrepreneurial journey and want to rest.

A lot of these problems are to do with the different levels of ambition
in the team and tolerance to the new situation at each level of achievement. Sometimes though, it is much simpler than that. Many of us are
just driven by the opportunity and the excitement that goes with it. We
know a winning situation when we see it and go for it like crazy.

The final thing to say on this subject is that there is a natural assumption that the fact that people want to grow at different rates is a bad
thing and this will cause a team to splinter and disintegrate. It might,
but it is also a very positive team dynamic and one that often helps in
avoiding those dangerous delusions of competence or feelings of
invincibility.

Ageing and Einstein with e-mail

How does the ageing process of directors lead to dilemmas or influence
their course? There is so much silly ageism about these days it would
be easy to feel you were a business geriatric once you have reached 45.
Relax, I'm not about to add to it here. Right from school and through
the media we are conditioned to think that the age of our body and our
attitude of mind are inextricably linked. Nowhere is this more evident
than in the way the media communicates with teenagers and geriatrics.
However, having met as many 70-year-old teenagers as 30-year-old
geriatrics and witnessed as much *'young fartitis'* as *'old fartitis'*, this
seems to me to be a very silly assumption to make. So here are just a
few points, some observations and of course, a sprinkling of my own
personal prejudices.

'And when the time comes the company will put you to sleep at its own expense.'

What dilemmas emerge from the ageing process of directors? Several are obvious. Succession is the most obvious of all. Menopausal angst and frustration are two more. Dashed expectations and the questioning that goes with deciding what to do in the second half of one's life can lead to odd behaviour. Insecurity or anxiety arising from this can also make us less receptive to change in our business life. We might look for business security to compensate for personal insecurity.

A sad group are those who refuse to accept they are getting older and in order to make it appear that they are not, do very silly things to display their vigour. Most of these are tiring for them and pretty tiresome for others.

When directors are too close together in age other problems can emerge. If they are all reaching retirement the succession issue can often force a sale of the business. If they are all younger, over-competitive behaviour can arise. The 40-year-old star who is determined to be a chief executive but works for a chief executive who is only 42 presents an obvious situation for tension. This issue is heightened by the trend for chief executives to be appointed younger and for their tenure in the job to be shorter.

An unscientific poll of directors I've undertaken reveals what may be one of the most important causes of dilemmas for directors today: *'tiredness'* and the fact that there is *'now so little time to relax'*. Being almost permanently on duty is not the only factor; the degree to which directors can control their time, despite their name, seems less and less. Reasons differ from person to person but here are just a few from my friends:

‹ *It's tiring because of...* ›

■ *Increased internationalization. The travelling that goes with it, the stress of screwing up in another country, managing people at long distance and the whole mix of cross-cultural challenges.*

■ *Press attention. Your every move is analysed. You need to be immediately available. Most times it is very friendly and enjoyable but it matters hugely. One slip can destroy you.*

■ *The breadth of subjects on which you must be knowledgeable has been increasing. I can't possibly know all this stuff.*

■ *Customers, suppliers and employees. They are becoming ever more demanding.*

■ *Technology. We are now contactable everywhere, across more time zones than ever before. Sure we all need and are keen to be easily accessible, but freedom and time to think are a big price to pay.*

The older we get the more wearing these things become.

Charles Handy has become the authority on how to deal with these key changes in working life, and the 50s in particular. His excellent book, *The Empty Raincoat*, sums up well some of the major shifts that occurred in the working patterns of 50-something directors in the 1990s.

One group who turn early retirement into a huge opportunity are those who take on investing chairmanship roles, or what are known as 'business angels' in the United States. They often end up being more active than in their previous roles and occasionally make a lot more money.

As we get older we are supposed to become more cautious and conservative, but do we? Does increasing age lead to increasing financial prudence? The financial service company advertisements would lead us to think so. I'm not so sure. I think there are as many people who want to enjoy the fruits of their labours as those who want to pass everything on. Indeed they may feel their children will be far wealthier than they were, so without being reckless why not go and enjoy?

There is another phenomenon, which I call *'Final fling syndrome'*. It happens in business as much as in people's personal lives. Every now and then one of life's prudent people will do something really adventurous late on in life. They make a dramatic transition from the spectator who sits on the sidelines watching everyone else have a great time, and turn into the active participant. In the process they can surprise, embarrass or even outrage their colleagues and family.

A marvellous little book called *Tolstoy's Bicycle* is all about people who achieve great things late in life. Several of the heroes described are final-flingers, including Ray Kroc the founder of Macdonald's. The title is because Tolstoy only learnt to ride a bike in his 70s. This was due to the fact that this is when they came out, but he was so thrilled at the prospect of racing around at his age in a way that was a bit safer than his horse that he became determined to learn how to ride. Today's high take-up rates of the over-50s on the Internet would suggest Tolstoy's spirit is alive and well and that you can be a *'screenager'* at any stage in life. This led me to wonder what Einstein might have been able to achieve with e-mail and what can be achieved if we get rid of all our silly misconceptions. Would he have dramatically increased the number of brilliant thoughts he had with this amazing new tool? Or would he have had no time for great thoughts as he struggled with responding to e-mail?

'When to call it a day.' This is one of the hardest decisions to make and one so few time well. Some of the most effective directors I know are well advanced in years. The collection of all that knowledge and skill combined with great judgement is a joy to watch in action. Their judgement usually means that despite the great personal pain to some of them, they know when their sell-by date is coming up. They also save everyone else the embarrassment of having to tell them. The critical thing is recognizing when it is starting to happen, and going before it does. Succeeding successfully must be the ultimate demonstration of successful leadership.

I'm doing fine

'Edgar, why do you insist on living in a fantasy world?'

Who wants to admit they are a failure? Most of us like a little sympathy but we hate to be ridiculed, to lose credibility or to be pitied. Self-esteem and pride are probably higher than average in directors. True feelings and fears are seldom expressed in case they send out a signal of weakness or under-performance. Consequently millions of little white lies of the *'never been busier'* type are told in business every day. As a problem gets bigger, sometimes these little white lies get piled on top of each other.

You may be doing badly but feeling fine, determined not to let a tricky situation get you down. Equally you may end up feeling bad but doing fine. You might be worried about falling off your perch. What people say about how they are doing and feeling may not be the reality and this may have nothing to do with them being raving liars.

While most of us are a little shy about revealing our problems, there are people who break with this general rule. Behaviourally they might be described as *'the business hypochondriacs'*. To them disaster is perma-nently imminent, yet they appear happy in their helplessness, content to blame others for their misfortune and often prone to martyrdom. A natural reluctance to do anything about their plight will gradually remove any initial sympathy we feel for them.

Helping someone who doesn't want help can be immensely frustrating.

Experimenting

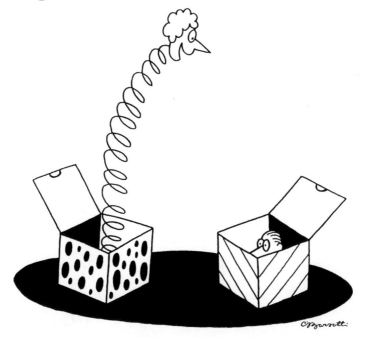

'Come on, Louis. No risk, no reward.'

Fascination with flight as a boy meant that my heroes tended to be the great pioneers of aviation – the Wright brothers, Charles Lindbergh, Louis Bleriot and so on. By definition all of these pioneers pushed the boundaries through constant experimentation.

Successful experimentation has as much to do with the power of observation, the measurement of effects and patience as giving it a go to see what happens. Thomas Edison's quote, *'I know fifty thousand things that won't work'*, gives us a clue as to his patience and determination.

One of the keys to unlocking the ability to control a wing in flight and several other aerodynamic principles came from the Wright brothers' powers of observation. They watched birds obsessively to see what they did as they landed, turned and manoeuvred. There was no fear of getting it wrong, despite the fact that going down the wrong track for a couple of months might have lost them the race for the first powered flight. It was worth it. Watching what happened and wondering why it happened that way made all the difference. Their skill then was to hold on to the working bits and add to them.

Directors have many inhibitors to experimentation – the press, analysts and lawyers to name but three. Pride is another. It's a shame so few of us are prepared to say:

> **'**Look, I haven't a clue if it will work. I sure as hell think it might and if it does the rewards will be well worth it.**'**

The transition rollercoaster

'I used to think it was cruel to keep a dog in the city, but Homer's made a remarkable adjustment.'

What happens when there are one or several new members on a board? It inevitably changes the relationships and the group dynamic. Does a new role for an existing board member do the same? Of course it does, even if they are well known to each other beforehand. Ask any sales or finance directors who have become chief executives. Then for a little bit more fun ask their colleagues.

A piece of work which struck a chord with me many years ago was a paper called 'Moving up... how to handle transitions to senior levels successfully', written by Chris Parker and Ralph Lewis at Cranfield. Their research was focused on people entering new senior positions in companies. So not necessarily board positions. It was centred on what people felt like as they went through the various stages of entering a new role. It has high applicability to merger or take-over situations.

Parker and Lewis came up with what they called 'The transition curve' (see below). Interestingly, whenever 3i has conducted research into what happens to managers involved in management buy-outs through the buy-out process it follows a similar pattern. We labelled this 'the emotional rollercoaster'.

Parker and Lewis describe eight stages to the transition for those who get through it:

1. Rosy positive picture: 'I'm out of here, the new role's going to be fantastic.'
   This stage is usually before you start.
   The position has been oversold.
   As you make your way for the last time around the track of activity of your old role it feels good to be moving on.
2. Immobilization: 'This isn't the job they told me it would be.'
   Natural feelings of shock.
   You become overwhelmed.
   There has been a serious mismatch between expectations and reality.
   The person who persuaded you to take the role has gone. There may be a lower budget.
3. Disbelief: 'I'm not having this, they'll have to sort it out.'
   Temporary retreat. It's someone else's responsibility to help me.
   False competence. I'll just carry on doing what I'm good at.
   Better explain why, so 'In my last company we...'.

4. Incompetence: *'Now everything is going wrong. It could be me.'*
   Awareness of the need to change.
   Frustration at not knowing what to do.
   Sink or swim time.
5. Accept reality: *'Forget what's happened. I've got to sort this out.'*
   Let go of the past.
   I can see where I am going wrong.
   I need to find the solution.
6. Testing: *'I think this might work.'*
   High energy. Determination to find the way out.
   Anger at the fact you have to and for all the false starts.
   Wonder if this is the way we should do it?
7. Search for meaning: *'Hey, it's working.'*
   Understanding how it all fits together.
   What works here?
   Post-rationalizing a little experimental success.
8. Integration: *'Everyone else thinks so as well.'*
   Getting your act together.
   Gaining credibility.
   Doing it naturally with people understanding why.

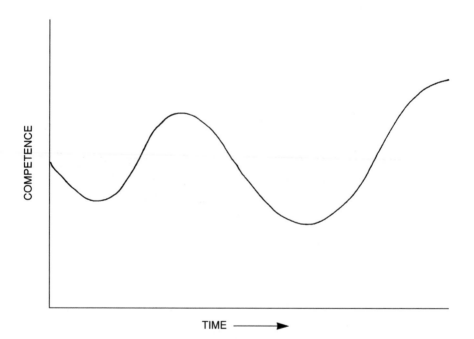

Figure 1.1 *The transition rollercoaster*

Imagine if several people were going through this at the same time. What happens if they all reach the valley of incompetence together? The rollercoaster doesn't fit everything but the basic principles are interesting. Just by talking about this beforehand with someone new helps.

Teenage boards

Ever wondered if there is any comparison between the behaviour of a board and that of a bunch of teenagers? I have. One night I was asked to speak after dinner at a 13-year-old company's board awayday. As an experiment I asked them all to close their eyes and think back to when they were about 13 or so. They reacted well so I asked them what they remembered it felt like at the time. I've tried this with many groups since in companies of all sorts of sizes. It usually works. That is except for groups of accountants: they are always a little suspicious about closing their eyes.

So what words did they come out with?

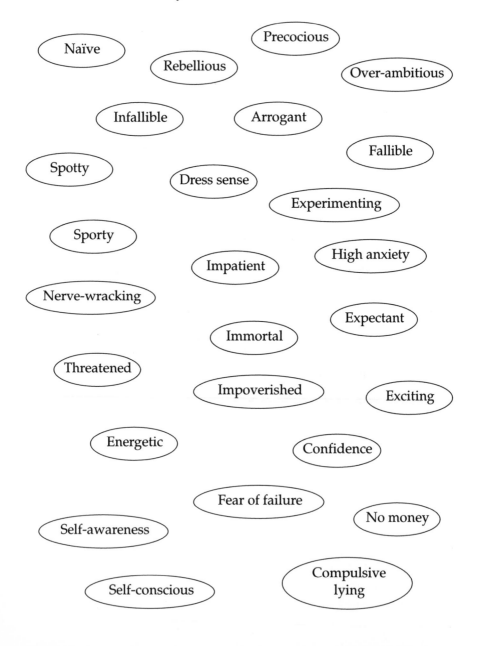

A balance of the positive and the negative. A blend of anxiety and expectancy. A huge number of different emotions, all strong, all going on simultaneously. The interesting questions to ask are how these feelings manifest themselves in a teenage company and how do you deal with them?

Most of the words used above translate straightforwardly into a business context. Wacky dress could manifest itself in poor promotion, usually resulting from a confused strategy. Compulsive lying, that natural reluctance for your parents to know everything that you are doing, in business could be different stories to the bank, venture capitalists, suppliers, customers, staff and so on.

How do we deal with them though? For our children, what we are trying to achieve is to turn them into successful adults. Most of us attempt this through a mix of nurturing, love, encouragement and education, giving exposure to a wide range of experiences and an appropriate level of discipline. For the teenagers themselves, they have to move from pretending they are an adult to being one. The same is true for teenage businesses. At some point they have to behave like grown-up ones, which may remove a lot of fun but doesn't really need to. They are more likely to make this transition successfully with a caring parent or two than without. An astute and caring parent may also recognize that sometimes the message is more powerfully communicated by an uncle or a friend of the family rather than themselves. This can be a painfully arrived at recognition. The same is true in business, where maybe someone from outside the company saying exactly the same thing will have more weight. In business a mentor, an independent director or other business friend may well be fulfilling the parental role. It doesn't just have to be your boss.

Festering and fostering

'After 34 years of marriage you thought you knew me, didn't you?
Well, welcome to the real world!'

The cartoon above was used to illustrate a character called the *'silent seether'* in *Running Board Meetings*. The silent seethers became the most popular characters in the book, especially with journalists. They were described as follows:

> ‹ *These are usually very clever, very shrewd people who sadly lack either confidence or arrogance enough to get themselves heard. Instead they sit there seething whilst others do all the talking and make the wrong decisions. Their attempts at interjecting are often too late and the momentum of the debate too great to take their view on board. Later amongst their colleagues or at home, they vent their spleen, often threatening to resign if it happens again. Of course they never do. They just continue to sit there and seethe. Until they snap.* ›

In terms of dealing with seethers, or those who will let a problem fester and get bigger, the best advice seems to be to use all your chairing or mentoring skills to get them to open up and engage in conversation about it. Weak chairmen will let the seethers seethe. Dreadful chairmen won't even notice that there is a seether in their midst. Sometimes a problem just eats away at someone for a long time before it becomes evident. The resulting insecurity is likely to lead them to withhold information from the rest of the group. Another danger.

When it comes to fostering, some people are just naturals and others have to learn the art. Those that have a talent for it can engender self-belief in the most depressed and unconfident of people. They can also calm the most dramatic over-exuberance with a couple of light remarks. Yet, *'It is always much easier to calm a bit of zip than to put it in'*, and this is particularly true of those who have reached the level of a director in a company.

'Seethers', unlike *'silent seethers'*, are very open wounds. They need dressing quickly if they are not to infect other parts of the board body. One of the things these guys do a lot is project their frustrations onto every issue. This means they are almost permanently talking at cross-purposes, which makes them even more irritating.

Divisive chief executives or chairmen who subscribe to the divide and rule school will engender festering and then probably fostering as someone will inevitably see it as their role to compensate.

Vive la difference

'Mitchell, we should be more like the Japanese.'

For all of us these days the internationalization of business means we spend a lot more time with people from other countries. Travelling around the world on business it would be easy to make the assumption that the world is homogenizing. CNN in every hotel room. Hollywood, pop music and the Internet making us all speak English as a second language. Especially the English. Despite the fact that the similarities are becoming bigger than the differences, there still are big differences. If you have a large and growing international business you will inevitably have a large and growing number of dilemmas as a result. If you haven't, you probably don't know what's going on.

Running an international business presents some other obvious dilemmas. For example, do you run the group as an integrated multinational or a collection of national businesses, ie a multi-domestic? Do you organize the business in terms of product, geography or customer type? How do you deal with remuneration disparity and so on? There is also the knowledge transfer dilemma. As Nail Fitzgerald, the Chairman of Unilever, put it so well at a speech recently:

‹ How do you turn local knowledge into international expertise?›

Time presents another challenge. If you are not careful you can become the 24-hour director if you have business in the USA, Europe and Asia.

One of the hardest things is gaining consistency for your brand while legitimizing diversity and keeping the flexibility to adapt to the conditions of the countries you operate in. This is dealt with well in *Managing Across Borders* by Bartlett and Ghoshal.

Understanding the different cultures and commercial frameworks in a new country can take a very long time. Just when you think you've got the hang of what works in a particular place, something happens that makes you feel you haven't really got a clue. So it is wise to be modest about your knowledge. Elizabeth Marx's book, *Breaking Through the Culture Shock* is a useful guide on this subject. Another useful piece is the work done by Rene Mauborgne at INSEAD on *Fair Process*. Although this work is not written with international issues in mind, the thoughts it stimulates are relevant, because if you attempt to implement decisions in a way that is considered unfair to the people concerned, they are less likely to be implemented successfully. What is considered fair in one country may not be in another.

Situations change

Those who can manage to align a company's strategy and resources perfectly to the situation that it faces as it grows, possess a quality of judgement and timing rarely found. More commonly we find ourselves permanently adapting, occasionally in advance, more often as it is happening, and frequently as a retrofit. Predicting the future is tricky even with the best market intelligence we can buy. The best we can do is to be the leader in our industry and try to shape it to our advantage. If we miss a trend, or make a poor judgement, then we need to act with great conviction and change the moment we recognize it. In his book, *Business @ the Speed of Thought*, Bill Gates talks about the way Microsoft almost lost the plot with regard to the Internet. The conviction shown by Microsoft in recovery was amazing. Especially so when you consider the huge public about-face required to make it possible.

Is the rate of change in business increasing? It is according to Bill Gates. Also in *Business @ the Speed of Thought*, he states that he believes that the velocity of change is driven by information. No surprises there then, but given that far more information is available every day and that it is transmitted more rapidly than ever before, he is almost certainly right. The time you get to have product advantage is much shorter. In technology businesses the speed of knowledge transfer can be as scary as it is exciting. Yet, having said all of the above, even the most progressive changers will feel that Mahatma Gandhi had a point when he said:

There is more to life than increasing its speed.

For a board, dilemmas may arise from a changing market or financial position. They regularly change because of the human aspects. They may also change because the business itself is reaching a new stage of development, and this is not just to do with size. A common problem for start-up company boards when they are successful is that the reasons they started up in the first place may be the reasons why they don't like managing a bigger business. Few start-up managers make a Bill Gates transition. Those moving from growth strategies based on organic development to acquisition-led growth find similar disconnections occur. The nature of the ownership may change, or if it is a public company the state of the stock markets may cause a significant change for a business. Ask any smaller quoted company in the UK. Most of the dilemmas in Part 3 of the book have a major element of a situation changing.

Recognizing reality

'How do you know you've moved if you don't know where you are and where you were?'

'Easy – because of the sensation of movement.'

It is natural to sense change rather than analytically observe it. We don't spend our days plotting our coordinates on the global corporate geo-positioning system. Our common sense also tells us that while we wouldn't have started here, we are here and we'd better get on with our new situation.

A common feeling for new entrants on boards is that while they see the board, the company and the characters are in one position, the incumbents have an entirely different perspective on where they are. This in itself is a dilemma.

A kick in the stomach is better than cancer

I don't know what it is either, but it's almost up to here.

People tend to deal with external shocks better than the slow malingering problem from within the board or the business. Why?

An external threat or attack often forces us to concentrate on survival rather than analysis and blame. They seem to have a unifying and galvanizing effect. There are few divided loyalties and the spinning bottle of blame is put away until we have emerged from the crisis.

Malingering problems can easily be put off to another day in the hope that they may go away or reduce in significance. A company's intelligence about its market, its people and its financial position may be inadequate. If the job of the board is principally that described above, then the board members will need to be very well informed on a wide range of issues to do their jobs. They are heavily dependent upon other people.

In their book *The Paranoid Corporation*, which looks at the causes of major corporate disasters, the authors William and Nurit Cohen refer to loss of contact with reality as a major factor. I guess a bit like hair, gradual loss is more likely than sudden loss; perhaps another reason why the external shock, where reality is very clear, is easier to deal with.

How can heavy hitter boards lose the plot?

This is something I have often wondered about. How does a board comprised of renowned business heavyweights get into horrendous problems? When they do, the reputations of most of those involved suffer terribly. Every time I hear of a big, apparently self-induced corporate hiccup, this question recurs. It would be an interesting area for someone to do some proper research. None seemed to emerge from my brief searches, so here are some personal views that are posed as questions.

■ *'Is it because the board of heavy hitters is usually assembled for a big business?'* They are all busy people and the business is complex. They can't possibly be on top of the detail. They may miss the signals that there is a problem emerging.
■ *'Is it because they always think someone else has the problems thought through?'* The high degree of mutual respect they have for their boardroom colleagues may mean that things fall between the cracks. Is everyone thinking, 'It must be OK if Joe hasn't said anything'?

- *'Is it because their skills and experiences are not relevant to the company concerned?'* They may be wise and wonderfully warm human beings but simply not relevant to the issues of the particular situation.
- *'Does the arrogance that sometimes goes with prolonged periods as a heavy hitter numb their antennae?'* Persistent preening and grooming may dull the senses.
- *'Is too much focus placed on the chief executive and the finance director in terms of information flow?'* If board meetings become a carefully organized show for the non-executives this is a possibility.
- Perhaps the most difficult question though is: *'Is the heavy hitter's reputation deserved?'*

'Oh, oh here's one of them paradigm shift thingies'

'The real me is on Internet.'

' The US economy thrives on paradigm shifts. We are the best at capitalizing on them in the world. Just look how we are dominating Internet trade.' So said a US marketeer at a conference I was at. *'*

' That's right buddy,' said another delegate, *'but look how you've slaughtered my industry and my community.'*

' What the ****'s a paradigm shift? Sounds like I need one,' said the Texan next to me.

' You know one when you see one,' said the management consultant on the other side. *'*

' But he only sees them when they've passed us by,' said the client sitting next to him. *'*

Your view as to whether a paradigm shift is a good thing depends very much on whether you are a beneficiary or not. Before we go any further though we ought to answer the Texan's question properly:

' A paradigm shift is when the established principles and framework of a market undergo a dramatic shift.'

Jean Claude Larreche, the marketing guru at INSEAD, uses Swatch as one of the best examples of this. By looking at the watch as a fashion accessory rather than as a timepiece, it was able to massively expand the market. People might want to wear different watches for different occasions. By being the first and keeping its innovative spirit, it took a significant position.

How can you spot one coming? Dealing with the consequences is a frequent business dilemma. No matter what sector you are in there is likely to be a major shift at least once during your time as a director. They are inherently more difficult to see coming the more we become absorbed in today's business. I am convinced that the only way to see them coming is to get out more and explore a bit. Don't become a corporate tourist; rather, listen carefully to people from other industries and other countries. If you see or hear about a shift in another industry, ask yourself if it applies to yours. The real trick in this is to do it before it has become a fad. However, the most obvious way to benefit from these shifts, like Swatch, is to be the one creating the shift.

Whip up, whiplash and tailspin

Humans, when gathered together and in the right humour, can whip up enthusiasm for almost anything. They don't even need to be intoxicated. For most of the time this is healthy. Occasionally though it can lead to a temporary or permanent losing of the plot as we end up believing our own hype. In order to avoid this, you have to have at least one good healthy cynic on the board who can keep that sense of perspective and bring everybody back to the real world. Nowhere is this more necessary than in the highly successful business. The board that worries about falling off its perch is far less likely to than the one that thinks it doesn't need one anymore.

Whiplash is a little different, as anyone who has been involved in a car accident knows. Although the initial damage of a minor incident may appear inconsequential, the knock-on effects and reverberations may be much more significant and not apparent until much later.

It only takes a momentary loss of control in an unstable aircraft or bad weather to result in tailspin. Tailspin in the context of a board is a rapid loss of confidence and unity of purpose and a feeling among the directors that they are not in control. Tailspin is a common emotion at strategy awaydays when we have difficult dilemmas to address. Good boards will be very mindful of the competitive threats the business faces. However, over-analysis of competitors and of risks can lead to feeling that *'we are all doomed'*.

Another thing about whip up, whiplash and tailspin is to do with the rate at which momentum gathers. The well-known corporate governance speaker, Bob Monks of Lens, was quoted as saying that for good corporate governance to flourish,

> *People only have to change their patterns of behaviour a little.*

My experience with people in business, especially those in senior positions in companies and even more so with entrepreneurs, is that whatever device it is that is used for adjusting behaviour, it has pretty big steps in it. Incy wincy little changes are difficult in practice.

Probably the most important thing to remember about people's ability to whip up a crowd or induce a tailspin is that it has nothing to do with the quality of their judgement.

You're not the man I married

It would be negligent not to mention joint ventures under the heading of situations changing. About a year ago we ran a number of events for our Independent Directors Programme on internationalizing businesses. During these we spent quite a lot of time on market entry strategies and inevitably we came to the subject of joint ventures and strategic alliances. Experience of joint ventures was almost universally disappointing, but at the time you couldn't go a day without reading about a new strategic alliance between two major corporations. Amusingly, I have tried to get a definition of the difference between a strategic alliance and a joint venture from those announcing them. There is no real consistency; the only recurring themes appear to be that:

> *A strategic alliance is effectively the same only we won't have to announce it has failed when it inevitably does,* and

> *Strategic alliances are about understandings rather than commitments.*

Why do joint ventures seem to have such a bad name that they are being given the new one of 'strategic alliances'? I suspect it has something to do with the fact that neatly aligned objectives at the start will inevitably diverge as the organizations involved develop themselves. They may find that the thing they wanted their partner to provide they are now able to do for themselves. It may also be that in a lot of these situations no one is in control and where joint agreement is required at a moment of crisis for the joint venture, the inertia produced by the decision-making process is a killer. More importantly, I think it has much more to do with the fact that the people who had the vision and commitment to put them together and make them work at the outset inevitably move on to do something different. Any marriage requires enormous commitment and sacrifice. The 'not invented here' side of any director makes any transition of joint venture responsibility risky.

Money

It's a personal thing

'I can't sleep. I just got this incredible craving for capital.'

‹Money doesn't change men it merely unmasks them. If a man is naturally selfish or arrogant or greedy the money brings it out that's all.›

Henry Ford

The five 'money' dilemmas specifically dedicated to financial greed and envy explore some of the many issues around the motivational effects of money. What is clear to me is that money does seem to affect people in different ways. The important thing as a director is to be clear about how it affects you and, just as importantly, how it influences your colleagues in their behaviour and approach to making decisions.

Apart from posing the questions below I have chosen to focus on three aspects of money which are rich in dilemmas for directors. These are the pay of others, stock options and what is known as 'hurt money'.

- *Why does money motivate you?*
- *Does the motivational effect of money change the more you get?*
- *If it drives you because of things you want to buy, why carry on when you've got them?*
- *Have you figured out what getting a lot of it does to the psychology of your family?*
- *Does the rate at which capital is acquired affect its value?*
- *Will gaining wealth reduce your ambition?*

The pay dilemma

What about other people's money? An area fertile in dilemmas for directors is the remuneration policy for the organization as a whole and the myriad of related issues. Here are just a few of them with some points beneath. The subject of share options is worthy of its own section.

How do you arrive at the most appropriate approach? Balancing good rewards, which will attract the best staff and shareholder value, is not always easy. What's fair?

> *Get yourself some clear objectives and settle on some key parameters and comparitors. Do you want people to stay for the long term? Are they being paid for just a job? Market salaries, long-term performance bonuses linked to the individuals, their teams and the company's performance together with a piece of the equity.*

If only it were that simple.

What is the role of the remuneration committee?

> *To determine on behalf of the board and the shareholders the company's broad policy for executive remuneration and the entire individual remunera-*

tion packages for each of the executive directors and, as appropriate, other senior executives.'

How do you link pay with performance, one of the hardest pay dilemmas? The toughest part of this is coming up with performance measures that stand the test of time.

' Pick measurable measures that the person can influence and that link in to the strategy. This isn't as daft as it sounds. You'd be surprised at what people pick.'

Can you fix the loyalty elastic with money?

' Ever tried to fix a snapped elastic band? Almost impossible. Once it has snapped it is never the same again. Most employees' loyalty can be pulled and stretched a hell of a long way before it snaps, but once they reach that point where it has snapped you can't win it back. When you think you have with money, it is usually short lived.'

Lawrence Katz at Harvard, an expert in this field, was quoted in The Economist magazine as saying that pay diversity is now greater than ever in the USA. The same job, even in the same industry, receives widely different rates depending on the employer. He believes it is becoming harder for many jobs to be easily compared:

' Pay diversity is perfectly legitimate. Organizations are different and the same described role may have very different conditions and environment. One reason jobs are less comparable is because of differing organization cultures.'

The virtuous circle of the most successful companies being able to attract the most successful people holds as true in business as in football. The local market for their role determines most people's pay. Having said that, increasing numbers of jobs are becoming more mobile, software engineers being the best example. They can find their rate instantly on the Internet.

Pay is made up of many components: salary, bonus, long-term incentive plans (LTIPs), share options, pension and other benefits. It can become a very complicated business and the administration of pay can become expensive.

We have a natural compulsion to make pay overcomplicated. Keep it as simple as possible, don't let it become too tax-driven. The tax rules will inevitably change. A balanced package may also just mean more of everything. If you are going to go in for lots of components, especially if there is pick-and-mix as well, then give people a detailed personal benefits statement at least once a year with a total on it. All but the monthly cheque is easily disregarded.

Does benchmarking talk it up? It sure does but you won't be able to avoid it.

Is the impact of internationalization and the euro effect in Europe making pay transparency easier?

> ‘In some respects, yes. Yet I heard an interesting remark from a German corporate financier during a debate over the relative strengths of London and Frankfurt as stock market locations. Several other Germans were convinced that London had had it and that Frankfurt would within five years become Europe's major market. They were interrupted by the corporate financier who said, to the disgust of his compatriots, 'You are forgetting one major strategic advantage that London has over Frankfurt.' He let the silence hang for a moment and then in the driest of German accents said, "Frankfurt is a **** place to live. The traders will prefer to live in London."
>
> 'Seriously, the answer is yes, but there is a lot to consider when making comparisons between locations. One thing often forgotten is whether you are simply paying the local market rate or whether it is an expatriate deal. The challenges of moving people are considerable.’

Does variable pay penalize the team players?

> ‘Often, but it doesn't have to if you reward team behaviour. Variable pay does, however, shift some of the risk from shareholders to staff.’

What about using remuneration consultants to help?

> ‘Great idea if you can get a good one who can avoid making it too complicated. Awful if you get a dud. So take very careful references.’

The stock option dilemma

Stock options have been described as the best way of aligning shareholder and employee interests. They have also been used enthusiastically in many early-stage businesses as a component of salary because they don't consume cash. Their growth has been extraordinary and they have generated significant capital wealth and a sense of ownership among groups who were unlikely to experience it any other way. Just look at the impact on the housing market in northern California. Their *'heads you win, tails you don't lose'* quality has made them extremely popular with those receiving them. No downside, only opportunity cost, has proved easy to sell.

However, there has been some questioning in the *Wall Street Journal* and elsewhere about their effectiveness in their spiritual home, the United States. The concern is that contrary to their objective, they are in fact causing job-hopping and short-termism. The high technology companies in Silicon Valley are given as an example. Young avaricious technologists have been job-hopping from company to company on the basis of where is likely to show the highest stock appreciation, cashing in their chips when there has been significant growth and moving on quickly. I really don't think such practice is that common and I haven't observed it myself, but it is an interesting thought.

One other share option myth is that they are free to the company. Sure, they don't consume the business's cash. They do, however, result in dilution for shareholders. A good scheme is one that has been carefully considered with regard to the basis of their grant, their pricing and the manner in which they can be exercised. It is also likely to have performance hurdles that must be met before any exercise can take place.

Realistically, the growth in value may come more from timing, the growth in the stock market and the contribution of others than the individuals' own contribution. A scheme may confuse brilliance with a buoyant stock market. In this way they are aligned with shareholders.

Hurt money

‹ *If this goes down I want it to hurt.* ›

So speaks a classic venture capitalist. I remember causing some considerable embarrassment early on in my career when I was working with a couple of seasoned campaigners from another institution and asked them, *'Why? Why do you want it to hurt?'* My question was treated with disbelief, almost as if I'd accused the most experienced of the group of raping his chairman.

'When you are a bit older and you have done as many deals as us, you will understand' was all I apparently deserved. What was difficult for me to understand was what they gained from the other guy being hurt. It was easy to understand why they wanted someone to invest a significant sum so that they were committed and wouldn't walk away at the first sign of trouble. Easy also to see how the spectre of losing all might motivate an entrepreneur. Yet this was not what they meant at all. They were talking about when it had failed.

Even then, at that early stage, it seemed obvious that venture capitalists spent more time trying to persuade people to get out of things that weren't doing well than persuading them to stay. If something fails I'm much more interested in protecting my own downside than delighting in the misfortune of the entrepreneur. Research conducted at the beginning of the 1990s for 3i's management buy-in business also showed that there was no correlation between how successful managers were and how much of their own money they had invested in the company.

So, once people are making a significant commitment, what is the point of squeezing a bit more? Money clearly brings out the sadistic side in some.

Part 2

GENERAL PRINCIPLES FOR DEALING WITH DILEMMAS

Out of clutter find simplicity.
From discord find harmony.
In the middle of difficulty lies opportunity.

Albert Einstein's three rules of work.

WHAT? HOW? WHAT? HOW?

Wouldn't it be nice if there was a universally applicable process for resolving dilemmas and everybody approached dilemmas with Einstein's positive perspective? Life appears not to be that simple. However, I have found a general approach to resolving dilemmas which works pretty well for me most of the time. Whenever I think 'Oh God not now', I immediately try and think, 'What? How? What? How?' What I mean by this is the following:

- *What's the dilemma?*
- *How am I going to decide what to do?*
- *What am I going to decide to do? And then,*
- *How will I communicate what I have decided to do?*

By addressing these basic questions you can usually make progress. If you are trying to help someone with a dilemma it can be a great way of taking some of the emotion out and getting them into resolution rather than desolation mode. Asking questions is better than stating answers. Endorsing is easier than proposing.

What's the dilemma?

How has it arisen?

Figuring out how the dilemma has arisen may help you solve it and avoid leaping straight into blame or victim mode. Thinking about the four key drivers of dilemmas in turn – the board's role, humans, situations changing and the power of money – should result in a clearer picture of what the dilemma really is. For those with wonderful gut feel this can be helpful in coming up with the rationale you will need to convince others later.

Even if you are absolutely convinced that there is a dilemma and that you know exactly what it is, others may not have spotted it yet. When they do will they agree with your analysis? The same goes for the issues involved and the consequences arising out of the different options in resolving the dilemma. It is going to be much easier to resolve any dilemma if there is agreement over these fundamentals. Agreement of course does not mean happiness.

Observing rather than participating

BOOTH

One way of seeing the issues and the effects of a dilemma more clearly is to try to detach yourself from the action and attempt to observe rather than participate. At its simplest level all this might mean is keeping quiet for a bit. Maybe playing the new kid on the block routine. If you are normally actively involved and you go quiet, this will also signal that you think something is wrong. You may or may not want to do this. However, it is generally much easier to see what the dilemma is this way, what the issues are and how people are likely to react to various routes forward. Perhaps this is also why sensible outsiders who enter a situation will often see more clearly what's wrong than those involved. They have to observe before acting.

An additional benefit of this approach is that it buys you time to think and removes the danger of you doing or saying anything inappropriate which may undermine your position. Understanding where you are, your own skills and their relevance, as well as what levers, real power, respect and influence you possess will also help. The trick here is being honest with ourselves.

One of the best ways of observing is to try to *draw the thought bubbles*. It can be a lot of fun and very instructive to quietly jot down what you think people are really thinking or feeling when they are making a contribution as a director. If you find it difficult to bite your lip for too long, try a few challenges with yourself like trying to go a whole meeting without showing any reaction to what has been said.

Issues and consequences

'Calm down, chief, it's not as bad as it first appears.'

Think of all the parties involved, what their position is, how they might react and so on. You will also need to separate cause from effect, and this is as true in the behaviour that is being displayed as in anything else. This is important because while curing a few symptoms may be pleasing and help you to feel you are contributing to resolving the situation, it seldom results in resolving the real dilemma.

Some people find it helps to write down the issues, then, taking each individual involved in turn, write down what you think their perception of the situation and the issue is. It may also be helpful to write down the view you think each individual has of the other participants. Think about who respects who. This may come in very handy later if you have to persuade people who don't respect you to change. Coming up with these perceptions will be easier for some than others. For a character like the late Bavarian leader Franz Josef Strauss, who is quoted as saying, '*I don't keep the dagger of my ambition hidden beneath my robes*', it must have been easy. For others who may have more in common with Machiavelli, it will be a little harder.

You also need to start thinking about the consequences of each of these issues for those involved and for the business itself. With regard to the business, focus on the market and financial positions. This invariably helps with prioritizing later.

How am I going to decide what to do?
Remind me, what are the facts and feelings?

IDEA MAN

A good place to start is to be absolutely sure about the facts surrounding the dilemma. The facts are helpful for all sorts of reasons and as Aldous Huxley is reported to have said, *'Facts do not cease to exist because they are ignored'*. In stressful situations they are easy to ignore or to forget, or they can become hazy. So a regular reminder is helpful.

Reminding yourself how everyone is feeling and likely to feel is also useful at this point. Remember, it is always personal to someone, and someone may be quite happy to be objective in discussing what the problem is but if they start to feel the possible outcomes may present a threat, their position can easily shift. Whether people share the same basic sense of ethics will influence how easy it might be to gain consensus. Therefore it is important to think about who you really trust and who you feel comfortable with.

A dilemma may rapidly result in chaos if you try to resolve it without having appropriate power or with mistaken information about someone else's position. This is one reason why it is more than helpful to know exactly your own legal position, responsibilities and powers as well as those of the others involved.

Whenever you take any directorship you need to get yourself a bible of key documents. Most directors have their own favourites but they are likely to include:

- Memorandum and Articles of Association.
- Last year's board agendas and minutes.
- The annual report and accounts for the last three years.
- CVs of the other directors.
- Your own detailed letter of appointment.
- Organization structure for the company.
- List of outstanding material litigation.
- Any relevant shareholder or investment agreements.
- Bank covenants.

This is probably the time to consider what professional advice might be needed, why, and who should be considered to provide it.

What's the relevant approach here?

Each situation will be different, so you need to decide what the relevant approach is for the specific circumstances you are in and for the particular people involved. Having got it clear what the situation is and given thought to the characters involved, the approach to adopt should become clear. For example, if you believe everyone will be in agreement about what the dilemma is and what the best way forward is, then a consensual style is obviously relevant. On the other hand, if there is considerable disarray then autocratic clarity has a lot going for it. However, for an autocratic approach to work, whoever is leading needs a mandate and a base of respect. They will need to remind themselves whether they want to get the credit for resolving things or not and whether there will be a continuing role for them once the dilemma is resolved. This can have a major influence on the approach they take.

As part of deciding what might be a relevant approach, deciding what is solvable and what's not can be important. This reduces the wasted effort and resultant frustration in trying to solve the insoluble. It may also be perfectly legitimate to come to the conclusion that the particular dilemma has nothing to do with you and that you should not get involved. A popular approach by negligent directors is to hope the problem will go away. So if you decide it isn't something you should be getting involved in, it's well worth being clear why.

If you can get a process agreed with everyone involved that is completely out in the open, the dilemma is much more likely to be resolved. While this is impossible in many situations because of the very nature of the dilemma itself, it must help if the process is clear to those whose support is required.

It's always worth asking:

‘ *Where have I seen this before?*’ and

‘ *Who do I know who might have seen it before?*’

One of the people who is likely to have seen it before is your lawyer. If you have a good commercial lawyer it is often worth a quick call just to chat things through. Involving lawyers at the right stage is important. Consulting them is very different to instructing them.

The dangers of mass debating

How consensual do you want to be in resolving your dilemma? You could of course assemble all of the participants together with every conceivable adviser you might need, then explore the dilemma in great depth. Having obtained everyone's input and looked at all of the possible options available, you might then vote on the possibilities. If there weren't humans involved with something to lose or something to gain this would be the obvious way of resolving all dilemmas. It rarely works in practice.

Dilemmas relating to external threats or shocks can be a tremendous way of unifying the team. However, for internal board member issues they are more likely to be a disaster.

If you are going to debate a dilemma with several others there has to be a point to the debate. If it is to inform those involved and get their input then that's perfectly fine. If it is to try to decide together then the more people involved and the more personal it is the less likely there is to be a successful conclusion to the discussion. It's more likely to become an endless debate with the clarity over whose decision it really is, lost in the process.

Be cool

NEVER LET THEM SEE YOU SWEAT

There is a lot to be gained from having a calm exterior when you are trying to resolve a dilemma, even if inside you are frightened, angry or far from certain what to do. Your mandate to be the one to resolve the dilemma may simply come because of your cool head. Unless you are in one of those rare situations where you need to inject some sense of panic to get people to face reality and the only way is through losing your temper, it is by far the most useful personality to possess. That is, of course, if it is combined with good judgement and an ability to persuade others.

You have obviously got more time to think if you are not talking. In many dilemmas a huge amount of time is spent with people getting things off their chest. While this can be useful in reducing pressure, it generally doesn't do anything to solve the problem. People almost always say something that others will use against them later. So if everyone else is talking away, calmness and quietness make it easier to think.

Psychologists believe that there is a relationship between how effective people are and what sort of pressure they are under. No pressure, no output. A reasonable amount of pressure and they perform well; too much pressure and they crack up. Often in a dilemma where there is a reasonable amount of pressure there will be some people making it worse by increasing the pressure. The dilemma resolver needs to find ways to reduce it and create space for a solution. Buying time creates space and reduces pressure.

The funniest moment I had in using this analogy was when giving a seminar one night. I drew it as a simple normal curve to get the point across. Someone in the audience got very upset and started to argue about the shape. Trying to calm him down I said, *'You're absolutely right, the shape will differ from person to person, but it doesn't matter that much, it's the basic principle that's important'*. This had the undesired effect of getting him more wound up. *'Of course it matters,'* he said and it took a few minutes to pacify him. My mistake was to be casual about something that seemed to matter a lot to him. Making light of things when other people are under stress, or about things that are deadly serious for them, can easily undermine you.

The other reason that buying a bit of time and creating some space is useful is that you may need time to turn your instincts into rational arguments. You may sense the solution before you can prove it.

The *'no sweaters'* are often good at another useful resolving skill – that of enlisting support from others. Some of that extra thinking time can be used to figure out what support can be enlisted from friends, advisers and others.

When putting together a board it is very important to work out whether you have one of these types of characters in the mix. 'A chemical reaction', the dilemma about the explosion in a chemical factory, refers to a serious disaster. A dilemma is not a disaster, but the consequence of any disaster is to present a number of dilemmas. This is certainly true in this case. Those who have the steel and nerve to cope with disasters are probably also good at dilemmas.

3i's chief executive Brian Larcombe is definitely one of the masters of the *'never let them see you sweat'* school. Cool as a cucumber, I've seen him sort out a lot of difficult situations through his calm approach. A wonderful exponent of the power of silence, his other talent seems to be picking the right moment to decide. *'When to decide?'* is another important trait of dilemma resolvers. They seldom peak too early.

What am I going to decide to do?

Depending on how much thought you have put into how you will decide, and the specific nature of the dilemma you face, what you decide will either be very straightforward or a highly complicated iterative process. There are three things that matter most in deciding what to do:

Judgement, judgement and judgement.

Some seem to possess fantastic commercial and human judgement and appear to have been born with it. Others have to develop it. While I think it is possible to improve the quality of your judgement through experience and training, there is a large proportion that comes naturally. When we are placed in a stressful position where a quick decision is required, our natural instincts will frequently rule. Judgement will always be the deciding thing in terms of getting it right, but here are a few factors that can combine with excellent judgement in helping to obtain a satisfactory outcome.

Seizing the moment

One approach to resolving dilemmas is waiting for and then seizing that ideal moment when the atmosphere of the situation is just right to make the required intervention or when the circumstances prevail to make a decision easiest to bring into effect. Often it isn't a matter of waiting and planning but simply recognizing a pivotal moment and forming a judgement. Prevaricators of course will use the *'the moment isn't quite right yet'* argument as an excuse for their indecisiveness. The judgement as to how much damage is caused during the time before what needs doing becomes obvious to everyone, is key.

Getting a mandate

It is much easier to resolve difficult situations, particularly those concerning the relationships on the board, if you have a clear mandate to do so. Figuring out what sort of mandate you need and then ascertaining whether you have it already may result in the simple realization that all is required is to make it stronger. All those bible checks you did earlier will come in very handy at this point. However, checking your authority in terms of the legal aspects, appointment letters or other contracts is only a part of it. The most important thing is the relative respect you are held in. I have seen many situations superbly resolved by people with little formal power to do so. They were just very strong personalities who seized the moment.

If you have got the mandate to resolve, there may be one or more disruptive influences on the board which need to be dealt with. I call this *'neutralizing the Ws'*. That's worriers, whingers and wreckers. Not dealing with them may weaken your mandate. Dealing with them will give you extra power and reduce the pressure for everyone. You will also reduce the risk of *'tailspin'*.

How do you deal with these people if their removal isn't an option? A useful ploy is to keep them extremely busy. Views differ on whether you should give them things they are really good at so they'll be happier, or things they aren't so good at so you'll put them under the sort of pressure they are putting others under. If they are the sort of people who don't know what they are doing and just can't stop doing it, get them busy on researching something. Anything that keeps them away from the heart of the dilemma and the people dealing with it will help.

Sometimes the mandate to resolve a dilemma comes simply from taking it in the absence of anyone else doing so. As discussed in the 'Do you want to be the solution?' section earlier, before you set out to build a position of authority to resolve you have to be perfectly sure you want to.

Working through the board

The most straightforward way to work is through the board, despite the practical and logistical difficulties sometimes involved. As chairman or chief executive this is much easier to do. Your influence on the agenda and the board meetings themselves is obviously greater than for other directors. But what happens if you aren't the chairman or chief executive and, worse, it is one of them that is part of the dilemma? You could be lucky and have a weak chairman who is happy for you to feed him his lines as long as you don't embarrass him. But this is not that common. The following comments are more frequently heard and the issues below them the ones that go through your mind in trying to make progress.

‹ The chairman may not see that there is a dilemma at all.›

Why? Is it a denial or a recognition issue? Either way, if you have high-lighted the issues as clearly as you can and provided good reasons for accepting that there is a dilemma and still got nowhere, then you will need to play 'hunt the confidant'. Once you have found the confidant you will need to persuade them.

‹ The chairman may agree with you in private that there is a dilemma which needs resolving, says he is working on it, but there is no evidence of any progress. It hasn't been discussed at the board and the non-executives are unaware.›

You have to decide whether this is serious or not and whether you want to be the one to do something about it. Building support diplomatically from the other executive directors is the obvious and easiest way forward. Galvanizing the executive through a common purpose will be powerful as long as their support is genuine. Beware assuming commitment from those colleagues who always say the right thing but would never, ever risk jeopardizing their position.

If the executives aren't in agreement or are not prepared to take the risk then you have a number of options that vary in risk. You could focus on the non-executives. If they are effective and you have a sufficiently good relationship with them, you can send them a diplomatic signal without undermining the chairman. If the non-executives aren't effective, it's much more difficult. So the shareholders may be the next group to focus on if they aren't the board members. This could really increase the stakes and jeopardize your own position on the board. The final-straw strategy for those in public companies of using journalists or analysts seldom works and usually ends up with the reputation of the company and the individual suffering as a consequence.

‹ As an executive I don't want to embarrass the chairman or the chief executive in front of the non-executives. Our board meetings are generally a show for them and we don't normally ask questions.›

There are two issues here. One, the chairman and chief executive don't recognize or accept that there is a dilemma; and two, the board meetings aren't effective. If it really is a serious dilemma, and the chairman or chief executive won't listen outside the board and the non-executives aren't aware, you sound completely alone. We have already covered this above. Show meetings are largely a waste of time, so you have to find a way of helping to make them more useful. Few companies ever review the board meeting process. It is a very worthwhile exercise to undertake, even if all you do is brainstorm around what the point of them is.

‘I'm a new non-executive. I'm sure this must have been discussed before. Better wait until I've checked with the company secretary.’

Before taking the appointment you will no doubt have reviewed last year's board agendas and minutes. So if the issue is older than a year, what's wrong with a brief interruption to check? If it was discussed but not minuted for some reason, there is no embarrassment. It is generally better to be an embarrassed non-executive director of a company than a non-executive director of an embarrassed company.

‘I can't seem to get the issue put on the agenda; it always gets crowded out.’

It might just be that your burning issue is not a priority. You feel it is, so list the other items that you feel did get airtime but shouldn't have, and discuss it with the chairman or the company secretary. A good company secretary can be very powerful here and may, depending on the company, have a useful and healthy influence over setting the agenda. Is the problem a general one and not just confined to your specific issue? If it is then ask yourself what really are the five or six most important things for the board to discuss in the year ahead and try to make sure they are planned in. Reviewing last year's agendas and seeing what could have been removed may help.

‘I suppose I and the other non-executives could force the issue, but I'm not sure what they think and it's really not a big enough issue to deal with in this way.’

Will it get bigger? If not, the quiet word later sounds appropriate. If it will become a much bigger issue, then not to do anything is negligence. Effective non-executives take the time to get to know their colleagues. They develop enough knowledge and rapport to sense or read the body language.

If the composition of the board is right and the board is led by an effective chairman, then of course none of the above would happen. Sometimes it is impossible to make any progress on any of the above issues until you have changed the board and the way it operates.

How good are you at chess?

A little chess-playing ability may also come in handy. Having a clear objective, thinking ahead, anticipating responses and having your moves planned for various outcomes reduces pressure and confusion. Chess masters also recognize the value of all of their players and it is not simply about force. Victory through a lowly pawn is tremendously satisfying.

Money and success versus sleep

By the time we get to be a director, most of us will have a good sense of what, for us, is right and wrong, what things might make us feel very uneasy and what it is that we would find difficult to live with later. At the heart of many dilemmas we are forced to make a difficult choice between what we think is the right thing to do to resolve the dilemma, what is in our own best interests, furthering our position or reputation, and our own morals and comfort zone. Occasionally, in the heat of the moment we may not think enough about what it is we will have to live with. Sometimes this may make us decide we don't want to get involved. Occasionally, withdrawing from a situation may be the thing we regret afterwards – *'If only I'd helped'* and so on.

A good tip I was given many years ago as a final thing to do before going ahead with a decision is to write down the dilemma, the facts as you see them, then what you have decided. Then check whether it looks sensible, defendable and sellable.

How will I communicate what I have decided to do?

Communications experts all agree that excellent communications depend on two things:

1. *Understanding the audiences you want to get your messages across to.*
2. *Being clear about your messages.*

This has a hint of a suggestion that communication is a one-way process. In resolving dilemmas it clearly mustn't be. Understanding your audience and coming up with the right messages will require a lot of listening.

Get yourself connected

'You calm down!'

Why is it that we can sometimes put an enormous amount of preparation into giving a message, the audience and message are exactly right, yet we fail? Probably because we just haven't connected. There may be no empathy at all between us and those we are communicating to. We may have been better letting someone else give the message simply because they will be listened to, and painful as it might be to accept the fact, we won't. In dealing with dilemmas we need to think about the connections and be prepared to let others deliver our messages when appropriate. You may be able to do it satisfactorily yourself, but could someone else do it even better?

It is much easier to get someone to open up to you on a difficult personal issue if you have a strong relationship already and they trust you. The same goes for giving difficult messages to people. This is obvious, but how do you get yourself connected if you are, as frequently occurs, new to a situation? How can you generate empathy in an atmosphere of suspicion? Avoiding the spiral of a defence–attack

'I suppose you know you're doing that all wrong.'

style of conversation can be difficult if you have critical remarks to make to individuals under pressure. What do you do if you don't have a good relationship already well established?

If you have time and you feel you have a personality that will fit, then the answer is easy: you have to be patient and focus on building this rapport before you can start to get near the topic you want to discuss. If you really believe that no matter how much time you had you won't be able to connect, then you need to play 'hunt the confidant'. If it's just time that's the problem, then you need to be spending as much time as you can with whoever it is, show you listen, empathize with their situation and look as if you might be the one who will help them. For this to work it must be genuine, you must keep confidences and you have to be very careful in your choice of words. As I write this it sounds so trite and obvious. I've deleted it three times thinking the average reader of this book will be thinking a big *'So what?'*. Yet in the end I put it back in because it seems that so often in the dilemmas that I've observed or been involved in that someone has rushed a situation or assumed empathy when it isn't there.

Gaining empathy is easier if you understand the pressures that people are under and what the consequences of the various outcomes will be. This also reduces the danger of trying to enlist support for a specific solution that may be a great overall outcome but a disaster for the particular person we are trying to persuade. Assumptions need to be tested before they are made.

Think also about the influence of place and time on the communication. Formal and informal settings, familiar and unfamiliar places, travelling times, using already scheduled meetings for a different purpose, how the meeting is set up or convened – these are all important factors affecting expectations and mood.

One danger of having an especially good relationship is that when you have to be the bearer of unwelcome news or views, feelings of betrayal can be quite strong.

A final point on this subject. If you are a real cynic and don't believe in any of this softer stuff, just remember:

‹ *Do unto others, it makes it easier to sell.* ›

Is what you've said what has been heard? Is what you've heard what they think?

In most good negotiations courses we are taught that before proceeding to the next step of a negotiation we need to check that the assumptions we are making or the things we have agreed are as we think. One of the things which strikes me about situations where I have been in the tricky spot of being a confidant to two people who have fallen out, is that what they hear is seldom what the other person said. It seems all too easy to make the words or the tone sound like something different.

Exactly the same goes for when you are trying to find out how people really feel about something or what they want. They may over- or under-estimate feelings for effect, to avoid embarrassment or simply to frustrate a solution that is disagreeable to them. If you are dealing with people from different countries it is even more important to calibrate your hearing. Many a visitor to Japan has been innocently misled by hearing the word 'Yes' and taking it to mean agreement, when the Japanese person simply means yes, he or she heard what you said.

Painting pictures

'OK, let's try <u>this</u> scenario…'

This well-known technique for persuading someone to do something is very useful when you get to explore the alternatives and what you might actually do. It is especially relevant when dealing with high emotions and people who are more instinctive. The sort of people who aren't going to read a carefully argued, rational paper will be far more inclined to listen to an appeal to the senses and emotions. So what does painting pictures involve?

In its crudest form it's just painting an image in someone's head of what it will be like if a particular outcome emerges – describing in an *'Imagine Joe, career in tatters, forced to move to a small house, children moving schools…'* kind of way. A more sophisticated use involves giving the person you are trying to influence the brush and asking them to paint *'What it might be like if…'*. You then build on the picture as you go. This is much more powerful and will appear far less manipulative.

Of course it only works if you can paint verbally and if you have a good feeling as to what their sense of taste is. Their sense of taste in this case is driven strongly by the things they value most. Gaps in age can produce some interesting issues here. The language you use to paint your picture will have a big effect. Words can be taken to mean different things. Just as with the flavour of their food, those who are advanced in years might like their colours stronger.

On the subject of dealing with a business teenager, remember that the picture you are painting which you feel is awful, they might like. A friend of mine was telling me how lucky I was to have three boys and not three girls like he has. His biggest problem now they are teenagers is the boyfriends his daughters come home with. One daughter in particular likes to shock. To start with he had terrible problems dealing with this, while his wife just shrugged it off, expecting the relationships to be short. He couldn't deal with it that way no matter how hard he tried. However, recently he has learnt a new tactic that seems to be working well. Whenever his daughter brings home someone he thinks is entirely unsuitable he makes a particular point of being friendly, and when the young boy has gone says, *'I must say he was a particularly nice boy'.*

Teenagers need support and encouragement. Confrontation doesn't generally work and you frequently have to use reverse logic.

Good signalling

This is simply what some people would call *'setting expectations'* or others call avoiding the *'Why didn't you tell me earlier?'* complaint. If you are trying to change behaviour or make a change it will be easier if those involved know it is happening and what is expected of them in the process. This is especially true when there is under-performance or unacceptable behaviour. Whether or not you think that the inevitable end result is removal, it is still worth the effort to send clear signals about what is expected and what the consequences of under-performance are.

Idle threats undermine our position and reduce the respect we have. Repeated idle threats reduce your respect to zero. Whenever we get the urge to threaten to provoke a change, we need to remember that we must follow through. Your decision over whether and if so, when, to involve lawyers is an important signal to someone. The timing and way in which you communicate this will have an impact. Remember as well that letters from a lawyer are inevitably more formal and serious in tone. Make sure you understand how your lawyer communicates.

Another important aspect of signalling is to:

‹ *Think about the viewers.* ›

Influencing the viewers may be more important than influencing the one you are directly communicating with. Thinking about the signals you are giving out to others by what you say to someone or the way in which you say it can be instructive. There are people who spend too much time thinking about the viewers to the extent that it becomes so obvious that they have no influence over the person they are supposed to be talking to.

A little impact therapy

One group of people who definitely wouldn't make an idle threat are the 'impacters'.

A sudden impact is useful for gaining attention. A shock can be a legitimate signal that things have changed and a different behaviour or standard is expected. Presumably this, as well as exacting punishment, is the justification for slapping children. However, more often than not, just as with kids, the giving of a shock has more to do with the frustration they may have caused than any premeditated signalling. None the less we hope our sudden action will get attention and break a cycle of bad behaviour. It may follow a period when we tolerated something wrong and may have even reinforced it either by ignoring or condoning it.

In a boardroom setting a little impact therapy can go a long way. Someone who has been relatively quiet and has built up a store of respect suddenly becoming angry obviously has more impact than the permanently angry person. Your kick has more impact if you can cuddle as well. A group of non-executives who have consistently conceded to a rampant chief executive's plans but then vote against one will do likewise. We have to be careful, though, that our sudden impact isn't and isn't seen to be simply an outpouring of frustration. Likewise, most of the interventions we will be looking to make will be positive.

Removing directors

MANKOFF

'You're fired, Bingle!'   'I'm sorry, I don't get your drift, sir.'

Removing directors, thankfully, is not something that we get regular experience of. The logistics and the communications involved are complicated. It is one of the most stressful things directors are involved in, but there is precious little training available on the subject. Practice and effectiveness in doing it therefore varies enormously. So does the damage done in the process. As well as seeing some real masters of this particular art, I have witnessed and heard second-hand some real howlers. Those who take it upon themselves to remove a director without having the authority to do so, or try to do so without having thought through the legal, compensation or succession issues, are the most common. Some people just lose the moral high ground completely through clumsy implementation, such as the man who tried to fire someone over the telephone or the one who attempted it over lunch.

Why should removing a director be any different from removing an employee of the company? Obviously, much that applies to removing anyone or making them redundant will also apply to this situation, but there are some differences when it is a director. The fall in status may appear more dramatic to the recipient. Their removal may be reported on in the press. Even if this is just in the trade rather than national papers, the embarrassment can naturally be hard to deal with. It may be a lot more personally charged for all sorts of reasons. If they have been the founder or one of the founders, their identification with the business is likely to be much stronger than for others. They will normally have a longer service contract. Acting through the board is vital.

The process of removing a director can be made less stressful and there are many people who do it an extremely effective fashion. So what is it that they do? One of the privileges of working at 3i with such a big portfolio of investments and with our pool of independent directors is the ability to observe some real star performers in this area. What follows is a summary of some of the things they do. *'Preparation, preparation and preparation'* seems to be the lesson.

An important starting point is to be absolutely clear of the commercial decision: that the business will be better for the person concerned departing. There is a clear and objective assessment of performance to support the decision. Clear signals will have been given about under-performance. Holding the commercial high ground makes a big difference. Why someone is being removed will impact the manner and ease of their departure. Obviously the easiest situation is where there has been clear misconduct or fraud. However, it is important to recognize that one man's clarity is another's matter for debate.

The best have it as a clear objective that no matter how painful for those involved, on reflection everyone will feel it was fair and handled as effectively as it could have been. One of the best operators in this area that I know has as his simple objective: *'The person going should end up thanking me afterwards for the way it was done'*.

They also ensure that they know what the legal ground is and that any necessary powers or approvals are in place. It will normally be the case that the person is being removed as an employee and possibly as a shareholder as well as a director. Appropriate shareholder support for what they are proposing to do will have been obtained. There needs to be clarity over which lawyers are acting for who and whether support is provided for the proposed departee. Major contracts will also have been checked to ensure none is jeopardized by the removal of the director concerned.

Few will embark on a removal without a clear idea of the consequential reshaping of the board, and if external replacements are required, some idea of which head-hunter will be used, how long it will take and how they will manage in the interim.

Thought will have been given to the terms of any settlement and, if shareholdings are involved, the alternatives for dealing with it. Their objective is to present a fair and reasonable offer verbally and in writing that it is hard for a lawyer to consider worth contesting. The small practical details such as what is happening about the car and other company property will be included. They will have gone through every possible objection and have prepared a response. Communications will have been prepared for all those who need to be informed – staff, shareholders, press, customers, suppliers, advisers, etc.

But what about the meeting itself? For the most part, traditional redundancy communication advice is relevant but there are some extra things to think about in terms of the where, who and how. Is it better to do it off site? You certainly shouldn't do it in a room with big windows that others can see into. This needs to be as private as possible.

Convening the meeting may prove challenging. You need to make it as immediate as you can. You need to signal it is a serious meeting but not state that 'I'd like to meet you to fire you'. Most times people are expecting it.

With regard to who, it should be the chairman of the board, unless of course he is the one being removed, in which case it should be the representative of the lead shareholder who has the support of the majority. One of the objectives of the suggestion by the Hampel

Committee on corporate governance that there be a lead non-executive director, was that this person would fulfil such a role when required. Then it is obviously easier to state:

‹ *You have lost the confidence of the board* › or

‹ *You have lost the confidence of shareholders.* ›

Having a mantra like this is helpful because it makes it clear it is not negotiable. Most people find it difficult to remember anything immediately afterwards other than that they've been fired. It is wise for the chairman to have a witness; many prefer this to be the company secretary in a larger business or the company's lawyer in a smaller one. Few put the departee through the embarrassment of doing it with the entire board present.

In terms of the how, you need to be absolutely clear and calm and state that this is not a debate, but a decision that has been taken by the board with the full support of the shareholders. It should be kept brief. You need to get on with it and not dance around the subject beforehand. This is not a meeting you start by talking about last night's football or wasting time over who had the decaf coffee without sugar. Making the statement as formally and briefly as possible will increase its clarity. This doesn't mean that it needs to be without empathy. It makes sense to have prepared the necessary termination letter and offer of settlement, repeating what has been said. As to what might be offered, this is covered later on. While you may be calm and clear, the person receiving the bad news, understandably, may not. What they hear may be quite different from what you say. Calm words are likely to be met with an emotional response. They should be given plenty of opportunity to speak without interruption. All very well, but here are some typical objections:

‹ *You are making a terrible mistake.* ›

‹ *You can't do this without hearing my side of the story.* ›

‹ *You didn't give me any warning.* ›

‹ *It's not fair.* ›

‹ *It's not my fault, it's market conditions.* ›

‹ *I've worked my butt off for you and this is my reward.* ›

‹ *You promised to support me.* ›

'*You don't have the authority to do this.*'

'*You can't do this now when it's about to come right. Just give me another month.*'

'*What do the other directors have to say?*'

'*How long have you been plotting against me?*'

'*You never gave me a chance.*'

'*You'll regret this.*'

'*The customers will switch.*'

'*The rest of the team will leave.*'

'*Who's going to replace me? What makes you think he'll do a better job?*'

'*What am I going to say to my wife?*'

'*You can't afford to get rid of me like this.*'

'*You don't expect me to take this lying down do you?*'

I guess the response to most of these will be in straight bat form along the lines of:

'*I'm sorry you feel that way, but the board has considered this matter extremely carefully and come to the conclusion that I have outlined to you.*'

Having the company's lawyer present should help emphasize that what you are doing is legal and fair, but given the psychology of the moment it probably won't. It is important to advise the person that he or she should take good legal advice and that this should be from an employment specialist. It is often worth getting some well-respected local names. This can be a very shrewd move and avoid the person, through lack of experience, picking an inappropriate lawyer. Over-adversarial lawyers can ruin the best of intentions.

What about the settlement? What needs to be considered?

- Employment contract terms. There will normally be good and bad leaver provisions. There will also be a notice period, but you will usually not want them to appear on the premises during this. Briefing the company's lawyer and getting their input before you take any action are essential.
- Shareholder agreements. There will normally be clauses for such eventualities, including pre-emption rights and valuation procedures. These are likely to involve independent auditors' valuations. The auditors will often come up with surprisingly high valuations for minority stakes in private businesses. There is a natural desire to be generous to the departing director. I suppose they are more likely to sue them successfully later as well!
- The car. Sometimes this has a high emotional value. Neighbours, children, friends don't need to know.
- Other company property (computers etc).
- Access to premises and systems.
- Pension arrangements.
- Agreed but unpaid bonuses, often a point of contention.
- Agreement over what will be provided by way of a reference.
- Restrictive covenants, return of proprietary information and other related potential competitor issues.

Obviously the resultant settlement will be a negotiated package of items, but it is helpful to split the contract and shareholder aspects right from the outset. But what is the best approach? Should you try and get away with as little as possible, or overpay and get it sorted out more quickly? Most people believe it is better, however much it grates if someone has seriously under-performed, to pay out generously and quickly so that the board's attentions can be focused not on the battle but on the future. You want their lawyer to be saying, *'You've got a very reasonable offer, we can negotiate a bit more, I'm sure, but this is not worth a big fight'*. When there is equity involved then valuation is usually the hardest part, especially if the company overall is under-performing. The seller of a minority shareholding in an under-performing company is clearly not selling at the best time, and many forget that a minority holding doesn't carry a majority premium. Weak shareholder agreements that have no provision for leavers or independent valuation processes can cause no end of frustration for all parties involved.

With the major focus being on the person who is being removed, it is very important not to forget about the communications with everyone else. It is possible, particularly if there has been 'taking of sides' in the run up, that the removal of a director may have knock-on effects in terms of close colleagues who will find it uncomfortable to stay. These issues should be dealt with swiftly, otherwise disharmony continues.

The final thing to say about removing directors is that it often removes considerable pressure, signals a new start and clears the air. That is, of course, if you have made the right choice.

Conclusion

Dilemmas are challenging but they can be tremendously satisfying to resolve. As I said in the Introduction, all I wanted to achieve with this book was something thought-provoking and fun. I hope I have met this goal for you.

Part 3

SOME DILEMMAS

DAVE'S DREAMING IS DISTURBED

Dave, a busy chairman of a number of companies, is musing content-edly in his garden. He has just returned from a four-hour drive back from a board meeting at his most recently acquired chairmanship at Aceco.

'What a smashing evening. For once, home on Friday in time for tea. The garden looks great and Sarah seems very jolly tonight. Expect she can't wait for this time next week. Guess we'll be half-way there by now. Wonder what a three-week holiday is really like?

'Funny, we were half-way across the Atlantic this time last year on our way to that amazing retirement weekend Globeco laid on for us in Florida. Still, 20 years flogging around the world sorting out messes for them, they should have been grateful. Must write that "Retirement Relief Counsellor" a note, smarmy little git. Just to think I almost fell for that, what was it he called it, ah yes the FLP, a "Future Life Plan" ':

'Two months' holiday with your partner, time to reflect and get to know each other again. Two months hypernetworking to get yourself into the new opportunity superhighway. Then a highly recommended refresher visit to me to reorient the plan. In a year's time you'll have built the ideal balance in your life. A day for your partner, a day for golf and a portfolio of interesting but not too challenging consultancies and directorships.'

'Complete tosh!

'Sarah did seem a bit fed up when we had to cancel the cruise so I could chair Ritco. She's obviously right to be a little brassed off that we've not had a Saturday together so far this year. But at least everything's under control now. The holiday will be a great chance to make it up to her. She needs a break as well, she's been so busy with the Events Company. Who'd have thought it would have taken off that quickly?

'Ritco's been such good fun, great team and if that whiz kid venture capitalist Paul has got the numbers right, I reckon I'll make as much from that as the 20 years at Globeco. He's all right, Paul. I'm sure I wouldn't have got Wimco without the glowing reference he gave me on Ritco. Aceco looks to have got off to a cracking start as well. Best managing director I've seen in ages that Ian. I'm sure we'll be able to build a good team around him in time. Probably ought to start with the finance director. Wurry by name and worry by nature.'

Dave's dreaming is suddenly disturbed. Sarah calls:

Dave, Daaave, it's that Jim Wurry on the phone again. Says it's urgent. Must be, he hasn't even had time to get into Uriah Heep mode. Please don't be long, dinner will spoil.'

'Hi Jim, what's up?'

'I'm afraid I've got some terrible news, Dave. Ian's had a brain haemorrhage this afternoon and Helen [his wife] has just called me to say they don't think he's going to pull through. I'm sorry to disturb you, but I thought you ought to know. To be honest, I'm really not sure what to do. It's hit me hard as well. I suppose I need to take charge now. Ian and I were off to Atlanta on Sunday to close the Coke deal.

What would you do now if you were Dave?

What are the issues?

Dave has several things to consider. How deeply involved should he get? Should he leave it to Wurry or does he need to own the problem? How much time does he want to devote? What about his other directorships? The logistics of home and where Aceco is located are far from easy. Wurry's on the phone and he needs to give some sort of initial response. Does the rest of the board know? If not, how should he let them know and when? What should he do about the trip to Atlanta? What should he say to the institutions? After all, they own a majority stake between them. Who is going to inform the company's advisers and what should they be expected to do to help? Then there is the matter of the holiday. What does he say to Sarah when he puts the phone down?

The managing director and his family have their own concerns. How ill is he really? Dave only has the naturally pessimistic Wurry's description to go on. What support do his wife and family need immediately? What was Ian's role? Managing director's roles differ from company to company. Are there any other things that he was working on which need to be dealt with?

The business itself will face some new challenges. Is there a contingency plan already prepared? How damaging is the loss of the managing director at this critical stage? Is there any temporary or permanent successor from within? Wurry doesn't feel like a natural leader and it sounds like there are issues with him in his current role.

If it isn't known whether Ian is coming back or not, is it appropriate to start recruiting? Should they get an interim manager in? Could they if you wanted to? What's the company's financial position? Is their key man insurance in place? How does the company manage public relations? What public relations issues are there now?

How to decide?

What are the facts? Given Wurry's disposition he may want to check. Dave is unlikely to know Ian's prognosis, which is fairly critical to any decisions that are taken. He is reliant on Ian's wife for this.

Dave will also have to determine what it is he can decide on his own as chairman, what things he must put to the other directors and what he needs to discuss with the institutional investor. He needs to decide whether he needs to seek their guidance or whether he should develop a plan and make a clear recommendation. He also needs to think about how much time he's got. How can he create space and relieve the pressure, particularly on Wurry? Luckily he has got the weekend. Gives him some time to prepare communications and to talk with people who are bound to be upset.

Dave may also be thinking about other people he knows who have been through this situation before. If he does know someone, a quick call to see what they did could prove well worthwhile.

There is a need to exercise control, introduce calm and provide an *'It's OK, we can work through this together'* sense of security to those unsettled. For Wurry this is vital. He is on the phone and needs a response now.

Dave also needs to decide whether Atlanta is a red herring or not. A decision on going is needed and he will have to find out whether a week's delay will have an adverse effect.

The views of the institutional investor will be important. Should Dave contact them, or Jim? Does this need doing over the weekend? Will whoever it is ask them what to do, or make a recommendation?

What to decide?

Let's look at some of the options.

‹ Not now Jim, I'm having my tea. ›

A little insensitive and irresponsible perhaps.

'This must be very distressing for you, Jim. I don't think it would be a good idea for you to take Ian's role. I think I should until we can get a proper replacement.'

Almost as bad.

‹ OK Jim, I think you're right. You should take over. I'll come and see you on Monday and we can decide what to do. ›

Irresponsible and negligent. The cynical may think that this option is ok because he could always be fired later if he doesn't work out.

‹ I'll be there as soon as I can. It'll take me four hours. Let's meet for breakfast at the hotel. We can both sleep on it. I'd particularly like you to think about internal communications; you know the people best and how they're feeling. ›

Very supportive, makes no commitments and buys time to think what to do. Dave probably plans to assume control with a view to recruiting a new managing director, assuming there is no internal candidate. At this stage Dave will delay the decision on Atlanta.

What to say to Sarah when he puts the phone down?

‹ Sarah it really is awful news this time... I know this may jeopardize the holiday but I'm chairman. I don't think Jim can cope on his own. They need me. ›

The decision over whether anyone should go to Atlanta and if so who, can be made when the directors get together.

How to communicate it?

First of all, who needs communicating with? There are lots of people. Sarah, Wurry, Ian's wife, the other directors, institutional shareholders, key advisers, key customers and suppliers, the public relations company.

In what order? The order matters as well as who talks to whom. In this case it is reasonably straightforward. He has to speak to Wurry – he's on the phone – then to Sarah his wife, Ian's wife, the other directors and then the lead institutional investor. The decision over who should speak to the staff can be made when the directors get together. Given that, of the directors, Dave is likely to be the most effective communicator and he is chairman, it probably should be him. However, it may be a good thing for Wurry to do.

For most of these conversations he will have to have given serious thought beforehand to what he is going to say. He probably won't need much beyond a brief statement of the facts and what the board proposes doing.

How to say it? Remember, Jim Wurry is likely to be losing his mentor and his friend, someone he's been through a lot with. His normal anxiety level will be taken higher. The chairman will be looking to reduce the pressure for Wurry rather than increase it. Uncertainty will no doubt raise it, as will telling him to relax.

Using the common purpose to galvanize is entirely appropriate here: *'We owe this to Ian and his wife. It's what he would have wanted'*.

If Ian dies then many of the staff will understandably want to grieve. They may need a symbol, however simple, to help with this. A special edition of the company newsletter, a memorial service, a plaque, or a collection and donation to his favourite charity – whatever is appropriate and sensitive to his family.

Honesty about the process of replacing Ian will be important. Getting the other directors input to the brief for the head-hunters may help gain commitment.

What did Dave do?

This situation in some ways is one of the more easy dilemmas for highly committed professional chairmen to deal with. This is because of the high sense of ownership and responsibility they generally feel for the board and the future of the business. Dave had no doubt that he had to assume control of the situation, that any other priorities he had, whether they were domestic or commercial, were lower than this one for the next few months. He was certain that his wife Sarah would understand and be supportive. Absolute conviction is the hallmark of those who sort things out.

After Wurry had finished speaking, he paused for a moment and said in the most genuinely sensitive of tones:

> *Jim, I'm extremely grateful to you for letting me know. I can appreciate what a terrible blow this must be to you. You two seemed joined at the hip. It's an awful shock. How are you feeling?*

Wurry talked for a while and was naturally very upset. He intended visiting the hospital after he had spoken to Dave and would go into the office tomorrow to prepare for the Atlanta trip and write the necessary communications to staff and so on. Dave was very careful to sound supportive throughout. It was obvious that Wurry was terrified at the prospect of being the front man, and his proposal to become managing director was more out of duty than desire.

Dave then told him that he would come down to Aceco later that night and suggested that they meet for breakfast the next morning. He asked if Wurry could give him the mobile number for Ian's wife. He told him that he wanted to call her and convey his sympathy and offer to have the company arrange for relatives to be put up at the local hotel if necessary. Dave may not have done this had he not met her before and felt some rapport. He also asked if Jim could contact Ian's secretary and ask her to come in tomorrow, there was bound to be a lot to do. He suggested that they shouldn't decide on what to do about Atlanta until they'd chatted it through the next day.

What did he tell Sarah?

> *Well, this time it's serious. Ian's had a brain haemorrhage and isn't likely to make it past the weekend. Wurry sounds gutted. Not surprising – they were as close as you could get. Poor bloke needs some help. I think I should get down there for the morning. What do think?'*
>
> 'You've got no choice have you? I think you should get a car to take you. You're not driving yourself. I'd take you but I've got the event tomorrow afternoon.*

Sarah didn't mention the holiday, but the next day when it was clear to Dave, the holiday was postponed for him. Sarah's sister went instead.

Dave took Sarah's advice and booked a car for the journey. This was a tremendous way of reducing pressure. During the journey he spoke to Ian's wife to convey his sympathy and ask what logistical support she needed. He bought tickets and arranged travel for relatives. He used Ian's secretary to do this; she was a real trooper.

Dave then called other directors to let them know what had happened and to ask if they could attend a short meeting at 5 o'clock the next evening to discuss the situation. Unsurprisingly, all of them agreed. Dave was glad Wurry had given him that handy little sheet of all the directors' numbers when he joined.

At the meeting with the directors Dave started by thanking them and offering sympathy. He then set about building a galvanizing purpose – *'What Ian would have wanted, we must show we're in control'*, etc. He told them that he would be taking over as chief executive until either Ian recovered or a successor from outside was appointed. They agreed on this instantly, it has to be said with some relief. The fact that he made it clear that the successor would not be from within immediately reduced the pressure again, particularly for Wurry who was terrified at the prospect of being in charge. Having got that agreed, they then spent some time agreeing and planning the communications.

On Monday morning Dave told the institutional investors and the managers briefed staff. A short statement was prepared for all staff. As it was clear by this stage that Ian wasn't coming back, this contained a sensitively written tribute to him.

They decided that the trip to Atlanta could be postponed a week and that Wurry and the sales director would go. They informed Coke who were perfectly understanding.

Sadly, Ian died a few weeks later. It took nearly nine months to recruit his successor. He turned out to be highly effective. Not quite as capable as Ian, but the company has prospered. So the managing director died but the company didn't.

What about Sarah? Well, she forgave Dave instantly. After all, she knew what he would do. He did make it up to her later. The institutions were very impressed by the way Dave had handled a difficult situation and particularly by his commitment.

THE DEPARTING DIRECTOR

You are a longstanding independent director of LPJ.

The three directors who founded LPJ, Liz, Paul and John, have much to be proud of. Their business has grown from start-up six years ago to sales of £10 million. Profits are healthy at over 10 per cent net. Until recently the team have got on very well together. They have shared the many highs and lows during LPJ's formative years. However, the stresses and strains of growth are starting to show. John, the sales director, and Paul, the operations director, just don't seem to be able to agree about anything any more.

Liz, the managing director, has performed extremely well, driving through the change and holding the team together through a major expansion. However, it's obvious that this has been at a cost and the team has reached its limit. She is a wonderful mix of visionary and manager and is capable of running a much bigger operation, and plans to do so. Liz is convinced that LPJ will double in size in the next three years. However, her analysis is that the business has outgrown Paul and although he's done a great job so far, he is finding it hard to keep pace with recruitment, planning and control, and it's time to face reality and make a change.

Liz, Paul and John invested £150,000 from savings in the first couple of years to form and fund the early development. Liz has 30 per cent of the equity, Paul and John each have 15 per cent, you've got 5 per cent and a well-known venture capital company has 35 per cent. They've done well and the business could easily double in value from here.

Happily you are seen as a trustworthy, reliable confidant by all the team and Liz has asked you to chat to Paul to get a feel for how she might best handle it. She wants to do everything she can to treat him well. You're sure John will be delighted to see Paul go, but equally sure he may be difficult over the terms of Paul's departure. One area where you think there is bound to be difficulty is in valuing Paul's equity. You and Paul have a regular chat a couple of times of year. Fortunately one of these is coming up.

The chat with Paul got off to a great start. You didn't even need to raise the issue. As open and naturally engaging as ever, Paul raised it first:

'We've always had a good straightforward relationship, and I would welcome your input on something really important.'

'Yes of course, Paul. What?'

'I guess it must be pretty obvious to you that Liz and John want to expand more quickly than I do. To be honest, I'm not sure I'm cut out for what they've got in mind. I think it's best to recognize reality and for me to go before John and I cause any damage! Given the recent approaches we've had, my equity must be worth at least £2 million. That and a decent payoff should be more than enough for me. I'm sure I can count upon your support to make sure John's not too difficult over things. He seems to be getting more and more aggressive by the day. Frankly, I'm a bit worried he might stitch me up. I recognize my own limitations but he does seem to make a meal of them. It's not as if he's Mister Perfect. He just seems better at presenting his problems.

'Liz is bound to be embarrassed over things. She's been great all along. I want to make it as easy as possible for her, but I'm not going to let John force me out on the cheap. We all know he's extremely effective, but I reckon Liz will have to keep a close eye on him.'

How should you, the independent director, respond to Paul and then resolve the dilemma?

What are the issues?

The key issues relate to Paul, John, Liz and you. Starting with Paul: is his performance and potential really below that required? Should he really be going? Can he be trained for the larger emerging role? If he is under-performing or even if he isn't, is it right that he should go? How does he go with dignity and in a fair way? Does he need to go immediately or can there be a suitably long period of withdrawal to give time for his successor to be recruited/promoted and handed over to? What's the likelihood of getting someone better than Paul? Are they readily available? Would they be attracted to LPJ? How do they select an appropriate search firm and so on?

With regard to John: is he as good as he thinks, and as good as is needed? Or is he just the next problem waiting to happen? If he isn't a problem, how do you balance John and Paul's views over equity value?

There are several issues relating to Paul's equity. How will it be valued? It is after all a minority stake in a private company and the company is not being sold. If a successor for Paul is to be recruited, will the replacement be offered equity at the outset or later? Has the company got the cash to buy the equity in or are external funds required? What do the Memorandum and Articles of Association say about equity transfer? What about the investment agreement with the institutional investor? If there are good and bad leaver provisions, what is Paul in these circumstances? If the reason he is going is to do with his potential and his performance to date has been fine, then it sounds like good. If he is seriously under-performing in his current role, then obviously not. Occasionally this issue highlights the fact that none of the directors is appraised in a conventional sense or have objectives.

You need to be clear what your role in this is. Are you the key resolver, the honest broker? Or perhaps you should be Liz's main supporter. She is chairman after all. Liz's role also needs discussing. Is she showing sufficient leadership? It sounds like she is within the business, but is the board operating as a board? Should she continue to be chairman and managing director? Or is now the time to separate the roles?

Apart from these, there may be other more fundamental issues. Is it appropriate to review the whole strategy for ownership and for the business? What is best for the owners may not be best for the business. Armed with this review, the suitability of the current team will be clearer. It may be that the best option is a sale of the company.

You also need to find a response to Paul, which gives you time and Paul comfort without false hope.

How to decide?

This is a situation where the chairman, ie Liz, needs to take charge and be the key character in resolving the situation. However, you have a major supporting role. Agreement to any solution is needed from all parties, especially Paul, John and the institutional shareholder. Finding out what Liz, Paul and John really want will be critical. It may not be what they say.

Liz will need to determine the likelihood of recruiting someone stronger than Paul to replace him. She also must decide whether it is appropriate to undertake a proper review of the business, its prospects and its management. This could result in highlighting weaknesses in the rest of the team. It could prove necessary in any event if external capital is required to buy Paul's equity. Asking the institutional investor early on for an indication of the likelihood of raising capital might provide some useful input.

Clearly, with regard to an immediate response to Paul, you have to be brief and non-committal and, to give him comfort, he needs to be told that things will be dealt with properly and fairly.

What to decide?

Undertaking a review of the business will buy time and also introduce a measure of objectivity into the situation. However, given the description, it would seem that the likely outcome will be for Paul to go and for an external successor to be appointed. In the process a fair value for his equity will need to be arrived at and it is likely external funds will be required to fund its purchase and planned growth within the business.

You need to exercise your authority; you appear to have the respect of all concerned, which gives you pivotal influence. You may want to reinforce Liz's position and use the situation as an opportunity to send signals to John about acceptable behaviour if he is to develop. Liz and you will want to find a way for Paul to depart with dignity with a fair value for his equity. The starting point will probably be to get it valued as per the Memorandum and Articles of Association with the help of the auditors and the support of the institutional investor. The key will be whether Paul accepts the value is on a minority basis. He may of course wish to keep some of his shares in the company. Depending on how the relationships develop, this could be acceptable to the others.

If extra capital is required to fund Paul's equity then it might be worth considering raising growth capital at the same time, given Liz's plans to double the business. The extra capital could prove helpful in attracting top talent. With regard to attracting top talent, a decision will be needed over Paul's replacement's equity position. Keeping some equity by for the new person to purchase at the end of a probation period on terms and performance objectives agreed at the outset would be wise. Share options may be an alternative.

The final decision, if Paul is to be replaced externally, is to choose a search firm. You are likely to have had experience of this, so will know that it is important to organize a proper pitch, be clear about what the search firm will actually do and on what basis they will be paid. Your initial response to Paul is brief:

> ❛I can understand how you feel, Paul. I think the best thing is for me to reflect on what you have said and then have a chat with Liz. In these situations it is very important that things are done properly and fairly. I can't imagine Liz will want to do anything otherwise, either. So why don't you leave it with us for a few days and then we'll see if we can recommend a way forward?❜

How to communicate it?

The most important relationship at this point is that between Liz and you, the independent director. If you are at one then, given the respect you both appear to be held in, an amicable solution should be forthcoming. Consequently, you may decide to start by having a long chat with Liz, during which you need to face the issue of her own position.

You need to discuss the issues raised above and then recommend a course of action to the others. Before you have this discussion with Paul and John, you will most likely want to consult with the legal and accounting adviser and probably the institutional investor to ensure that any recommended process or solution is feasible. If you feel external funding will be required, this is essential.

When you make your recommendations to Paul and John, you should be entirely even-handed in their communication. To do otherwise jeopardizes the trust you have built up and endangers a solution.

In this case it will be very important that key communications are also written, ie use confirmatory letters. To communicate verbally with no record will inevitably cause problems later. To communicate solely in writing is inconsistent with amicable solutions.

What did the independent director do?

He had a long chat with Liz first. Because of their relationship, the discussion about her own role went well and indeed she raised the issue first of separating the chairmanship from the managing director role.

They both felt that it was right for Paul to go and that John probably could grow a lot further with the company if properly directed. Liz and the independent director agreed that a proper review of the business would be worthwhile. Liz quickly warmed to the idea of a properly constructed board and raising enough new money to reduce the financial stress of growth.

The review was carried out in three parts: a market, a financial and an operational review. It was felt that with it, it would be much easier to arrive at a value everyone could accept. It would also help in determining the right amount of money to raise, and it would be likely to confirm the independent director's view that there was nothing wrong with current operations, hence making it clear that the issue with Paul was to do with potential. A firm of consultants did the market and operational review and the auditors did the financial review. They were also asked to give an independent view of value calculated as per the Memorandum and Articles of Association.

While the review was being done, discussions were held with John and Paul and a good job was done of getting them to appreciate each other's strengths and positions more. Interestingly, the independent director decided that he didn't feel he was the right person to be chairman, but with their help he found a selection of possible candidates for the role. This helped considerably with fundraising. It also reinforced his position as the honest broker.

One thing which he and Liz did at the outset which helped enormously as they went through was to write a short board paper setting out what they thought the situation was, the issues, the options, the objectives of the board and a recommended process for resolving the dilemma. They also made sure that all of the directors had access to good legal advice

So how did it work out? Well, after a shaky start with John, the objectives were achieved. These were to strengthen the board, clarify the strategy and raise £5 million for the business, as well as to get Paul going on a high and receiving a good value for his shares. The extra cash for the company proved the turning point for John. Three headhunters pitched to find Paul's successor, who took six months to find and work his notice. He has worked out well, in fact so much so that he is the natural successor to Liz rather than John. The new chairman fitted in well and the company continues to prosper. The directors are currently contemplating a sale to a leading US business in their sector.

WHO WOULD HAVE THOUGHT?

Woodentop is a £30 million turnover company that is making £3 million profit pre-tax. The next few years will be much tougher, but the company is well placed in its sector and very well run. Bill Pale, the managing director and majority shareholder, is particularly impressive. His finance director Alice Evans, who holds the balance of the equity, has things very tightly under control.

Woodentop's chairman is just leaving the board meeting early in order to catch a train when Jane, Bill's secretary, asks if she can have a quiet word. She looks as if she has been crying and clearly something is up.

‘ *Yes, of course Jane. Why don't we nab Jim's office as he's away today?'*

'John, I'm not really sure I should be telling you this but I can't keep it a secret any longer.'

'I thought you'd been a bit subdued the last two visits, but I thought it must be something at home and didn't pry.'

'Well I suppose it is in a kind of a way. You see Bill and I, well, Bill and… .'

At this point Jane bursts into tears. He consoles her. She takes a moment or two to recover.

‘ *You'll never forgive me for this, but Bill and I have been having a fling for the last year.'*

'And it's this that's made you so unhappy?'

'Yes, but I'm afraid it's all got a bit messy. Bill promised to leave his wife last July and said we could live together. I even found a flat. Unfortunately Danny [her husband] found out before I could tell him. Stupid bloody estate agent! As you know, Danny's been redundant for most of this year and has been doing a great job looking after the kids while I was doing overtime to bring in more money. You can imagine how he felt. Anyway, he told me I had to move out, and who could blame him. He's let me have the kids at weekends. But Bill hadn't told his wife. He told me he couldn't possibly move out for a bit as her mother had become ill and she was going through a tricky spell.'

'Jane, I'm not sure how you want me to help.'

'Wait, it's even worse. Last week I was in the ladies and Abigail [the marketing director], that new hot shot MBA Bill hired a few months ago, was in there sobbing her heart out. You'll never believe it, but Bill had been two-timing me. Worse, she's pregnant. She was devastated. Bill told her it was her fault. Apparently he called her stupid and said she should deal with it. I

gave her some comfort, but I didn't tell her about Bill and me. She says she's going to make him pay. She's already told Sue [Bill's wife] and she's found out that Bill is sleeping with at least two other members of staff. She's going to blow the whistle tomorrow. Say's she's been up all night doing posters.

'Bill's a complete bastard and deserves all he's going to get. I just can't face another day here and even though I need the money desperately, I'm going to leave today. Who knows what Bill will say to everyone about why I've gone? You've always been so good to me, I thought you ought to know.'

All of the above has been a bit of a stunner to the chairman, who was under the misapprehension that Bill was a happily married guy devoted to his wife and children. He thinks the new marketing director, although much smarter than Bill and of obvious strength, is a bit feisty for the company.

Is this a matter for the chairman? If so, what might be an appropriate course of action for him to take?

What are the issues?

Is this a matter for the board and the chairman? This must be the first issue. For most of us it will depend on whether we feel, once we establish the facts, that Bill has committed an act of gross misconduct or that we feel his credibility and authority as managing director are undermined. Finding out the complete facts may not be that easy here. The situation is highly charged. Woodentop's chairman will also need to hear Bill's version of events. There are a lot of people in highly visible positions involved. The range of responses to this dilemma may be anything from nil to firing Bill. The chairman's own moral views may have an influence. Should they? What about the other shareholders?

There may also be the potential for sexual harassment claims, even though none appears to have been made yet. For Bill there may be other personal issues that emerge as a result of this disclosure. One interesting question asked by a lawyer friend of mine is, *'Does it make a difference if the alleged indiscretions happened on the premises?'* In the sense that this will then be a clear act of gross misconduct in most companies, it might. The company may have fired employees previously for similar conduct. Will this have an influence?

There is obviously considerable time pressure, given the plans to expose Bill the next day. Bringing some sense of order to a situation that is rapidly getting out of hand will be foremost in the chairman's mind. Urgent action seems to be required. Does the chairman need to do anything this afternoon?

Jane, Bill's secretary, doesn't want to continue a moment longer. Does the company need to do anything, or is it a personal matter? Is it a matter for the company? If it is, then what should they do?

How does the company respond to Abigail's demands? Again, does it need to?

If any compensation is to be paid to Jane or Abigail, who should pay? Does it come from the company or Bill? Whoever it is proposed, do they have the resources to pay?

What has already been circulated around the company? Whatever is decided, there needs to be careful communication quickly to avoid further damage to reputations. How these situations are handled will send a signal to the rest of the company about what is acceptable behaviour.

How to decide?

In this case a huge amount of instinctive judgement and common sense is required. The situation has emerged in a highly irrational and emotional way. Finding a decision that is palatable to all concerned may not be possible. The chairman may have had no experience of such situations. He has to decide quickly whether he will take responsibility for sorting it out. I think most chairmen under the circumstances would. If the managing director's authority is undermined then any responsible chairman will feel he must. He would also consider whether he needs to involve the finance director.

John might then try hard to establish the facts by talking to the three people involved. He may also decide he needs to speak to the other directors. In between this he may call a friend, if he has one who has been through this before. A call to the company's lawyers would be useful to make sure of the legal ground and also to seek their advice. In particular, they should be concerned to ascertain the company's position in all of this. He may decide that having a lawyer present would be helpful. He then needs to determine whether it is an issue for the company or solely an issue for Bill.

During all of this it will be important to take very good notes and to summarize the position at the end of each conversation.

If John does have time to reflect, he may be wondering about his own beliefs and prejudices. How will they influence him? He may also get an interesting reaction from his own partner.

Another factor in reaching his decision will be Bill's reaction. A contrite Bill will induce a different reaction to a *'What's all the fuss about?'* Bill. If Bill has acted as described, is he going to change? If he gets through this will he do it again? I'm no psychologist but it seems to me that if he has taken the risks he has, then he is more than likely to.

What to decide?

A quick decision is required. So what are the options?

- *Resign in disgust.* Not a terribly helpful response and somewhat irresponsible.
- *Summon Bill and tell him to sort it out.* Could be the easiest for John, but how feasible is this and is it likely to result in a fair solution?
- *Have a conversation with Bill and try and come up with a face-saving solution for him.* Loses effect on the others involved, even if he comes up with something fair. Being seen to be sorting it out with Bill may backfire in this particular situation. Moreover, does he have the time to do this anyway?
- *Let the lawyer come up with a solution.* Hint of abdication again.

■ *Get the three together and thrash out a solution that saves as much face as possible for all of them and does minimum damage to the company.* Looks like a high-risk strategy but it may just be one of those 'seize the moment' opportunities. It's high risk because it could just end up as a slanging match.

How to communicate it?

This dilemma is about as personal as it's likely to get and it's probably going to be deeply embarrassing for those involved to discuss. Consequently a calm, firm, sensitive listening style is probably the most appropriate. The ordering of conversations will be important, as will the place where John has them. The obvious order would appear to be Bill, then Abigail, then Jane again. Would it be wise to get all three of them together? A *'resolution à trois'* sounds risky.

What should he say? He obviously needs to hear the different perspectives first and establish not just the facts but the feelings. They may not all want to tell him. Partial disclosure is almost certain, making it difficult to get at what has really happened. If they disagree on the facts then there is obviously more judgement required in terms of who is to be trusted on the matter

Should he have a witness present? Views will differ on this. It makes it less likely for Bill in particular to be open, but it would bring home the seriousness of the situation and provide another interpretation of what is being said.

Given the high level of emotion around he would also be wise to hold any conversations in rooms that are private and free from interruption. A 'no windows' situation if ever there was one.

What did the chairman do?

In this case he did what probably few would do. He went for the risky option of gathering them all together. Recognizing that it really was deeply embarrassing for all involved, he adopted a paternal supportive manner:

> *Bill, I think you, Abigail, Jane and I should all have a cuppa and chat about what has been going on here.*

He clearly couldn't have done this without a position of considerable respect within the company, or without having made the judgement that Jane was telling the truth.

They joined him. He opened with:

'From what I've learnt today, it seems to me that you've all done things you probably now regret. We're all naturally fired up and emotional about the whole thing. I have a lot of respect for all of you and what I'd like to do is to help each of you get out of this mess with some form of dignity and livelihood intact. I also have a duty to try and ensure that you don't wreck the livelihoods of the whole company.'

Silence, which he took for quiet consent to continue:

'I would like to propose a solution and I would like it agreed at the end of the meeting. I have prepared a hand-written summary of it which, once we have discussed it, I would like you all to sign.'

Abigail interjected at this point somewhat aggressively:

'You can't do this. I'm not signing anything without my lawyer seeing it first.'
'I think you should wait until I've finished before you make that judgement, Abigail. No one will be forcing you to do anything. However, if you would like to leave the rest of us here, you are perfectly free to do so.'
'Carry on and we'll see,' said Abigail.

He carried on:

'As I understand it, the simple facts are that Bill and Jane have been having an affair, and during the last few months so have Abigail and Bill. Jane and Abigail feel aggrieved that you were two-timing them Bill, and they would no longer like to work here. There is no issue of any gross misconduct taking place on the premises, but you are all concerned about your reputations with your colleagues when they find out. As I also understand it, remarkably no one else is aware yet.
'Are these the facts as you all see them?'

He received three quiet affirmative responses.

'Well, we are all in agreement as to what has happened. What we're talking about is a damage limitation exercise. I can quite see how Abigail and Jane feel it would be better not to be here anymore. I also feel that it would be wrong for the company and anyone else to suffer as a result. So what I would like to propose is that Jane and Abigail tender their resignations and that Bill provides, personally, sufficient funds to enable you to survive for long enough to get another job. I am also prepared to give you both a very good reference with regard to your work here. However, I'm afraid if I am

asked why you left I would have to be honest and say that you sensibly decided to leave after entering into a personal relationship with the managing director. As to the reasons we give the rest of the company for your departures, I'd like to suggest we agree those now please.

He then proceeded to show them all his proposals, which were fair for Abigail and very generous for Jane. Remarkably, they all, including Bill, agreed.

He then asked to see Bill alone. Bill was absolutely furious:

‘How dare you humiliate me like that in front of them? You've suggested far too much. I can't possibly do that.'

'Bill, your whole credibility as managing director was at stake. To be frank, you are lucky they agreed to solve it this quietly and quickly. I think when you reflect on it overnight you'll think the settlement fair. The damage that could have been done to the company and your shareholding would have been far more.'

Bill calmed down and agreed. Abigail and Jane quickly got jobs elsewhere. People in the company found out later about Jane's real reasons for going but not Abigail's. They just assumed she'd got a better offer. So chaos was avoided.

Why did John decide to deal with the situation in this way? First, because the chaotic scene he witnessed made him convinced that if he didn't get rapid control then the company was in danger. Second, from the demeanours of Bill and Abigail in particular when they first entered the room, he knew he'd done the right thing. Had they taken a different stance he would have reverted to what he called his plan B, which was simply to make his first few statements and then ask to see them separately. Third, Alice was out of the country that day. Finally, and the main reason, it was simply what his instincts were telling him to do.

I think he was lucky; so does he!

THE FAMILY MAN

Jonathan is managing director of a family engineering company in the West Midlands. The business, JT Engineering Ltd, has been in the family for 60 years. Jonathan became MD five years ago at 34 when his father died. He had spent time outside the company qualifying as a chartered accountant with one of the big five firms. He is bright, likeable and had done moderately well with the business until last year.

Sales have remained fairly static in the last three years at around £30 million. Productivity since Jonathan took over has improved dramatically. In this year's budget meeting with the operations director it was agreed that the company had squeezed as much as it could out of the current plant and that revenue generation was the issue. Jonathan was struggling with how!

Another issue for Jonathan is the wide spread of shareholdings these days:

‘Frankly, those in the family who whinge most about low dividends and growth have shown least interest in the company. An increasing amount of time is spent explaining what we're doing to them.’

His uncle Paul is chairman but he takes no more than an 'interested guardian' role. He is very impressed by Jonathan and the resilience with which he dealt with the trauma of his father's death and assuming such an important job so young. He probably still sees Jonathan as a 30-year-old.

Jonathan has decided he needs a non-family independent director and has picked you because he thinks you'll tell him the truth and *'support me against the idiots in the family'*. He is also keen to listen and to solve the growth issue. You have been on the board a few months and until now you thought a softly, softly gradual coaching of Jonathan would be the most appropriate approach.

Events at today's Annual General Meeting have prompted you to rethink this plan. It is proving a somewhat traumatic day for Jonathan. His cousin David was particularly aggressive in questioning JT's strategy. Unfortunately, his questions were put quite personally. At first Jonathan was calm and professional if a little brief in his responses. However, this just seemed to make David even more aggressive. The final straw for Jonathan was when David said:

If you don't mind me saying so it looks as if you have run out of ideas, Jonathan. It's hard to imagine Uncle George [Jonathan's late father] would have got us into this mess. Perhaps it's time for a change.

Jonathan's response was equally personal:

Why don't you just shut up and go back to running that tin pot little accountancy practice of yours?

This had the effect of bringing David's emotional and not terribly articulate father into the debate. The situation deteriorated rapidly. Paul seems to find it difficult to interject and get control of the meeting as the insults from one side of the family are traded with the other.

You feel it is time for you to make an intervention. What do you say? What would you do following the meeting to help both the company and Jonathan?

What are the issues?

There are some obvious ones relating to Jonathan, David and Paul. With regard to Jonathan, his confidence and his capability are being questioned. How good is he? Is it simply a matter of training and coaching him? Is he really capable of driving the business forward? It isn't clear what David's position is. Does he have a significant share-holding? What influence does he have with other members of the family? Paul appears to be an ineffective chairman. Should he be replaced or stay? What about the rest of the board? Who is on it? How appropriate are they? What are their views?

The shareholders in general raise some more. Do they have a strategy for their ownership? Would they welcome one? This may matter as much as the strategy for the business. What can the family expect from the business and what can the business expect from the family?

Then there is the performance of the business. What's the reality? Is it really ex-growth or is it just ex-imagination or capability? What is the financial position? Does it have the funds to grow?

Your position as the new non-executive could be an issue. After such a short time you may not have the influence and familiarity with the business and the family politics you might need. Will not being a member of the family be a help or a hindrance? How much time will you have to do something?

How to decide?

There are some obvious facts that you will need, like a shareholder map. This is a simple chart showing who owns what and a brief state-ment of where you think they are coming from in terms of their current perspective and wishes. It may have lots of blanks in it, but is always a good starting point in a family situation. If possible, in the process of doing this make some assessment as to how likely you are to command the respect of each shareholder. It may come in handy later.

You will also find a read of the Memorandum and Articles of Association useful. It's quite possible that there may be some company-specific clauses to do with voting rights and board membership. Another document that will come in handy is your appointment letter and in particular any reference to the background and reasons for your appointment. This may be useful in clarifying any mandate required.

Do you know Jonathan well enough yet to judge whether he can solve the growth issue? If not, you will need to spend more time with him and the rest of the board. Many new non-executives use the excuse of a strategy awayday for just such a purpose, as well as helping to get to know the business better.

You need to decide how you are going to involve Paul in the decision-making process. It sounds like he'll be happy just to be consulted and fed his lines. However, it would be wise not to underestimate or offend him.

You will want to try and come up with a process that enables all shareholders to feel they have had the opportunity to express their views and that obtains as much consensus as possible. In doing this you will need to ensure the company's key advisers have been involved. They may have some useful insights. Even if they don't, you may need their reinforcement of proposals later on. Not to consult them may move them from helpful advocate to inhibitor.

Before any of the above, you will need to determine your own position and whether you want to get seriously involved or just give advice. How much spare time you have as well as how likely you think you are to command the respect of the family will influence this. These family situations can require a big time commitment and you won't get anywhere if they don't rate you.

What to decide?

This feels like a situation which could get considerably more destructive for the business and the family if someone doesn't get control of the meeting and the wider situation. It seems unlikely that the chairman, Paul, will do either. As the independent director, if you decide your role is to help the family and Jonathan overcome his current problems, then you have a clear choice. You either intervene in the meeting or wait until it is over and then act. A classic 'Let it wash or seize the moment' dilemma.

Interrupting is fairly straightforward and could be a good way of introducing yourself to shareholders you don't know. However, if you are going to do this, you need to avoid alienating David, undermining Paul or getting into an argument. The advantage of leaving it until after the meeting is that a number of people are bound to say things they regret, making it easier for you to come in as the calm objective one. Much depends on your reading of the atmosphere and the characters present.

With regard to the issues of the board, Jonathan and the growth issue. These look fairly straightforward once you have formed a view on whether Jonathan is capable of successfully growing the business with support and training. This may result in changing the planning process and reshaping the board once a new strategy has been formulated.

On the subject of differing shareholder requirements. If the majority are happy to support Jonathan with a new plan, then the others will have to be given a clear choice. Either they stay in or they allow themselves to be bought out. If the latter is necessary, then external funds may be required. The strength of Jonathan's new plan and the confidence he builds in his ability to deliver it will determine how feasible this is.

How to communicate it?

This is obviously an emotional and uncomfortable situation for the key participants. Jonathan and David are in danger of getting into a spiral of attacking and defending. The chairman is probably wondering what to do and ill at ease with the conflict. Other shareholders may feel David has a point, but might be offended by the way he is making it. Jonathan will have some loyal supporters, but will have alienated others. There will also no doubt be some who are undecided. Consequently, if you want to intervene, you must get into clear honest broker position first. You need to convey a sense of being integral to the solution, avoid taking sides and sound very fair and reasonable. You will probably want to say something to establish your authority and make it clear that you are not someone who is likely to be pushed around. You will want to keep it brief and not leave any loose ends to argue with.

How you develop your relationship with Paul and with Jonathan will be critical. If you have a successful intervention at the meeting, you should follow it up as soon as you can with a meeting with Paul and Jonathan.

There may be a few external confidants you need to strike up a good rapport with as well. Often in these situations the family lawyer or accountant will have considerable influence. You must be careful to ensure they don't feel you are usurping their role. Though quite obviously they haven't prevented the situation developing, they may be helpful in resolving it.

What did the independent director do?

He interjected with:

> *Excuse me chairman, I've been listening to the debate very carefully and I'd like to add something.'* [Silence, which he took to mean consent.]

'I have to say I share David's concerns and his frustration with the growth issue. After having been on the board a few months now, it seems clear to me that our business is a very robust one and has a number of options to grow. However, after hearing the debate this morning I am also sure that whatever route we take we will be severely constrained if the board and the shareholders are not united. Feelings are obviously running high. We mustn't let those feelings damage what has been a very successful business and what is likely to produce significant wealth for the family. I didn't know George, but I have heard a lot about him. I wonder what he would think of this morning's discussion?

'I would like to make a proposal. As the only non-family non-executive on the board, I would like to offer to support your chairman in reviewing the aspirations of each of the shareholders as well as the strategy of the business. The purpose of this would be to produce a recommendation by the board to shareholders of a clear way forward, which will enhance the value of your shares.'

Paul and Jonathan were unlikely to have difficulty with what he said. It was hard to see how David could rationally disagree. While there was unease with the situation in the company, few of the other shareholders wanted to be as aggressive as David. Although they thought he had a point, they were uncomfortable with the way he was making it. They therefore agreed. But what if David had disagreed? What would he have done then? He would have passed a note to the chairman suggesting that the meeting vote on this proposal and ask David for an alternative. As it turned out, his intervention was successful; he established his authority, took the steam out of the situation and bought sufficient time to enable a robust solution to the real issues to be developed.

Immediately following the meeting he met with Jonathan and Paul and said, 'Right, we have a mandate and a lot of work to do. Let's decide how we proceed from here'.

The first of the other shareholders he met was David, and he calmed him down by saying, 'You're absolutely right David, the board does need to move up a gear and I'm convinced it will following your intervention'. By keeping him well informed, David didn't cause any further problems.

The shareholding was widely split and there were very many different requirements. Some needed a secure source of income, others would have been very happy to realize their capital. Most didn't understand the business.

The independent director organized a strategy awayday for the board prior to which he had been to see most of the shareholders and had separate meetings with each board member. Apart from himself, two other non-family members took part in the awayday. The first was JT's marketing director, who was a very positive and imaginative individual. He had joined 18 months earlier, made a significant impact and got on well with everyone. JT's auditor was invited because of his knowledge of the business and his role as family confidant.

The awayday was split into two. First the strategy for the business and then the strategy for the shareholders. The morning was highly productive and everyone entered into it in the right spirit, except for the finance director who was a little subdued. Paul was happy to let the independent director chair the session on the basis that he was independent. During the day it became clear that the business had four significant opportunities in its market but was constrained by management's confidence. It also became clear that the finance director was a dead hand on the company. He was reluctant to invest any capital in development. Jonathan had obviously been overly influenced by him in the past. As an older cousin he had made sure the business was prudently managed during the risky period following Jonathan's father's death. However, he was locked in that mindset.

The afternoon went well. The independent director commenced proceedings by going through the shareholder map he had prepared following his one-to-one meetings. The result of this was that most shareholders were happy to support Jonathan if there was a likelihood of a growing dividend. A few wanted to sell their shareholdings. David really just wanted to shake things up and was quite happy to be unpopular for doing so. He felt most of the family would thank him in the end.

As a result of the awayday and a subsequent further analysis of the four growth options, Jonathan and the independent director produced a paper with a number of recommendations, which was approved by the board. These were:

- That the company pursue a strategy of geographical expansion, given the demand for its products in continental Europe. That a new plant be built in Spain and additional capital investment made to modernize the UK plant.
- To support this development the company will raise equity capital and increase its long-term borrowing. (The feasibility of this had been checked out before going to the board!) This capital raising would also provide the opportunity for those shareholders seeking an exit to do so at a minority valuation as prepared by the auditors. A dividend policy statement was also prepared.

- That the board be reorganized. A new finance director with international experience be appointed. The marketing director be appointed to the main board and allowed to purchase a 5% equity holding in the company. That the independent director be appointed deputy chairman with a view to succeeding Paul upon his retirement in a year's time.
- The company should fund a number of training initiatives within the company, including the board. For example, Jonathan attended the INSEAD owners–directors course with the objective of increasing his strategic awareness and knowledge of marketing. This course was also seen as helpful in enabling him to meet others in a similar position.

The company flourished and the independent director is now chairman.

BONE & SONS

Bones is a £70 million-turnover, family-owned business. It has a high reputation for its specialist engineering skills. Its products are known throughout the world, although market leadership now rests with a German competitor. The company has never made a loss throughout its history, but it has struggled in the last few years to make much more than £1 million profit.

The present MD, Jim Bone, is the grandson of the founder. His brother Joe is sales director. Both their wives are non-executive directors. Each brother holds around 20 per cent of the equity. An institution holds 35 per cent, which it acquired in the late 1960s after the autocratic son of the founder died, leaving a massive Estate Duty problem. Various family members hold the balance of the equity. They are not involved in the business on a day-to-day basis.

The institution has historically taken a 'hands-off' approach to the business, but has become increasingly concerned about performance. Jim has always sought to keep it at arm's length and it holds only ordinary shares with no special rights. The current investment executive has, however, worked hard on his relationship with the business and persuaded the executive directors that the company would benefit from the appointment of an independent chairman to help identify the way forward. The fact that Jim came under some pressure from family shareholders at the Annual General Meeting has also been of some help. It is difficult to tell how serious the discontent was, given the complicated voting rights of the different classes of shares and the heat and steam generated by a few with very little equity.

When the institution approached Simon, he was able to say that he knew the company and had dealt with them as a customer in his previous life. This helped to sell him to the Bone brothers, and he has now been in the chair for some six months.

What he found in the company was in line with his expectations. The Bone brothers, a mixed ability group aspiring to be average, had done little to develop the business or to identify where its profitable operations and markets lay. Instinctively, he feels that the company could be made much more profitable in the short term and that there is considerable scope for further development, given significant capital expenditure.

The company's finance director, a fairly recent appointment with whom Simon is quite impressed, has decided to analyse the situation and prepare a report for the brothers Bone. He has put together a well argued paper setting out a package of measures both to secure the short-term future and to go on to expand and develop the business – the latter at a cost of around £20 million. While the business has clear potential it has no cash, so any expansion will require a large element of additional equity funding.

The brothers accept that this must be the way forward and they appear persuaded that this will require a radical management shake-up. In his late 50s, Jim has already indicated that he'd like to take things easier and the proposal for (as yet unidentified) management change is also accepted. The paper is also shown to the institution, which shows some enthusiasm for the principle; it also gets into the hands of a number of family shareholders.

How would Simon deal with the following?

1. Jim Bone introduces Simon to his 28-year-old son. He is an engineering graduate who, after working for five years at a large engineering group, has recently taken an MBA. To Jim, he is the answer to the management change. Simon happens to know his former employer quite well and he tells Simon that, while the son is not without ability, he is very naïve and has a lot to learn commercially. Jim believes passionately that the current change programme, which his son is leading, will round out his experience and demonstrate to others just how good he is. Jim has told Simon he has no doubt at all that his son is the right person to be his successor.

2. Joe's wife talks to Simon after a board meeting. She tells him that Joe has never had the chance to show you his true worth, having always been in the shadow of Jim. Jim, she tells Simon, is only MD because of a cruel accident of history – the fact that he was born first. She hopes that Simon will now give him the opportunity to show what he can do as MD. She also tells him that Great Aunt Mildred, who owns an 18% stake in the business, would support his appointment (Joe was always her favourite). Simon admires her tremendous loyalty but it's rather a pity that he thinks Joe is hopeless.

3. Simon takes a phone call from Jeremy Bone, a cousin who has just under 2% of the shares. He has just lost his seat as a Member of Parliament so he is looking for something to do to exercise his talents. He tells Simon he is very well connected in the City and has

shown the paper to some of his contacts. He feels he can deliver the £20 million required for the development of the business, provided, of course, that he himself becomes chairman.

4. A very insistent and not very pleasant director of Vulture Co, an investment bank Simon has never heard of, persuades Simon to meet him. The wife of one of his colleagues is a Bone shareholder and has shown him Simon's plans. He tells Simon that what he really has is a massive problem and that what all the family shareholders want is to get out now rather than be diluted and take additional risks. He tells Simon that Vulture Co would be prepared to buy it now and suggests that Simon, as chairman, is duty bound to give shareholders the opportunity to consider this.

5. The finance director goes to see Simon. He has been talking to his old colleagues at one of the big five accountancy firms and they say that a management buy-out is the answer. He is therefore letting Simon know as a matter of courtesy that it is his intention to lead an MBO of the company. He has done so immediately after informing Jim likewise.

6. Some of the family members are so incensed by the finance director's suggestions that they have written to the chairman and asked for the FD's immediate removal.

7. The investment executive of the institution rings up and asks Simon how things are going.

What will the chairman do?

What are the issues?

There are a large number of issues in this case. The really serious ones, such as the capability of the board, the position of the business and the disunited shareholder base, are being made much more difficult by the emotions involved and numerous minor issues. We have a situation that has got out of control in a major way. Snatching at a solution is likely to be a mistake. A great deal of thought is needed before any action is taken. The situation is, however, much easier for the chairman than had he just been a non-executive director. So what are the issues?

Well, Jim is obviously a problem. He's operating like it's his company and not the family's as a whole. We know he only owns 20 per cent of the equity, but how much do his supporters have? How capable is he? He appears to be ready to hand over but hasn't prepared for succession. What's the relationship with his brother really like? How strong is his view that his son is the right successor?

Jim's son presents another issue. Is he really a capable successor? Even if he is, is this the right way for him to become the leader? The process may make it impossible for him to be successful. Does he want to anyway? It is so terribly hard to be objective about someone you love, so who is going to manage the succession process?

Joe is a problem as well. It sounds like he shouldn't be in the job he has, never mind being managing director. We don't know whether he shares his wife's feelings towards Jim or her ambition. If not, then he may not be the problem he first appears. How easy will it be to deal with his wife?

The finance director may be the only really competent member of the board and seems very frustrated. What if he goes? But has he overplayed his hand? Is his position with the family recoverable? He says he wants to lead the buy-out; is he capable of being managing director? How easy will it be for him to get funding? Which of the family members want him removed? Are they being reasonable? Even if they aren't, this needs responding to.

We then come to Jeremy: a real danger or a red herring? Much depends, obviously, on how much of the equity he and any of his supporters have and how the rest of the family and the institution see him. How good would he be as chairman? How real is the £20 million? Even if he has no real power, he could be a very disruptive influence and hamper a resolution of the company's problems.

The institution is clearly becoming frustrated. The chairman has a few communications issues to resolve with them. For example, what do they expect from him as an independent chairman, what should he tell them about what has just happened, and how involved in any resolution process should they get? What rights do they have with their 35 per cent stake? The fact they introduced Simon sounds like they might have significant influence. What is their relationship with the finance director? Would they be interested in funding the buy-out?

Can the chairman now play the honest broker? How good is his relationship with Jim and Joe? Does he have the time that will now be required to sort things out? Does he want to? How is he motivated, given that he seems not to have any equity interest in the company? On what basis was he originally appointed? How much did he know when he took the assignment? Does he need to strengthen his powers? If so, which ones and how will he achieve it? Is there any common ground upon which he can build? Would any of the proposals involve a continuing role for him?

Who actually owns the balancing 25 per cent not owned by the brothers and the institution? We don't have a clear picture of how this part equity is split. Who can make the decisions necessary? Can Simon get a sufficient block of shares together to support any plan? How well do the shareholders know what is going on? Is there a constitution for ownership? Is there a declared dividend policy?

Is there a general family confidant? Someone who has the respect of most of them and someone they will listen to? Perhaps the family lawyer? This leads us to wonder what the family's advisers have been doing. Have they been as aware of the situation as they should have been? Are the family all advised by the same people?

Then there is the business itself. What's the real performance? Has it got a strategy? If so, is it appropriate? Has it got the resources to achieve it? How vulnerable is it? Is it really invest or die? What damage is shareholder disunity doing? How capable are the management beneath the board?

In summary, a wide range of issues.

How to decide?

This certainly doesn't sound like one that can be ignored in the hope that the dilemma will go away. Sometimes you do need things to get a bit worse before you can act. In this case it's probably got there! However, Simon may make the process of coming up with a resolution easier if he can organize a cooling-down period to enable a more considered analysis of the issues to take place.

If I had to pick three things to focus on in terms of deciding, I think I would pick the board, the board and the board. Lack of an effective board has got them into this pickle. It is hard to see them getting out of the mess they are in other than through changing the board or its process. The chairman probably knew what he was getting into when he took the appointment, so we are assuming he is capable of making board change.

Although a shareholder map will be needed to determine exactly who owns what and what powers they have, the brothers, with the institution, have control. So if Simon can find a solution acceptable to them, which Great Aunt Mildred supports, he will get there. No doubt he realizes that where there is such disunity it is rare to find a solution that will keep everybody happy. He'll need to understand who will come out of it worse off and be well prepared with how to deal with it. What is fair may be tough to get at. What is in the best interests of the shareholders and the company will be driving his thinking.

Separating the facts from opinions, particularly in terms of the capabilities of the Bones, will be vital. Backing up his own judgements with supporting evidence as well as the views of others is essential. Whether Simon can now play the honest broker is not clear, nor is it clear what power he really has. These are key factors in how he decides to tackle the situation.

If he can establish what might be a sensible strategy for the owners first, then he is more likely to build support. As there appears to be no family constitution, this will have to be done by speaking to people, canvassing their views and their objectives for their shareholding. A careful inspection of the Memorandum and Articles of Association as well as the investment agreement with the institution will be done beforehand. Particular care will be needed in the matter of different rights for different classes of shares.

Simon will have to form an early view as to whether he can organize a resolution himself or whether he needs some form of external catalyst. As chairman he should. He will probably already know the family lawyer; if he has a strong relationship with him, they may be able to decide a lot together. If not, or if the lawyer is linked to one side in particular, then he may need to consider a new independent adviser to advise the company.

A finance director would normally be a key player in resolving a situation like this. The chairman now needs to decide whether to allow him to make a buy-out bid, in which case he can't be involved in assessing other proposals. Can he continue to work at the company? Should he resign in order to make his bid? Whatever the chairman decides, he needs to make it clear at the outset to the finance director and those who are pressing for his removal. If he is going to support him in staying, this will need doing with strong conviction. It will, however, become even more complicated if the finance director proposes that Simon is chairman of the buy-out.

What to decide?

Simon's first decision is to be clear about who he feels he is working for and how involved he wants to get. Then in order to be able to work through the board, he needs to organize a board meeting. He must also allow the board to consider the various options proposed. Yet how can they consider them properly without a clear understanding of the owners' objectives? This is what will give the chairman the real excuse for a cooling-off period in which to consult the shareholders individually. He must buy time and move the decision making to a rational plain. In order to do this he may have to use the simple mantra, *'Let's not destroy the good name of the family or the business'* as his unifying common purpose.

He will need to speak to the finance director to gauge how serious he is about a buy-out and how feasible it is. If it looks like a non-starter but the finance director is as competent in his role as suggested, the chairman will need to find a way of defusing the pressure for his removal.

He could instruct the company's key adviser in undertaking a formal review of shareholder objectives, the position of the business and the options proposed and possible. He will obviously need to decide who he is going to speak to directly. It sounds as if there aren't too many shareholders. He may therefore decide to speak to them all himself. This might be not just for hearing what they think firsthand, but so that they feel more involved and taken more seriously.

Having bought time and analysed the situation, the solution should emerge, whether it is one of the current proposals or not. He then needs to decide which option to put his authority behind. Some of the solutions may involve him more intensely than others. Some, because he feels strongly that they are not in the best interests of the company, may make him consider resigning.

How to communicate it?

If the chairman is adopting the independent arbiter role he will need to be extremely cautious and probably quite formal in his style and tone. Casual remarks can easily come back to haunt you in these situations. He will need to ensure he appears to treat Jim and Joe with equal respect, not appear too close to the finance director and also show Great Aunt Mildred considerable respect. The ordering of communications shouldn't be too difficult. The key players appear to be Jim, Joe, Great Aunt Mildred and the institution. He will need to take careful notes at each point.

What did the chairman do?

The person who was chairman in this case was a man of considerable presence who was very well respected in the city where the company was based. He had sold out of his own company a few years earlier and had one other appointment locally, as well as being on the board of a small public company. Jim was somewhat in awe of him and had become more and more insecure as the chairman got to know the business. Joe enjoyed the increased pressure that Jim had been under but didn't welcome the same feeling himself. The institution regarded the chairman highly, having made a considerable sum through backing him before. It was happy to trust his judgement but wanted things to be done properly. It was more than fed up with Jim and Joe, but rated the finance director highly and had been impressed by what he had achieved at the company. As for the chairman himself, he relished a challenge and thought it would be great fun to sort out Bone & Sons.

The company's advisers were not that useful. The lawyer really acted for Jim and his side of the family and had not been particularly friendly to Joe, his wife or Jeremy. The accountants had shown no interest beyond doing the audit each year, and the audit partner was not someone to express an opinion knowingly.

The finance director was determined about his buy-out and the chairman and the corporate finance advisers felt he would gain financial support to do it. He had some interesting ideas to grow the company free from the constraints of the family, which included scenarios involving a lot less than £20 million.

Jeremy was generally despised but also feared. A personal litigation lawyer by background, he had no business experience to talk of, but always knew the right thing to say and was highly devious.

Given this situation the chairman decided to exercise the authority of his position and the respect in which he was held. He had reviewed the formal documents carefully before taking his appointment in the beginning, so knew that all he had to do was to get the two brothers to agree and he had a solution. He took the view that Joe would be happy if he had sufficient funds to leave his wife and Jim would be happy to play golf. Neither Jeremy nor Vulture Co had any real substance behind them, but it would be important to give their approach very careful consideration before rejecting it.

So what did he actually do? First, he convened a board meeting with one item on the agenda: consideration of the various proposals that had been put to the company. At the meeting he explained that due to the composition of the board, the nature of the specific proposals, and the absence of a clear strategy for the business or its ownership, it would not be possible for them to vote on any of them. No one disagreed. Prior to the meeting he had agreed with the finance director and the Bone brothers that if the finance director wanted to pursue the possibility of a buy-out, he should be allowed to do so. However, if he were to do so he would have to resign from the board. The finance director was happy with this. He saw it as an all-or-nothing opportunity and was convinced it was the right thing for everyone.

The chairman then proposed that a formal review be undertaken by an independent corporate finance adviser who was acceptable to the brothers and the institution. The scope of their work would be to review shareholder aspirations, the position of the business in its market, the strategy, capital investment requirements and funding options, and then review the proposals that had been suggested, including the buy-out. He made it clear that if one of their recommendations was a sale of the business, they would not get the mandate for this sale. He did this to ensure an impartial approach. He then proposed three firms to do the work, which he felt the institution would be comfortable with. He proposed that each of them come in and make a presentation to the board. They agreed this as well and didn't propose any other firms.

He suggested that the board approve a budget for the work and a time scale of eight weeks. Costs should be met by the company. If the brothers agreed then he would seek the institution's consent before informing shareholders that the exercise was taking place and that they should expect a call. So he got his eight-week cooling-off period.

The three firms pitched. All would have done a good job. Jim and Joe had a strong but different preference, so the third was picked as a compromise. This is why the chairman picked three, not two. A consultative process was agreed as well as commitment to the decision that the status quo was no longer tenable and that the board would make one recommendation to shareholders following the review.

The firm chosen did an excellent job. All the shareholders were canvassed and they produced an insightful review of the company's position, its likely value and its outlook. They found that, of the family shareholders, only Great Aunt Mildred felt passionately about the business remaining in family hands. It was clear that neither Jim nor Joe had a strong desire for a fight or to develop the business. Life was all getting a bit complicated for them. However, all of the family, with the exception of Mildred again, were deeply concerned about how much the company was worth. Most of them would be quite happy to realize their shareholdings if they received a sufficiently big sum. None of them had any appetite for putting any more money in or increasing the risk profile. The institution saw considerable potential in the business but only with a much stronger management team. They didn't want to sell out yet as they felt they would realize much more if the company could be developed.

So the advisers reviewed the various options for giving those shareholders who would be happy to sell the chance to do so. They felt that the two best options were a management buy-out or an outright sale. Great Aunt Mildred then became pivotal for a few weeks. At first she had been seriously opposed to the idea of a buy-out and deeply suspicious of the finance director. However, when Joe told her that he didn't really want to be the managing director, her thoughts turned to the family's reputation. She was torn between feeling that a sale was a failure for the family and the risk that the finance director would get the company on the cheap. In the end it was Joe who persuaded her that by letting the finance director bid against a trade buyer he would have to pay a full price.

At this point the institution became the key player. It was keener on the management buy-out, even to the extent of organizing an institutional purchase of the business and syndicating a part of its shareholding. This made the family worry that the institution, which had introduced the chairman, might be taking advantage of them. This was only softened by the fact that it offered 5 per cent more than the trade buyer and allowed Mildred to keep a 5 per cent stake. She thought it was bound to sell the business within 10 years and wanted a share in the upside.

The buy-out took place and the chairman was re-appointed chairman. Mildred ended up being delighted. Her 5 per cent became worth considerably more than her original 18 per cent. The Bone brothers are happily playing golf, though not with each other. Joe has left his wife and she now runs a successful small business, which she bought with the proceeds of the settlement.

THE BID CONFLICT

Snazzyco is a £40 million turnover specialist engineering company. The team who run it are a lively bunch who have exceeded their own and everyone else's expectations. They have received a number of approaches in recent months to buy the company. The industry has entered a period of consolidation and globalization driven by the demands of customers to enter into global supply arrangements. The chairman of Snazzyco has persuaded the board not to deal with approaches in an opportunistic way but to arrange a formal marketing of the business to enable all concerned to realize the most for their shareholdings.

The chairman is delighted at the interest that's been shown by trade purchasers since the sales memorandum was issued. Frankly, he was sceptical of the initial price estimates but there seems to be tremendous demand for the company and the auction is going really well. One slight concern is that he thinks management's forecast are a bit optimistic, but he is down to the last two and the time has come to decide which offer to go for.

Snazzyco is owned 60 per cent by a group of institutions and 40 per cent by the directors. The directors got their stakes through a management buy-out eight years ago. The chairman has a 2 per cent stake for which he paid £15,000 – one of his better investments. The relationship with the institutions is very good. Snazzyco has been an excellent investment for them and no relationship issues have emerged throughout the time since the MBO. Following the promotion of the guy from the lead institution that did the original deal, there has recently been a change of relationship director. The new woman seems sensible and ambitious. Both the team and the institutions believe now is a sensible time to sell, given the industry's consolidation internationally.

Offer one is from USINC, which wants to fit Snazzyco into its global network. Despite its sales pitch, the chairman doesn't think it wants to keep the directors beyond a decent handover. Its offer is a very straightforward £42 million, all cash. It is a multibillion-dollar business and Snazzyco will fill a gap in the strategic plan for Europe.

Offer two is from a UK plc, Smallcapco, which is about twice the size of Snazzyco. It is keen to keep some of the directors. Indeed it has even asked the chairman if he would be interested in joining its main board.

He suspects that the reason it is keen for such continuity is that it seems a bit stretched itself. Snazzyco is a perfect fit but would test its management, given recent other acquisitions. The financing is also a stretch. Its balance sheet looks a bit tight, even at the £40 million it has offered. This is why it has structured its offer for the retiring Snazzyco directors to take cash and the continuing ones paper. £10 million of its offer is in shares. Management warranties are much lighter than USINC's. The chairman of the UK plc has asked Snazzyco's chairman for lunch in a few days time.

Management, and particularly the managing director, prefers the UK plc's bid. He and the two who want to stay are only in their 40s and highly ambitious. They think they'll end up running Smallcapco before too long. They also think the UK bid will be better for employees and customers. If they stay they'll be issued with some new options. The chairman of Smallcapco has apparently also recommended that Snazzyco's chairman stay on and be given a substantial increase in emoluments to reflect a plc appointment. He feels the offer is far more than generous.

Before the lunch with the Smallcapco chairman, Snazzyco's chairman thought he'd have a chat with the lead investor.

What should he do?

What are the issues?

Foremost in the chairman's mind will be his own position. He will need to be clear about where his responsibilities lie. He will also need to have a good understanding of the different groups, what is in their best interests and what he thinks they really want. His primary responsibility is to the shareholders as a whole. Understanding what the institutions want is likely to be straightforward. Management may well want something different from the institutions and different from each other. How is the equity split between management and will this have an influence?

Does he feel like there has been an attempt to bribe him? Has there been? Is the increase above what would be commensurate with the new position? Bribery is often difficult to prove. What does he say to the institutions and management about it? What inducements are being offered to the management who are staying?

How will the board properly compare the two separate offers? Normally it would be on the basis of value, the form of the offer, the confidence in it being delivered, the process, the warranties and indemnities involved and the likely consequences of the sale for the business and its staff. Issues like *'Will the Americans salami the deal?'* will also need to be considered. They may have a superb reputation for standing by early offers or they may always cut the price at the last minute.

His feeling that management's forecasts are a bit optimistic will need to be reviewed. Late discovery of a significant difference could obviously result in a price reduction. Lack of disclosure, if significant, could result in a subsequent claim under the warranties. Is there the possibility of compensating good news?

The chairman's own stake will be worth in the order of £800,000, a significant sum. Will this influence his thinking? A sale will be good for his reputation. The alternative offers may be more or less favourable for him.

This ought to be a *'Heads you win, tails you don't lose'* situation. However, if the sale process is aborted, what are the costs and will the result be a disunited board? Any business going through a sale process will lose momentum unless there is significant effort put into avoiding distraction.

How to decide?

Will he let what he sees as an attempted bribe influence him or will he just ignore it? His decision on this will affect how he and therefore the board rank the bids. The criteria listed above can be used to try and do it objectively, but no matter how hard they try, emotions will have a strong influence over the decision. Should he seek the views of the institutions before the management or vice versa, or should he try and do it as one meeting? This could easily affect the outcome. He will also need to separate strong preferences from fixed positions. For example, what will really be the management's reaction to USINC?

Someone will need to do detailed due diligence on the two potential acquirers and the results of this might change views on deliverability.

What to decide?

The USINC offer looks the obvious one to take from a shareholder point of view, but could it be improved? They could try to get the price up and increase the difference between the offers. They could attempt to reduce restrictive covenants, the warranties and indemnities and improve the offer from USINC in other ways. In deciding this it will be important to present a unified Snazzyco front. So, the chairman needs to decide how to carry the management with him. He might decide that he doesn't need all of the management to be in agreement. Deciding whether and how he might gain the MD's commitment first will be key.

Having checked the agreements he will be clear as to whether management have a veto even if the institutions have control. While they won't feel comfortable selling against management's wishes, they will have a duty to maximize value to their own shareholders and investors. Does he tell the institutions that the UK plc tried to buy him off?

How to communicate it?

The institutions will be straightforward to communicate with as long as it's clear how they want to be involved. Most institutions will feel this is where they have a considerable amount to offer. Particularly where there is institutional control, they will want to get involved in detailed negotiations. Tensions may arise during the rituals of negotiations and people assume different roles. Their relationship with management will have a strong influence. He may need to be the bridge if it becomes stressed. When he communicates he will need to be conscious of declaring his own views and the impressions that this gives. This is definitely a case for a simple mantra along the lines of:

‹ *This is heads we win, tails we don't lose. Our primary objective is to maximize returns for shareholders.* ›

How does he communicate with the managing director if he really is committed to the UK plc offer and strongly opposed to USINC? A lot depends on their past relationship. Should he try and win him over or simply take a more formal approach and tell him that, *'While I appreciate your concerns, this is in the best interests of shareholders'*?

The chairman also needs to think about how communications are managed with all of the other interested parties involved through the bidding process and at the time of the actual sale. For employees in particular this is a very tense time. Motivation is a challenge if people gain nothing from the sale and may lose their jobs.

What did the chairman do?

He pretty much followed the path above in terms of trying to move the consideration of the offers onto as rational a basis as possible. However, he had a couple of problems with this approach. The managing director really was determined to do the UK plc deal, even though the due diligence on them made everyone else even less comfortable with them. Essentially, he withdrew his co-operation from anything involving USINC, wouldn't meet with them and so on. In the process he ruined his relationship with the institutions, the chairman and the rest of the team, who couldn't understand why he was acting the way he was. The chairman made numerous valiant attempts to win him over. All to no avail.

The managing director's approach increased the resolve of the chairman and the institutions to sell to USINC. The chairman had to get a lot more involved in the detail than he would have hoped. However, the company was successfully sold to USINC and for £1 million higher than their initial offer.

The chairman subsequently learnt that the managing director had been promised by the chairman of the UK plc that if the deal went ahead he would fire the UK plc's existing chief executive and appoint him.

CHALLENGE PLC

Challenge is a broadly based manufacturing plc capitalized at £90 million, which had a turbulent 1990s, to say the least. Put together in the late 1980s, the group nearly collapsed at the beginning of the 90s, weighed down by debt and poor acquisitions. Fortunately, chairman Eric Gruff was brought in to save the group in 1992. Eric is essentially an 'up and at 'em' operationally oriented chap. His simply delivered autocratic clarity is ideal for sorting out messes but can be a bit stifling for more enlightened or ambitious managers. There have been two chief executives since Eric, who is now 70, stepped back to three days a week, three years ago.

Eric told the board at that time that he planned to retire as soon as the newly recruited chief executive was settled in. This was just after Charles joined the board as a non-executive. His remit on joining was to support Eric in building a stronger board and to be Eric's successor as chairman. At the time his instinct as a new boy on the board was to go along with the consensus, despite some misgivings. While Eric's failings were fairly obvious, he commanded the unanimous respect of the board and their key advisers. Sadly, the performance of the business has been lacklustre ever since Charles' appointment. The wide spread of institutional shareholders, who between them account for around 80 per cent of the shares, have a low knowledge of the business.

Without prior discussion, Charles is called to an extraordinary meeting of the directors. Eric has left a message on his ansaphone:

> *Charles, it is absolutely essential you make the meeting for tomorrow afternoon. I really need you there. I've decided to fire Jack [the CEO]. The rest of the executive directors are in agreement. We've simply lost confidence in him and his latest growth plan's a joke. I know this is a bit short notice, but I think you have appreciated for some time that I've been a bit unhappy. Of course it makes a right mess of my retirement plan, but needs must. If we don't get to speak before the meeting, the item I have down for you on the agenda is communication with the City. I'm sure I can rely on you.*

Charles manages to retain his composure and decides to have dinner before calling Eric.

He is just tucking into his meal and the phone rings again. He naturally expects it to be Eric from Challenge plc. *'Thank God! I must get a few things clear with him,'* Charles mutters just before picking up the phone.

‹ *Charles, hello, it's Jack. Thank goodness you're in. I can't tell you how angry I am.* ›

He decides to do the obvious and let dinner cool.

‹ *What's up?*'

'*Come on you know, I'm not that stupid. Apparently Eric has called an extraordinary meeting of the directors for tomorrow afternoon without me. It's obvious isn't it? I'm going to get fired. I'll be the third scapegoat in a row. I can tell you, Charles, I'm not going to take this lying down. I can't believe you would do this to me. I'd like to come over and see you tonight. I've got an alternative proposal I'd like to discuss. It will only work with your support.* ›

What should Charles do now?

What are the issues?

This is a classic potential tailspin situation. There are many issues and a high degree of logistical challenge.

The most immediate issue is how to respond to Jack. What should the non-executive say on the phone? Should he agree to a meeting? If he does, on what basis and should anyone else be there? Jack's statement that Eric has *'apparently'* convened an extraordinary meeting implies that Jack has not been invited to attend. This is at odds with Eric's message, unless Eric simply hasn't called Jack yet.

Eric is now a serious liability and not using his board. What is the non-executive's influence over him? There is a disparate shareholder base who appear to have given up on the company. Apathy can make resolution tricky no matter how much a solution is in the shareholders' best interests. Is Eric's assertion that *'the rest of the executive directors are in agreement'* true? Eric is used to getting his own way; who does he listen to? What is Eric's proposal for replacing Jack? Another obvious but potential practical issue is, how to contact Eric?

Board process and corporate governance are major issues for Challenge. It is not clear who is on the board. If Eric does have the support of the other directors, even if it is unjust, there seems little the non-executive can do. Even if Eric is right that Jack should go, the issue of Eric's conduct remains.

The non-executive has a number of personal issues to address. He is likely to be feeling angry at being put in this position and this may be the final straw for him. How involved does he want to get? What power does he have to do anything? He may be concerned about the risk to his reputation. Is the risk made greater by resigning or staying? What motivation other than protecting his reputation does he have? What is his view of Jack, Eric and the other executive directors? How confident is he of influencing them individually? What is his relationship like with the company's key advisers?

Where are the company's advisers coming from? How close are they to Eric and Jack? What have they been advising up to this point? Was it one of them that introduced him to Challenge? Will this have any bearing?

There are then some other issues to do with the business itself. Why has it under-performed? Should it really be a listed company? And so on.

How to decide?

He has to deal with Jack first. His view of Jack will determine this. If he hasn't got one, a meeting might help. Given Eric's behaviour he may well feel he should meet him. However, he may want to elicit from Jack what it is he wants to discuss. At this stage, disclosing Eric's call sounds risky, but depending on his view of Jack he may decide to do this anyway. He gives a non-committal response:

> '*Obviously you feel very strongly about this, Jack. I don't know what is happening but naturally I'd be very happy to talk to you.*'

What will be the consequences of declining the meeting with Jack? Probably that Jack will assume he supports Eric. By declining, Charles also loses the opportunity to get additional information.

He could accept the meeting but make it early the following morning to buy more time. The downside of this is that there will then be less time between seeing Jack and the board meeting if anything needs to be done.

As he is having the conversation, he will no doubt be considering his own position and may well have decided how involved he wants to get and why. When he puts down the phone, what should he do next? There may be things he wants to do – consult his lawyer, speak to Eric – which aren't possible because he might not have home numbers and so on.

He has to get his own position clear first. If he wants to try and sort it out he needs to know more than his own legal position. He will have to determine what support he can gather. Does he know the key advisers? Could he enlist their support as well as their guidance?

If he decides that Eric should go, is he happy to take on the chairman's role? If so, does he have the time and is that what he wants to do? If not, how is he proposing Eric be replaced? Having a proposal in such circumstances strengthens the argument for replacing him.

A judgement on Jack and knowing whether he has the power to do anything with or without him seem the crucial points.

What to decide?

He could just go along with it, not disclose anything to Jack, and let Eric have his way. The totally ineffective, token non-executive director might do just that. However, most non-executives would consider a more vigorous approach.

He could just resign in disgust. If he chooses to do this, how will he manage the reputational issues both for himself and the company?

He could ally himself with Jack and use whatever levers he has to persuade Eric to go. Painting a picture of *'wonderful career ends in tears'* versus *'honourable way out'* is only likely to work if the implicit threat is real.

He could remove Eric, let Jack go and then recruit a new managing director with a view to a 'sort and sell' unless Jack can come up with a credible vision and plan for the future. Who would be interested in taking the job, given the history? How would they be motivated financially?

How to communicate it?

Jack and Eric will be highly charged. For both, this is an emotional moment. Their reputations are at stake. Eric may or may not respond well to the direct, blunt approach he favours for dealing with others. He will probably respond well to flattery. It will be difficult getting him to face reality. Perhaps leading him to realize the danger to his own credibility may be the result, though. He will not like having any conversation about this in front of others. Do you know someone he really respects and listens to? Is there a role for them?

For most of the alternative decisions Charles could make on this one, he will need to communicate with the company's lead advisers. If they don't know him, then getting their respect first is the most important thing to do.

Jack may be the hardest to deal with. Supportive noises but no commitment to him will put Charles firmly in the Eric camp, and he will expect great commitment. Charles needs to be very careful in his choice of words and not over-inflate Jack's expectations.

This is definitely a case for careful notes.

What did Charles do?

The shareholding meant that there was no one he could turn to to decide, which in some ways was helpful. He hadn't made his mind up about Jack before this. It was early days; it was obviously a disunited team; Jack performed well in meetings but the company wasn't doing well.

He decided to meet Jack but did not disclose the call from Eric. Jack told him about several occasions when Eric had undermined him. Part of this was because Jack felt that the other executive directors should all be replaced. As Eric had recruited them, he took this as personal criticism. Eric had shared Jack's views of the other directors with them. Jack feels very strongly that he was misled on taking his appointment as he was told by the head-hunter and by Eric that Eric's retirement was imminent.

Jack's description of the circumstances came over as balanced despite the strong emotion of his delivery. Charles was convinced that he should not be dismissed. He then asked Jack what his proposal was. In summary, Jack had a somewhat complicated proposal in which Eric and the executive directors were removed, Charles became chairman and Jack led a public-to-private buy-out.

Charles decided that trying to resolve this situation completely on his own would be a mistake. He thought about what help he could enlist. The only people he could think of were the company's advisers and Jack. By acting together, perhaps there was a small chance they might be able to resolve the crisis. He didn't know how the advisers would view a proposal to remove Eric. So, he decided that he would try and meet the company's key advisers in the morning. Fortunately he had his own lawyer's phone number and so was able to speak to him that night.

The advisers included the brokers, lawyers and the public relations company. He told Jack that while he did not support the idea of the buy-out in the current circumstances, he agreed with him that Eric should be replaced. At this stage he had an open mind about the other executive directors. He told Jack that they would meet with the key advisers in the morning and propose that he replace Eric as chairman and that Jack should continue as chief executive. The positions of the other executive directors would be decided as a result of interviews with the new chairman. He also told Jack that the only way they stood any chance of persuading the advisers to support them was if he had as clear an articulation of Eric's misdemeanours as possible.

At the meeting of the advisers he laid out the situation and described the phone call he had had from Eric and the meeting with Jack. He explained that the only way to persuade Eric was for the company's key advisers, himself and Jack to unite. What he meant by this was for them all to agree to resign themselves if Eric resisted their proposals. While the advisers were very resistant to this at the start of the meeting, when he laid out the evidence and the alternative of supporting Eric and his own very public resignation *'over corporate governance issues'*, they agreed.

The next thing was how to tell Eric. The advisers decided that Charles should do it. He was perfectly happy as long as he had letters from each of them saying they would resign if Eric continued as chairman. They wriggled a bit but finally agreed. They reviewed Eric's contract and agreed that they would pay out the remaining two years in full. Jack was not happy with this, believing that this was over-generous in the circumstances. They all agreed, but felt that this would be the best way of ensuring Eric's departure.

Charles then called Eric and arranged to see him alone before the board meeting. Eric said, *'Great idea Charles, see you in half an hour'*.

When Charles and Eric sat down, Charles told him that he had a very serious matter to discuss. Eric was not a man to beat about the bush himself, so Charles got to the point as quickly as he could. He told Eric that he had lost the confidence of the key advisers and himself. It would be a shame after all Eric had achieved in his business career, and for Challenge, if it all ended in ignominy. *'Well, it won't,'* interrupted Eric. *'We can sort this out without you.'* Charles asked Eric if he could continue with a proposal, which he felt would result in an honourable way out. Ever pragmatic, Eric let him finish. When Eric heard what was proposed and that the advisers and Charles were prepared to resign so publicly, he became very annoyed. Charles managed to calm him down and get him to think about the proposal. After all, he could retire with dignity, no one need know about the events of the last few days, most people would assume he had decided to take it easier, and he'd be well rewarded despite the company's performance. But most of all he and his family would avoid the terrible embarrassment resulting from the press coverage. Moreover, if he accepted the proposal they would issue a 'fairly gushy' press release.

Eric said he needed time to think about what had been said and that he would speak to his lawyer. Charles said, *'Fine, but I think we need an answer today and before the board meeting.'* *'Don't worry,'* said Eric, *'it won't take me that long to come up with something better.'* Charles moved to a neighbouring office and waited. An hour later after Eric had made some calls and spoken to each of the executive directors other than Jack. He called Charles in and said:

> *Alright, I'll let you have it, but I want a bigger settlement than two years. I want my car thrown in and a one-off payment to my pension fund of £100,000.*

Charles was so amazed that he had agreed that he said:

> *I have to say, Eric, I have always admired your pragmatism and your ability to get yourself out of a hole. You can have the car, but £100,000 is too much. I'm sure £50,000 would be more appropriate.*

They agreed at £60,000. Charles managed to hide his disgust that Eric was so clearly abusing the company. He was delighted to have got Eric's commitment to go, but also conscious of the huge job that lay before him. Jack couldn't believe it, and this enabled Charles to exercise major influence over him. Only one of the executive directors remained. The company's fortunes have been restored, although it will never be a high flyer. Because of this, a trade sale is being contemplated.

ANOTHER FINE MESS, STANLEY

Nine months ago John was asked by Stanley Star, who was with a bank in Bristol, to consider taking the chairmanship of a struggling start-up business. The company was two years old and although it had run out of cash, was getting rave pre-launch reviews from potential customers for its new electronic telecommunications product. The bank's view was that while to a certain extent it was simply a matter of time before prospects turned into sales, financial management hadn't been as tight as it could be. Moreover, although the general marketing had been excellent, sales conversion hadn't.

John is a natural galvanizer. His name and reputation have been made through a highly successful start-up in a related sector with a similar customer profile. He liked the product, knows the market and was quite excited at the prospect. One snag is that he lives 200 miles away in Derbyshire. He got involved through the recommendation of his own bank manager. Nevertheless, after a couple of meetings, some digging around, a further £150,000 investment from the bank's equity finance arm and a chance to invest £50,000 for 15 per cent of the equity, John decided to go for it. He'd not had a failure yet, even though his own start-up came fairly close in its early stages.

Unfortunately, sales still haven't really come through. The customers, all major corporates, seem to be either having problems in Asia or going through internal reorganizations which are delaying decisions. John reckons the managing director, although not really that strong, is OK. He replaced the finance director with a part-time 'wise owl type' who is doing a much better job. There are still very positive potential customer references. However, cash has run out again despite John and the managing director not drawing a salary. They will be trading while insolvent if new money isn't found by next week. John is now very anxious, but on balance will put some more cash and time in to make it a success. He thinks it needs another £200,000.

Stanley has been promoted to go and run the Bank's Corporate Lending team in Edinburgh and the new guy, James Young, seems another very sensible chap. He is, however, new to the bank, which makes John a bit anxious. He's only been on the case for three months but has attended two board meetings as an observer. John decides to go and see him to discuss further funding:

'Hi James, how are you settling in?'

'Er, very well thanks. We've got a house sorted out and the job's been great so far. John, I'm afraid this isn't going to be a very easy meeting for me.'

'What do you mean?'

'Well, it seems obvious from the file and from the two meetings I've been to that you're doing a great job in very difficult circumstances. I've been amazed at your commitment.'

'Well, I've tried my best. My reputation matters a great deal. You can't just walk away.'

'That's the problem, John. I'm afraid we won't be able to provide more cash. I thought I ought not to beat about the bush.'

'But hold on a minute. You haven't heard my plan and I'm putting in some more.'

'That won't make a difference, John. I just don't believe it's going to make it. I realize how upsetting this must be for you. But we have to face reality.'

What next?

What are the issues?

There are not too many issues in this dilemma, just some very hard ones. Namely, that the company will fail if John doesn't do anything. His record and reputation are at stake. His judgement is called into question. He will be doing some soul searching. Then there is the potential financial loss. How significant is that £50,000 investment?

Is the sales position simply weak management or are there more fundamental problems? Will the company really be trading while insolvent next week? Has absolutely every option to reduce cash outflow or generate cash inflow been explored? Is the bank right that it's time to accept reality? What's the banker doing attending board meetings? Does the bank really think John has done a good job? What's the relationship going to be like with the bank after this?

When the banker says he is not prepared to provide more cash, it sounds like he is not calling in the existing facility. This little detail is well worth checking.

If John decides the company is worth saving and is prepared to put more money in, will he need to find a new bank? If he gets over the short-term difficulty, will the business be capable of real growth, or is it a trap?

How to decide?

The single most important judgement here is whether John thinks the company is worth rescuing. If he does, then the other matters to attend to, though not easy, are more straightforward. So, is it good enough to put more in or is this a case of good money after bad? To find out he will need to focus on the market opportunity and the capability of the company to seize it. Fundamentally, is the upside worth the extra financial and reputational risk? Time is likely to be of the essence and he will need to move very quickly. A reliable business friend's view may be helpful. It doesn't seem that there is time for an in-depth review, that is unless John decides to fund the company while this is being done. Revisiting any prior research and testing the original assumptions will be helpful.

John needs to consult a lawyer immediately to ensure he understands the legal consequences of the various options. He shouldn't ask the lawyer whether he should put more money in. If he or one of his colleagues isn't an insolvency expert, John will need to find one.

Trying to get a new bank will be hard. Sounds like he only knows one and he will probably have to match their funding.

What to decide?

John could face reality, cut his losses, agree with the banker and get a letter from him saying what a wonderful job John's done in very difficult circumstances. If they really think he's done a good job, the personal downside of quitting now is limited to wounded pride, a feeling of letting the employees down and of course the £50,000. If this option is chosen quickly, the overall damage might be less than a slow, drawn out death. What John needs to ensure if he takes this option is minimum damage to all concerned – employees, suppliers, customers and key advisers. One important part of this is minimizing the costs of closing the company, particularly with regard to professional fees and asset sales.

Funding it himself for a fixed period to prove sales is an option. John could try to sell the business, but this is obviously from a position of considerable weakness. Extra care will be needed to avoid the stalkers – those potential buyers who string you along, gathering all the information they can so that when you fail they can move in more quickly.

At the end of the day this one's a judgement call. There is little new information that will affect the decision.

How to communicate it?

If John decides to fund it himself, then a vigorous, enthusiastic approach that inspires confidence is necessary. Any half-hearted signals of a *'Well, we'll see how it goes'* nature will increase the chances of subsequent failure.

Choosing the 'call it a day' option calls for a different style. In this circumstance, a reasonable and calm professional approach combined with energy that shows John is trying his best to minimize the losses and pain for all concerned will have a big impact. Many people just walk away and give up and lose enormous respect in the process. At 3i we have made a lot of money from backing people who handled failure well the first time.

How John communicates with the bank is vital. Indignation will not be a helpful response, even if it is justified. An *'Oh yes it is'*, *'Oh no it isn't'* conversation over whether the bank should be more supportive will be a disaster.

Careful notes will need to be taken and regular contact with his lawyer vital. We're assuming that the company hasn't been trading while insolvent up to this point. Is John sure it will be next week?

This is bound to be a depressing time and he is unlikely to be a barrel of laughs at home or socially, so he needs to be aware of the effect on those not involved in the crisis. He also needs to put this setback in the context of his track record and not let it assume greater significance than it deserves.

What did he do?

He was extremely angry with James. He couldn't believe that he wouldn't listen to his plans. He didn't really know James, but was sure that talking further to him was pointless. So he asked James if he minded if he called Stan. James's response was:

> *Not at all. I spoke to him yesterday to let him know that this was the decision I had come to. Stan is in complete agreement with me. He asked me to pass on his regards.*

He asked James under what circumstances he would be prepared to put more money up. James was clear, if not helpful: *'None. I just don't believe the company is a viable proposition'*. This response made John pause for thought, and he told James that there was no point continuing the conversation. He would consider alternatives and speak to him as soon as he had something to report.

Following the meeting with James, he immediately called his accountant and his lawyer and asked if they could meet later that day for him to seek their counsel, and also if they could exert any influence on James. Unfortunately, they didn't know him either. Their advice was simple, and that was to ask him how much money he thought it really needed and then how profitable he thought it would be if he managed to save it. The lawyer then spent some time taking him through the consequences of trading while insolvent. Their view was that he should quit while the loss was small and that it wasn't worth putting in more money.

Although he respected the pair of them, John was determined to see if he could save the business. He still believed in its future even though he recognized at best it would become a *'nice little earner'* rather than a significant business. However, he felt that it was well worth another £50,000 to avoid the horrible embarrassment and feeling of failure of the company going under. He reckoned £50,000 was enough to improve sales, get the company stable and then put it in a position to be sold.

He was wrong. The £50,000 ran out six months later and the company went into liquidation.

FALLING IN THE STRID

Peter was appointed chairman of Trekkers Ltd a year ago, some six months after a management buy-out. Trekkers is led by the rampantly entrepreneurial Alex Strid. He and his management team own 40 per cent of the equity.

The glowing picture that the lead venture capitalist painted of Strid and his team before Peter's appointment has been confirmed. Trekkers is about to exceed its current year budgeted profit of £7.5 million on sales of £50 million.

The only blot on the landscape is the performance of the South African distribution business, which is well below budget. Strid has assured Peter that he is going to take personal responsibility for this and plans to go out there again next week. He has also told Peter that he wants to be able to free up more of his time to look at new opportunities. In order to do so he proposes appointing John Vicker, the operations director, to the role of UK managing director.

Peter supports this proposal at a meeting with the lead venture capitalist who sits on the board. He too is happy despite some reservations about the appointment of Vicker. Peter was able to reassure him. As he leaves the meeting, Peter jocularly confirms that Strid's wife will not be joining him on the South African trip this time – an issue he had queried when agreeing Strid's last expenses!

On the eve of Strid's departure, Vicker calls and asks to see Peter urgently. He agrees to meet him at a local hotel. It's a bit of a surprise when Peter finds all the executive directors apart from Strid are also there.

It proves to be a long and very difficult meeting, the summary of which is that:

- The execs think that Strid has 'lost the plot' and is no longer contributing to the business. He is not putting in the hours and, on the rare occasions when he attends meetings, he makes no contribution other than to rubbish the efforts of others.
- South Africa is a disaster and everyone except Strid wants to shut it down. Nothing is achieved by his frequent trips, where he is normally accompanied by Mrs Strid. They always fly first class.
- Strid's brother has just been appointed distribution manager for the UK at an inflated salary and without going through the

company's appointment process. Peter also learns that the company employs his daughter and son-in-law. The daughter is paid nearly twice as much as her supervisor and drives a company BMW Z3.

- Strid, a rugby fan, has committed the company to a £20,000 sponsorship deal with the local club where his son is a player and whose chairman is managing director of a major customer. The board has not approved this. There is talk of Strid joining the club board.
- The company electrician carried out the installation of electric gates at Strid's new house. No payment has been received.

Peter's first reaction is to ask why this has not been raised before. He is reminded by the finance director that the company has just passed the 18-month period since the buy-out. This is significant because before this date, any director leaving the company would have to sell his shares back at par and, *'We knew that the venture capitalists would always side with Alex'*.

Peter thanks the directors for bringing this issue to his attention and says he wants to give it some thought before giving them his considered view. As he leaves, a somewhat embarrassed Vicker takes him aside and says he ought to be aware that his daughter too worked in the business on similar terms to Strid's girl. Vicker became uncomfortable with this and she has now moved to another job.

Plenty to think about as he drives home! What should he do?

What are the issues?

There is a lot going on here. The reality is hard to get at from what we know so far. So the main issue must be to find out what is actually going on and then prioritize. Most of the issues are likely to revolve around Strid.

For instance, has he 'lost the plot'? Has success gone to his head? Has he lost contact with reality? Is he defrauding the company? If he is, how serious is it? Is it a matter of degree or should any misappropriation of funds be treated in the same way? He appears, if the allegations are true, to be confusing what is his money and what is the company's. How much of Trekkers' success is really down to him? His lifestyle indicates boredom, insecurity and that he may be a bully. Is this right? Will he change? Can he be influenced by any of the current board members?

There are also issues relating to Vicker, which make a quick judgement very risky to make. Can Peter trust what he says? Would he be capable of taking over? Does he really have the respect of the rest of the executive? He has gone out on a limb. If Vicker is telling the truth and Peter doesn't do anything, what will his reaction be?

The way the board is working also presents some problems. Trekkers' board is far from united and not effective. Strid appears to be 'a majority of one'. The chairman seems not to be fulfilling the role and to have no influence over him. Is this simply because he has let him get on with it, or is it that he won't be able to? He doesn't appear to have spotted these problems or the breakdown in relationships on his board.

Then there is the subject of the shareholders. What should be said to the venture capitalists and when? The potential loss in shareholder value could be considerable.

As for the business, that also faces some challenges, despite its tremendous profitability. Is the South African business really under control or is it a potential black hole? Is there malpractice through the company? The atmosphere at the top can't have gone unnoticed and must be affecting morale generally.

If Strid has to go, how will Peter deal with the matter of his equity?

There is also a logistical issue, no matter what perspective Peter comes from. Should he speak to Alex before he departs for South Africa or should he let him go and speak to him when he gets back?

How to decide?

In this case the decision as to whether Peter wants to resolve the various dilemmas involved looks easy, assuming he is highly competent. Perhaps he didn't have his eye on the ball because of the excellent financial performance. Not to grab hold of the situation and sort things out would be to abdicate his responsibilities as chairman. His credibility with Trekkers' backers would be destroyed. Ironically, a chairman who isn't very competent might not realize it, but still try to resolve the situation anyway.

Determining whether or not Vicker's allegations are true is vital before any decision can be made. The chairman is unlikely to do so with the rigour required before Strid's departure for South Africa. If he is to conduct a formal investigation, what should its focus be? Is it into whether Strid has 'lost the plot', or into the financial irregularities and abuse of his position, or both? Should he also ask the auditors to confirm the latest financial position just in case the bad news is even worse?

He needs to find out what the alternatives he has are. Even if he lets Strid go before saying anything, time is still short.

He may want to get a better feel for Vicker and his colleagues.

It is hard to see any decisions being reached without the involvement of the company's lawyer. He may also need to consult an employment specialist if any of the directors will need to be removed.

What to decide?

Any decision should be dependent upon the emerging facts.

If Strid is innocent of the allegations made, then the chairman may decide to fire all or some of the rest of the team. Replacing an entire team will be difficult. However, it is obviously a high-performing business. This means Peter has time to do it properly and Trekkers will probably be attractive to candidates.

What if Strid is guilty of the financial irregularities but certainly hasn't lost the plot? He could be just plain greedy. He may be thinking he's the one who makes all the money and that no one would sack him for what to him seem relatively minor amounts. Should he be sacked? Should he be asked to put back the money involved and sort out the other issues?

A scenario where Strid has lost the plot in terms of running the business but where the allegations over the money aren't true is the most difficult. In this case Strid would have to go and the rest of his colleagues would be in doubt as well. Keeping control of that situation would be tricky.

The chairman's decisions will no doubt be based on what is ethically right, what is best for the business and what is acceptable to the shareholders.

How to communicate it?

Communications in this case need to be very serious and probably quite formal. Careful notes will be required and the chairman will not want to have any of the important meetings on a one-to-one basis. His most important meeting at the beginning of the process is with his key shareholder. If they either panic or don't support him in continuing as chairman then he will have no role. In order for them to have confidence in him he needs to appear calm and to be crystal clear about what he intends to do. This needs to be carefully considered, fair and highly professional.

So who needs communicating with and in what order? I suppose Peter needs to tell his partner at home that he's going to pretty busy for the next few weeks. He needs to speak to the venture capitalist, the company's lawyers and the auditors. Having informed them, he may decide to convene a meeting of these people with Vicker and the finance director for the allegations to be repeated and for a plan of action to be approved.

Vicker will be highly stressed by the circumstances, whether he is trustworthy or not. So he needs to be spoken to regularly throughout.

As to what to communicate to Strid when he returns – if he emerges with honour from the investigation then it is straightforward. If not, and it is decided he should go, he should be dealt with swiftly and professionally.

What did the chairman do?

He decided not to speak to Strid before his departure because the 10 days that Strid was away would give him the time to investigate the accusations being made. He kicked himself for not having got as involved in Trekkers as he should have. It all seemed to be going so well. Strid was so persuasive and the others hadn't given him any clues to how they were feeling. The chairman was actually a very high calibre man. Peter cleared his diary of everything so that he could spend the entire time dealing with Trekkers while Strid was away.

Vickers and the other directors were told that the allegations they were making were very serious and that if they proved unfounded they would be dismissed. The auditors were then instructed to undertake a formal investigation as discreetly as they could. They confirmed the following:

- That there was no authorization for the rugby club sponsorship. Business with the club's chairman had also increased by 30% to a rate of over £1 million per annum.
- The electrician did carry out work at Strid's home. The electrician's time-sheet showed that he had spent a total of seven hours on the work.
- Strid has been to South Africa five times, always with Mrs Strid and always travelling first class.
- The terms on which members of his family were appointed were unclear, but certainly appear outside company procedures. The auditors point out that the company's systems are not really adequate for a business this size and helpfully offer to undertake a separate review.

While the investigation was going on, Peter spent a lot of time with Vicker and the other directors. The main purpose of this was to form a view of them and in particular Vicker's capability as chief executive. His time was well spent and he discovered a great deal else that was not right in the company. The most useful was revealed by looking at Strid's diary for the previous 12 months. This showed that Strid had spent very little time on company business other than playing golf with customers and suppliers.

The chairman became impressed by Vicker, his grasp of the business, the respect felt for him by the rest of the team and the way he was conducting himself in this difficult situation. He was less impressed by the finance director who had been bullied by Strid and hadn't the personality to stand up to him or to ensure that others, who could, knew what was going on.

At the beginning of Strid's trip, Peter contacted the lead venture capitalist, the company lawyer and the auditor. All were told of his plan of action. All were as amazed as he was, as well as being equally embarrassed. The lawyer helpfully produced a review of Strid's contract. The venture capitalist cleared his diary for the two days between the completion of the auditor's investigation and Strid's arrival home. He did this so that if the consequence was Strid's removal, any necessary approvals, particularly in regard to Strid's equity, could be obtained.

Vicker had impressed the chairman so much that he decided that his plan of action would be to remove Strid immediately upon his return and appoint Vicker chief executive. Although he wasn't told at this point, the chairman also felt the finance director would have to go as well.

The chairman was at the company the morning Strid arrived with the lead venture capitalist. Meeting off-site was considered and this was actually felt to be the better idea, but they all thought that Strid was bound to go into the business first, whatever time they fixed a meeting. They asked to see him immediately. Strid was in a very relaxed mood and had no idea what was coming.

‹ *Alex, I'm afraid we have some rather serious and very bad news for you. You have lost the confidence of the investors and you are being dismissed both as a director and as an employee of the company. This is not a debate. We have the full support of the board and all of the shareholders, that is apart from yourself. The reasons for this are as follows. We have been made aware of some serious financial irregularities in the company. These have been investigated by the company's auditors and confirmed to be true. We have also been reviewing your contribution to the company and believe that you have not been undertaking the obligations of your contract.*

'However, we do recognize the contribution you have made to the business in the past and although we are under no obligation to do so given the circumstances, we are proposing to make the following offer by way of settlement. A copy of this, the auditor's report and the papers relating to your termination will be given to you in a moment. We have made provision in the settlement for you to receive proper legal advice. The company's lawyers have confirmed that what is being done is perfectly reasonable and feel sure that if you seek either their advice or the advice of another competent lawyer they will recommend you accept.

'We will offer to pay out the full terms of your two-year employment contract, including the value of all benefits. If you decide you would like to keep your car, then it will be valued and this amount will be deducted from the settlement. With regard to your shareholding in the company, we are proposing that the company purchase it under the provisions in the investment agreement with the venture capitalists. An auditor's valuation will be obtained as quickly as possible.

'In summary Alex, the investors and I have lost confidence in your ability to manage the business and there is no alternative. We would like you to leave the premises immediately and hand over your keys to the offices.›

Strid was stunned. He listened incredulously before erupting when the chairman had stopped speaking. He then became highly emotional and had to be physically restrained by the lawyer.

Wisely, Strid picked another good lawyer to advise him. His advice was that there was little he could do, as the offer in respect of his contract was so generous. Subsequently, the lawyer advised challenging the valuation that the auditors came up with. Strid refused to sell his equity back to the company at the price they suggested. Trekkers' investors and the rest of the management decided that the best tactic was to let him keep his equity for the time being. Realizing quite what a high spender Strid was, the chairman felt he was bound to be back before too long to negotiate. This proved very shrewd.

The board recovered from the trauma. Vicker turned out to be an excellent leader, even to the extent of remotivating the finance director enough for him to stay. Strid subsequently started another business in direct competition, which although small is highly profitable and keeps him and his family in the style that he considers appropriate.

MONEY, MONEY, MONEY

This is a series of five dilemmas to do with remuneration.

Money 1

You are a non-executive director of a small quoted company capitalized at around £250 million. There is a well-constructed board comprising a part time chairman, a chief executive, three other executive directors and two non-executives.

The company has a discretionary bonus scheme. The chairman recommends awards to the remuneration committee. The committee is made up of the non-executives and the human resources director. Although not a formal member of the committee, the chief executive attends every meeting to provide guidance. He is, however, always absent from the meeting where his own salary is discussed.

A take-over bid is in the wind and the executive directors want their bonuses guaranteed at the capped maximum for the year ahead. They also want to avoid having to make an announcement about this to the stock exchange when the bid is announced. The directors therefore want a non-formal but effectively binding understanding from you as chairman of the remuneration committee.

What should the remuneration committee do?

What are the issues?

Why is there a possible take-over? Has the company under-performed? Who are the likely acquirers? It sounds like they think the acquirer will remove them. What leads them to think this, or that their bonuses wouldn't be paid by the acquirer if they stayed?

What is the remuneration history? Have the directors been paid appropriately in the past? Have they been reasonable in their demands or permanently trying to get more? Are they proposing for the bonus to be pro-rated so that if the bid arrives half-way through the year they will receive half of it?

Does the performance of the company to date suggest that they would be likely to receive the maximum? This might be hard to assess if the year has just commenced.

What is the scale of the bonuses under discussion? Do they relate to a longer-term performance scheme or solely to the year under discussion? Does the level matter? Is it the principle that is at stake?

How will the executive directors react if the proposal is rejected? Some may consider their relationship with the management an issue. Clearly, accepting their proposal will be more likely to strengthen it than not. Others will feel this has nothing to do with it; for them it is a simple matter of corporate governance.

There is an issue of process as well. The non-executive shouldn't give a view either way or make any promises without discussing it with the remuneration committee. To do so will undermine its authority. It is not a good idea for the chief executive to be attending all the remuneration committee meetings and this may be the ideal opportunity to set some new ground rules.

What do they mean by 'non-formal but effectively binding'? A side letter or a verbal promise? How enforceable are either?

How to decide?

There are probably two key drivers of the decision here. First, the performance of the business and the reasons for a possible bid; secondly, whether or not you think it is morally acceptable to guarantee a bonus given that it appears to have been intended to be linked to performance. You may also feel that such an undisclosed arrangement is not appropriate for a public company. Some might try to compromise and avoid a fight by linking the bonus to the price at which the business gets taken over, ie linking it to shareholder value. This is generally only relevant where there is a clear objective to sell.

You will also need to consider how the other members of the remuneration committee will react. You'll face another dilemma if you disagree, but they are more relaxed.

Most decent chairmen would reach for their lawyer in these circumstances. Even if you know what is right commercially, the manner in which the process is conducted is crucial to a successful outcome.

What to decide?

The first decision is as to whether you feel the issue should be put to the remuneration committee. Even if they personally felt it was totally unacceptable, most non-executives would probably decide to do this. Why? Because it makes the decision non-personal and because this is exactly the sort of issue the remuneration committee should be discussing. If no scheduled meeting were to take place in the near future, a special meeting may be convened.

You then need to decide how the issue is framed for the remuneration committee. The most straightforward way is to ask the chief executive to write a proposal stating the reasons why the remuneration committee should give their consent. You should make it clear that the issues are fairly straightforward and won't require a presentation or the attendance of the chief executive at the meeting.

How to communicate it?

In terms of the tone of your response, a lot will depend here on the history of your relationship with the others and the performance of the business. You may or may not want to disclose your own view initially. So perhaps, *'Let's discuss it at the remuneration committee'* should be the response to the executive directors.

The next piece of communication relates to how you introduce the issue to the remuneration committee. Do you normally leave your view on a matter unclear until it has been debated, or do you state your position, overtly or otherwise, in your introduction?

If the decision is to support the executive's proposals, then the communication of it sounds easy. However, they will need to prepare for media or analysts' questions when it becomes public.

If the decision is not to support the executive, then the important thing is to communicate it decisively and not get into another debate.

What did the chairman of the remuneration committee do?

The situation was that the executive directors were all reasonably new to the business. The chief executive had been brought in two years ago to turn the company around. At that time the business was capitalized at only £120 million, under half the current market capitalization. He was paid a relatively low salary of £100,000 but stood to make approximately £2 million from his options at a pre-bid price. The view of the board was that the turnaround had been highly effective and the company was now poised for major growth, something that was not fully reflected in the share price.

The chairman's view was that the executive directors had done a tremendous job and should be rewarded handsomely for their efforts. However, he felt that the way to do this was through the options that they had. He felt the guaranteed bonus was unacceptable.

He recommended that the proposal be put to the remuneration committee with a paper from the chief executive. He suggested that as the issues were straightforward, there was no need for a presentation from the chief executive. The remuneration committee declined the proposal. He then asked that the executive directors' salaries be reviewed by the company's remuneration advisers to ensure they were at the appropriate level.

How did the chief executive feel about it? It wasn't actually too difficult to deal with. He was given a *'That's life, Jim'* message. His reaction was basically, *'Ah well, it was worth a try'*.

The remuneration consultants recommended a modest increase in base salaries.

Money 2

Zipco is a £400 million capitalized company listed on the London Stock Exchange. Due to a fall in the share price, 50 per cent of executive share options are hopelessly under water. The share price would have to double before they became worth anything. A new director is about to be appointed with two times his salary in options at today's depressed striking price.

Existing directors are delighted for their new colleague. However, they feel passionately that the option scheme needs reviewing. They have a proposal that they would like approved by the board immediately so that it is in place before the new director starts.

The proposal is that the current directors sacrifice their existing options, which would be cancelled, and receive a new allocation on the same terms as the new board member.

How should the remuneration committee of which you are chairman respond?

What are the issues?

Why has the share price performed so badly? Is it management, sector blight, stock market fluctuations, or something else? How have they performed relative to other companies in the sector? Whatever the reason, if the options were intended to tie in management, they won't now. This may be fine if you don't rate them, but what if you do and they have performed relatively well? If you want to keep them, how mobile are they? What will they do if you don't give in? Would they leave? How de-motivated will they really be? If you give in to them, what will they ask for next?

The option scheme is part of the overall remuneration for directors, so the issue needs to be considered in that context. What is the overall remuneration scheme like? Are there any targets to be met before the options become exercisable? It is unlikely that if there are, these will have been met, as most schemes with targets involve relative or absolute share performance. What about the rest of the employees? If there are other employee share schemes, are these working or do they need considering as well?

If you choose to agree with the executive directors, could you do what they want, legally? What shareholder approvals would be required and how are shareholders likely to react to such a proposal? Is this an issue that is likely to be picked up by the press? If so, should this have any bearing on the deliberations of the board? What knock-on consequences are there?

How will the relationship between the existing directors and their new colleague be affected by the decision you take? If you agree and the shares continue to under-perform and someone else joins, will he expect the same opportunity to renegotiate his options?

Fundamentally, you have to decide two things. First, is this something you wish to put to the remuneration committee or reject out of hand? Secondly, if you do decide to put it to the remuneration committee you need to consider your own views on the matter as well as how to manage the discussion properly. There may also be a personal issue if you have equity or options.

The issue over how quickly something needs doing also needs resolving. If you support their proposal, does it really need doing straight away?

How and what to decide?

Putting it to the remuneration committee, or not, is the first decision to take. As with the 'Money 1' case, even if you are strongly opposed to the proposal yourself, you may feel that if the executives are serious then the committee ought to consider it. Some might offer to sound out the other members of management so that they know whether it is worth doing the work to put up a properly prepared paper.

If the remuneration committee does consider management's proposal seriously, what should it take in to account? Most of the issues above will need to be thought through. The members should also be clear about their purpose as a remuneration committee and seek to balance the potentially conflicting interests of motivating management and protecting shareholder value.

When it comes to what to decide, the alternatives appear straightforward. You could reject the idea out of hand and refuse to allow it to be discussed at the remuneration committee. Another suggestion might be to tell the executive that while you don't agree with their proposal, you would be happy to discuss it at the remuneration committee.

Perhaps you could give a non-committal response and tell them that you will discuss it at the remuneration committee if the executive directors could prepare a detailed paper arguing the case for and against their proposal. Some might indicate their support for the proposal, but tell them that the performance targets will need renegotiating alongside.

You might tell them that while personally you think it is a great idea, you are not sure whether the rest of the remuneration committee will think likewise. You could helpfully suggest that you would be delighted to sound them out and see whether it is worthwhile pursuing.

Finally, you could make their day by telling them that you think the proposal is a wonderful idea and that you will have no problems getting it through the committee.

Before taking any of these alternatives you may want to consider talking to the company's advisers to see how other companies have dealt with this issue. Your lawyers or remuneration advisers will no doubt know. This is not an uncommon issue, particularly for smaller quoted UK companies. Of course the remuneration consultants may see this as another opportunity to introduce a new scheme and earn some more fees.

How to communicate it?

This is one of those subjects where people tend to have strong convictions either way. It is also a highly emotive issue for the management. So, if the decision is taken to reject management's proposal, it is the executive who will need communicating with carefully. Even if you feel very strongly that the proposal is outrageous and that they need a very clear message to that effect, you will not want to alienate them.

If you feel supportive of their proposal, then the communications with management are obviously easier, but the issue then is how to communicate with shareholders and the press. On the face of it this looks like a tricky job. The upside for shareholders, other than having a happier management team, is hard to see. The process for gaining shareholder approval needs considering carefully. Is this a company that is watched or has a history of press comment over remuneration?

How should the remuneration committee respond?

This is very similar to the previous dilemma. While you may have sympathy with them, the principle of cancelling options and issuing new ones when the price goes down is something most of us feel uncomfortable with. The company's other shareholders don't have the option to go back and pay a lower price. The directors are hardly likely to come to the remuneration committee and offer to pay a higher price if history suggests their options were cheap.

Many businesses fall into the trap of releasing all of the options available for granting as soon as they possibly can. It is much better, unless someone new is being appointed, to drip them out over time. In this way the pricing tends to be fairer and the above situation less likely to arise.

This may be a good opportunity to carry out a company-wide remuneration review, both in terms of the structure of the schemes and their levels.

What did the remuneration committee do?

The background to this situation was that although they had worked hard and profits relative to their UK competition were good, on an international basis they were below average. Overall remuneration for the directors was comparatively good, both domestically and internationally. The chairman of the remuneration committee personally thought that the proposal that the directors had made was outrageous and felt they needed to know this. However, he did not want to ruin his relationship with them, so they were given no indication of his own position at the outset. It was agreed with them that this was a very important matter for the remuneration committee and that it should be reviewed immediately. He had decided that the distractive potential of this issue was quite considerable, so the sooner it was resolved the better. The chief executive was asked to prepare a paper for the meeting. The company's remuneration consultants were also asked to prepare a short paper on the proposal.

The remuneration committee met a week later and unanimously decided to reject the proposal. They did so on the basis that it was not in the interests of shareholders. The chief executive decided to force things and made it a resigning issue. This was despite advice from the chairman that he shouldn't. He told the chairman that all of the executive directors would resign if the non-executives didn't agree with their proposal. The non-executives called their bluff. They didn't resign. The new director joined and was made aware of the issue. Twelve months later the chief executive who had unfortunately let the issue affect his performance was fired, and the new executive took over.

Money 3

Hipco is a small, progressive two-year-old technology business. It designs Web sites and Web community platforms for major corporates. Hipco has a tremendous reputation but due to the rapid increase in staff required to match the growth in contracts, it is still loss-making and consuming cash. All staff are paid partly in cash and partly in shares.

In order to build a stronger board in readiness for a potential flotation in two years time, Hipco has been searching for an independent chairman, a new chief operations officer and an independent director. Luckily they have found what appears to be a chairman with the perfect profile, Al Dink. Al has started up a company, grown it successfully and then sold it for £50 million. He has a lot of experience in the USA and in fundraising. Getting an equity stake in Hipco is the way he wants to be motivated.

Initial discussions with the proposed new chairman have gone well, that is until this morning when Al shocked Hipco's managing director, Simon Hip, by saying:

> *Well Simon, you have a fantastic opportunity and I'd be delighted to be a part of it. The only issue now is how much equity I'll be getting for lending my name and giving my time.'*
>
> *'Great news,'* said Simon. *'How much would you like to buy?'*
>
> *'Buy, buy? I assume you're joking, Simon. I'll be adding at least a million of value to your company. I'm not buying anything. What I have in mind is you issuing me options which, if the float happens in two years' time at the values we talked about, will realize a million for me post-tax.'*

How should Simon respond?

What are the issues?

There are two big issues raised by this situation. Is the chairman the right man for the job and if he is, how should he be rewarded?

Al's manner appears somewhat high-handed and arrogant. Simon needs to consider carefully the characteristics he is looking for and match against them. For example, while Al has had one very big success, which he can fairly be proud of, he hasn't got public company experience. This could be very useful given Hipco's plans for a listing. More importantly, Simon needs to feel he can trust and relate well to the chairman and that there is a feeling of mutual respect.

One thing that isn't clear from the description of the situation is, who is helping Simon find candidates? Is he using a search firm, a potential venture capital investor, or someone else? If he is, then it would be normal for the basis on which the chairman is to be appointed and the rewards on offer to be discussed before the search gets underway. Outline terms, particularly whether there was equity on offer or not, would also be made clear to candidates when they are approached.

Assume for the moment that Al is the right candidate. Is what he has proposed fair? There is no doubt that the right chairman could add enormous value to the business. But over a million? Well, in a business that is poised for explosive growth, yes, potentially they might. Coaching Simon through the challenges of growth, helping to organize funding and helping with making the right senior appointments could be well worth it. However, should Al buy his shares or get options? My experience is that views differ markedly on this. In the US a 'name', usually someone who has led a successful NASDAQ issue, could easily command such a sum and options would be typical. In the UK it would be more normal for the shares to be purchased.

There is an assumption that equity will align interests between Simon, the rest of the staff and the new joiners. It is obviously more likely to than not. However, to make the assumption that it automatically does would be wrong. One common problem for young high-technology companies is that equity gets spread around too quickly and not always to the appropriate people. Problems then emerge when new equity needs to be issued or board changes are required. Early on, when the value of equity is low, the cost of dilution is deemed to be negligible. Later on the real cost becomes apparent.

Management by committee can take over. This may already be an issue for Simon. He will need the support of other shareholders. If Hipco is also about to enter successive rounds of fundraising, the dilution for the new chairman and new investors will inevitably reduce Simon's stake. Fundamentally, he has to decide whether a smaller piece of a much bigger pie is what he really wants.

Another issue is to do with what happens if Al doesn't work out and he proves to be an inappropriate choice of chairman. How is his equity dealt with? If he has options, will they automatically lapse on cessation of his appointment as chairman? Perhaps there should be a probation period before the equity is purchased or options granted.

At the end of the day, these things are always open to negotiation, so Simon has to decide how much of a difference a new chairman could make and how much he wants to reward him for that difference.

Al has to decide how big an opportunity this is and how much he wants rewarding for what he will do for Hipco.

How to decide?

The first decision really relates to whether the potential chairman is the right candidate. Then and only then is it worth considering whether the terms are reasonable or worth paying.

It sounds like Simon may need some professional advice from an investor or search consultant, or both. We don't know whether Hipco will be self-funding until float or whether it will need additional capital. Perhaps raising external funding now will give the company the opportunity for more choice of chairman and then the VCs can negotiate with the potential chairman. It is always better to pick from a choice of more than one.

If Simon and the team do decide that they think the chairman is right, then rigorous referencing will be vital. It may be that this is the going rate for this chairman and it really isn't negotiable. It does seem to signify an inflexible approach though, so this aspect of his character in particular should be researched.

What to decide?

There are a number of obvious alternatives:

- Simon may think Al is the right person for the job, but try and negotiate the cost down.
- He could simply tell Al that he is one of a number of suitable candidates but that he is too expensive, and see what happens.
- Simon may decide that he can't work with someone so apparently inflexible and just end the discussion amicably.
- He could use the excuse of having other shareholders' views to take into account before making a decision, to buy himself some time.
- Rolling over and saying yes is an alternative, one that sets the tone of the relationship and may not engender respect from his new chairman. It's also one that may turn out to be at a significantly higher cost than other alternatives.

What did Simon do?

One of Simon's mentors was a friend who owned a company that was moderately successful without having an independent chairman. He told Simon not to bother with getting a chairman now and certainly not at the price suggested. Simon put the decision off until Al got fed up waiting and got himself busy elsewhere.

Six months later, funding became very tight. Hipco was over-trading in almost all respects. Simon was finding that his life was a logistical nightmare. However, the future potential of the business looked better than ever. Deciding to combine raising money with recruiting a new chairman, Simon approached a leading venture capitalist in his area and asked them for help. They introduced him to six potential chairmen, all of whom could have done the job. Simon picked the one he felt he could get on with best. The new chairman then focused on the fundraising exercise, leaving Simon to focus on building the business.

Simon had told the new chairman the first time they met about his earlier experience. *'Tell you what,'* the new chairman said, *'let's not rush the equity. Why not work together on the fundraising for three months; that should give you a good idea of what I might be able to do to help you succeed.'* Somewhat ironically, he ended up with a stake that was worth considerably in excess of £2 million when Hipco floated and was subsequently taken over. The moral of the story, I guess, is that it isn't about cost but attitude.

Money 4

MAVCO's US business has been having a difficult time and is losing money. However, the recently installed US chief executive, Chuck Wabb, appears to be doing all that's possible to turn it around. After many years' frustration and three changes of US chief executive, there finally appears to be some light at the end of the tunnel. Chuck looks as if he might turn out to be a hero. He is, however, paid handsomely for his efforts. Indeed, he gets paid significantly more than the highest European director yet runs a business only two-thirds the size of the German subsidiary.

This morning he has come to you, the English group chief executive, and said he wants a significant salary rise. In his usual friendly but slightly menacing way he has told you that if he doesn't get what he wants he will leave.

Chuck took a long time to find and you think he has high potential, even to the extent that he could be a candidate for your job when you retire in three years' time. However, there is already friction in the ranks of the divisional managing directors and you are fearful of their reaction if Chuck is given a big increase.

PS. One small detail that hasn't escaped your attention is that Chuck's proposal implies he would be earning more than you.

How should this situation be resolved?

What are the issues?

Chuck's ability, potential and style are obviously issues. How good is he really? How sustainable is his turnaround? Is he capable of growing the business once it is restored to health, or are his skills restricted to sorting things out? Is he claiming all the glory? What about the contribution made by the rest of his team; are they by implication to be rewarded better as well? How effective would he be in the role of group chief executive? Does he command the respect of the other divisional chief executives, even though they resent his salary? How loyal is he? Is he winding up the others deliberately? How serious is his threat? What's your fall back position? Who else have you got to run the US business if he leaves? If you give in to Chuck, how soon will he be back for more? Do you need to assert your authority with him? You may well end up setting a dangerous precedent if you don't.

The remuneration issues relate to Chuck and to the company as a whole. With regard to Chuck, was his salary benchmarked at the outset? Is it the market rate locally and within the industry? What is the real cost of switching? Apart from search fees, what would be the risk of losing the turnaround momentum and would you have to pay more to get someone then?

From a group perspective, you don't want to demotivate the others, but they must accept that world pay is not homogeneous. On the other hand, if you give in to Chuck, what will be the effect on the others? Is there a clear remuneration policy? Does the company have an effective remuneration committee? Is it getting the right level of professional advice? Is the US chief executive's package a matter for the remuneration committee if he isn't on the main board? Is the balance between base salary, performance bonuses, capital incentives and other benefits appropriate? Are incentives structured to match objectives? Are there issues elsewhere in the business and at other levels? What about the impact on your own package? How do you feel about him earning more than you? If you are opposed to the idea, is this on principle or is it just an objection to Chuck earning more than you?

A final issue you will have to deal with is how you might feel yourself. Only the seriously weird enjoy being blackmailed. Anger and determination not to give in to someone doing this to you may well consume you. You may need to remember John Kennedy's wise words, *'Don't get mad, get even'*. This is one of the reasons that in these situations it is often extremely useful to talk to someone else before you say anything to the Chuck in your life. Your chairman could be ideal; maybe it's another mentor or chief executive friend. A little informed objectivity can go a long way.

What options do you have?

The three obvious options appear to be to:

1. Pay him more, but no one else.
2. Give all the divisional chief executives a rise.
3. Call his bluff.

There are also variations on these core options. For example, you could agree to pay Chuck or any of the others more, but raise the performance targets for them to achieve new levels of remuneration. You could try to duck the issue and say it is a matter for the remuneration committee or chairman and you are quite happy to put it to them.

What to decide?

This sounds like a situation where you will need to think things through carefully before deciding. An immediate, inspirational response may work, but there is an element of risk in giving one, especially since you don't need to.

Possibly the worst thing is to fudge the issue and try to give everyone a little more. The obvious danger in doing this is that it won't make any difference motivationally and will still undermine your authority.

Thinking about who you will consult will be important. Even if you have a very clear idea about what you will do, and your chairman may not want to be involved in the process, it would be wise to inform him of what has happened and how you plan to deal with it.

Fundamentally, you have to make a judgement about how good Chuck is, decide whether you want to keep him and then if you do want to keep him, how to satisfy him without causing either significant disruption or cost.

How to communicate it?

In the *'Pay him more but no one else'* option, the key communication is obviously with the other divisional chief executives. You could try this:

> *Yes, I know it's unfair, but he's paid the market rate. None of you wanted the job, you could have applied. The contribution he is making to the group is beyond the simple matter of the scale of his business. If we can be seen to be successful in the US, especially after all the criticism we have had, then the impact on our share price could be tremendous. I can appreciate how you feel, but there it is.*

Or the more conciliatory and defusing:

> *I can appreciate how you feel and I'll conduct an independent review of your packages. I'm not promising to increase them, but if it helps you feel that you are being paid fairly, then it's well worth the cost. If it shows that you are underpaid in relation to your performance, then naturally we'll consider what we can do to rectify it.*

For the *'Give all the divisional chief executives a rise'* alternative, assuming it is sufficiently large and that others in the company will know, then the communication issue is with others. Apart from the staff, stock market analysts and the press may well take an interest in the subject when the next results come out.

If it's *'Call his bluff'* that you go for, then how you communicate with Chuck is clearly crucial. What do you say to minimize the risk of him leaving or causing disruption? A *'Tough luck, buster'* response has the benefit of clarity and ends the debate, but has an element of risk about it. *'We'll see what we can do at the next pay review'* potentially takes the heat out of the situation. However, if he doesn't believe anything will happen or the review is a long way off, he may see this as calling his bluff. A more effective route might be to say:

> ❬ *Chuck, you look to be doing a great job and the business appears at long last to be coming round. But given our history, I'm sure you'll appreciate we don't want to assume too much too soon. If the turnaround is sustained, then it will be much easier to argue the case for a bigger package. As I've said before, you are one of the few who has the potential to run the whole group, and the rewards for that are clearly a lot greater than for running a subsidiary, particularly with the potential of our Asian businesses. I can appreciate how you feel, but it would be a shame to blow your chances by being a little impatient.* ❭

Although he still may see this as *'Tough luck, buster'*, it does have the benefit of being honest, dangling a bit of a carrot and reasserting your authority.

What did the group chief executive do?

The background was that the US business had never been a success since it was acquired. It had been a career killer for several high-potential managers. Finally there was someone who looked like they had sorted it out. Although the group CEO felt he couldn't trust Chuck, and he certainly didn't like him, he was loath to jeopardize the US business. The business until this point had been unsellable and all of MAVCO's European competitors had lost money in the US. Maybe, just maybe, he thought, if they could get it into a healthy enough state then they could sell it. He didn't dare tell Chuck this for fear of him either leaving or driving the value down to buy it himself.

His solution to this dilemma was to agree that the compensation should be reviewed for all divisional chief executives. The result of this review was a small increase across the board and the suggestion of a new, industry-comparable Long Term Incentive Plan for the USA linked to the growth in value of the US business unit. This scheme provided the US manager with the opportunity to make several million dollars if he hit his aggressive targets. The bottom line was that if he got the value up to $100 million in three years, he received $3 million.

The solution worked for the most part. Chuck got the value of the US business to $50 million in three years and received $1 million when it was merged into another business that was acquired. This business had a much more appropriate chief executive who became CEO of the combined US business. The part of the solution that didn't work out so well was that the company's German leader left in disgust and the German business has significantly under-performed ever since.

Money 5

From the City's point of view, the group chief executive of Temco has had a splendid second year. Profits are up 30 per cent and this is despite flat sales. Temco's market capitalization has trebled to £100 million since he took over. The balance sheet is in much better shape. A difficult capital expenditure project has been completed on time and within budget. This expenditure will reduce operating costs significantly. It has also reduced employment in the company by 1,500 people. Significant progress has therefore been made on a number of fronts.

Temco's chief executive, Jim Hind, is expecting a very big bonus as well as a major grant of options as a reward for his efforts and as an incentive to develop the business further. Wages elsewhere in the company have been constrained as part of cost-cutting and although Jim is a superb motivator, morale has still not completely recovered.

Jim joined on a relatively low salary of £80,000 a year. He did not get too many options and, being relatively young, he couldn't afford to buy many shares at the time of his appointment. So keen was Jim to get his first job as a plc chief executive that he wasn't that concerned about the short-term rewards. His current profit on options if he exercised all of them today would be £200,000 pre tax, an amount he considers derisory when compared with his contribution to shareholder value. Jim has grown considerably in confidence and his expectations really are very high.

As well as being chairman of Temco, your friend is also chairman of Zyball, another public company. Unfortunately, Zyball has had a rough time with the City and with the press of late. The reason for this is a profits collapse occurring after what looked like a fairly glittering five years. This coincided with the pay out of some large bonuses to the directors, including to your friend. These bonuses related to the previous five years' performance. To make matters worse, the chief executive exercised and sold a major part of his options just before the last share-dealing window closed. There have been calls for your friend's resignation. He is furious and highly embarrassed about the Zyball situation. He has lost faith in Zyball's chief executive whom you had always considered a little bit of a wide boy. At last he is about to follow your advice to fire him and recruit a new chief executive.

Naturally, the situation at Zyball looms large in your friend's thoughts. Although he thinks Jim has done a fantastic job at Temco and feels sympathetic to the argument that he should receive a significant rise and bonus, he is very worried about the reaction from the press and the city.

What advice would you give to your friend?

What are the issues?

Let's consider Jim first. It appears that he is clearly underpaid for what he has achieved. He is therefore quite reasonably expecting a significant increase in salary, a decent bonus and better capital incentives. This assumes, of course, that the results are valid, that the much-improved performance is sustainable, and that Jim is the right man for the next phase of development. I wonder if we would have added the previous sentence if the chairman hadn't been involved in Zyball. If the chairman were to be more concerned about potential embarrassment than Jim, he may end up losing him. Jim is bound to be highly marketable. How easy would he be to replace? In fact it probably wouldn't be that difficult to find a quality chief executive for a company that had had most of its problems sorted out and the benefits of a big capital expenditure programme starting to come through. Yet the impact on morale within the company if a highly regarded leader leaves because he hasn't been fairly rewarded could be quite considerable.

There are likely to be other people at Temco who are underpaid. So another issue may be the overall remuneration within the company. What would a full review show? How does Temco's pay compare with its industry and local job market? If it was significantly under the industry norms, what impact would normalizing it have on profitability?

For the chairman there are a number of other issues. Should the situation at Zyball influence what happens at Temco? Will the analysts and press make the connection? What if they do; how are they likely to react? Can he ensure that Jim and his staff are rewarded fairly and avoid attack? He may also be asking himself, particularly if he was chairman at the time, why Jim got such a poor deal on joining? Moreover, why wasn't anything done about it last year? Additionally, the reason Jim has so few options is probably because his salary is so low. Most option schemes link the amount that can be vested to a multiple of salary.

What about his own remuneration at Temco? If he is relatively well paid compared with Jim, then the problem might be worse. If his remuneration is in line with Jim's, then there may be the opportunity to raise Jim's significantly and his own modestly. It is always easier to defend in these situations if you are below the market yourself.

There may be some additional process issues. For example, does the company have a properly composed and functioning remuneration committee? Is there an annual pay review approach in the company? Is this linked to the year's results and so on?

What to decide?

Assuming this is someone you know well, then you may have the opportunity to influence the outcome of events at Temco. There is a degree of risk in most of the alternative courses of action.

Your friend could decide that what happens at Temco has nothing to do with Zyball. Then he might endorse a significant improvement in Jim's package and take the risk that either the press and City won't notice, that they notice and feel it is perfectly in order, or that they notice, there's a bit of fuss, but it quickly dies down. If this is the route he wants to take then he might, if he has time, use some intelligent public relations to ensure that the Temco record is well understood and applauded. The wrong judgement about this could result in exactly the sort of hostile reaction he fears.

In this scenario he still has to decide what to do about Jim's salary, how significant he wants to make the uplift and how it should be structured. He could take the balanced approach and give Jim more of everything so that all aspects of his remuneration are fair and in line with market. The benefit of this approach is that it avoids an issue later on. If he decides to avoid the 'more of everything' scenario, then which aspects of Jim's package should he focus on – salary, benefits, performance bonuses or capital incentives such as options?

He may fear the embarrassment so much that he decides to play safe and only countenance a modest rise for Jim. The embarrassment of losing a highly respected chief executive later might be greater, of course.

He could resign from Zyball or even completely withdraw and resign from both companies – not the way most directors would choose to end their careers.

How to communicate it?

The most important people to communicate with are Jim, the other directors, Temco's staff, advisers, institutional shareholders, analysts and press followers. He will also need to be mindful of communicating carefully with the board, advisers, the institutional shareholder and followers of Zyball.

Whatever option he picks, he will need to prepare a thorough communications plan to ensure he has addressed his key audiences with appropriate messages. Due to the pressures of such moments, this is sometimes not done and regretted later when one very important group has been overlooked.

If he goes down the 'tough it out' route, building support in as many influential places as possible will be important. Brokers' reports or press comment which is highly favourable about the company won't stop the critics, but it will alleviate the pressure.

In order to prepare for taking the above alternatives he will need to be armed with the details, so a full salary review and benchmarking exercise seems inevitable.

If he decides not to give Jim a significant uplift, it sounds like inspirational communication and motivational skills will be required. Jim may feel very angry and let down. He may lose confidence and trust in his chairman, and what sounds like a healthy board could become disunited. Some chairmen in this position would find a way to get Jim to share the problem and for him to come up with the solution. Perhaps this approach could be taken:

> *Jim, the board is proposing to give you a significant increase but we are very concerned about the PR implications of doing so, particularly given the background at Zyball. We would welcome your input on how to handle it.*

But is this approach acceptable and does it undermine the chairman?

What happened?

The chairman was a genuine man who had done his best to control a difficult chief executive at Zyball. When he fired him, he then discovered all sorts of other issues and Zyball was quickly in the position of issuing profits warnings. While the situation was chaotic, he remained convinced Zyball was a good business with high potential and was determined to restore its reputation. However, his own position as chairman was seriously challenged in the press – *'He has presided over one of the biggest messes of the year'* and so on. Consequently, his confidence and preparedness to risk more damaging profiles was just too great.

When he talked the situation through with you, you asked:

> *Have you thought of resigning?'*
> *'I'm not going to walk away from a mess. I've got a responsibility to sort it out. I'd regret it forever if I didn't at least have a damn good try.'*

> *'I don't mean Zyball. I mean have you thought of resigning from Temco? John [the deputy chairman] is perfectly capable of taking over. You could say you were resigning so that you could focus more on restoring the health of Zyball.'*

The chairman thought this was an excellent idea and the next day met John to discuss it. John tried to discourage him, saying that resigning from Temco was unnecessary and that he was overreacting:

> *'You've got 30 years of good reputation behind you. This is the first blot on the copybook. Why don't you put it in perspective? Sure there will be a fuss. Just tough it out.'*

He was, however, determined and then went on to talk to Jim. Jim did not want to lose his chairman, even to the extent of saying that he would tone down his expectations for this year. The chairman was touched by Jim's loyalty but still determined to resign. He told Jim that just because he was resigning didn't mean that he wasn't interested and he would still be available for advice.

He did resign from Temco and spent the next two years almost full time at Zyball. Zyball's fortunes were restored and more than that, it became a leader in its market. It has recently been sold to a US company in the same sector.

Temco has also flourished and through some good acquisitions has built a commanding position in its industry. Jim's shares are currently worth around £10 million. His former chairman sleeps very well at night.

JOURNALISTIC LICENCE

Paul, the chief executive of NIMBO plc, is in a foul mood. He has just complained to you, his chairman, for the fifth time in three days about *'That bloody hatchet job in the* Financial Times *last week.'*

It seems that everyone he meets has seen it and wants to discuss it. Naturally you can understand why he feels uncomfortable discussing an article in which he was described as *'The charisma-free and deeply suspicious CEO of NIMBO'* and which went on to say, *'Although not liked by his industry peers and staff, he is envied for the way he has driven out cost.'*

The article also made a number of other specific criticisms relating to the group's inability to make an acquisition following several abortive attempts. In addition, it suggested that labour relations had soured because of a restructuring programme. On the other hand it did point out that NIMBO was the best performer in the industry and although it was not liked, it was a feared competitor and innovator.

Your own view of the chief executive is that he is highly capable if not highly personable. He has made a number of shrewd judgements, not least over people. He is not as bad as he is made out and lets himself down in the way he handles public relations. Previous attempts to coach him in this area have failed. You are also a little embarrassed over the fact that he is now on to his third public relations agency in as many years. He is normally good in front of a crowd and one-to-one, but has lost faith and confidence in dealing with the press. They make him uncharacteristically nervous.

In a rather unfortunate moment this morning he has, in his anger, fired off a fax to the chairman of Pearson to complain about the *'inaccurate and libellous reporting in the* Financial Times.*'* He has threatened legal action and wants the particular journalist to be removed from the paper. He called the journalist the day the article came out and said that he would never give another interview to the paper and that he would withdraw advertising immediately.

You think the matter is getting a little out of hand and feel the need to do something. But what?

What are the issues?

The obvious issue is that the chief executive has handled the press badly, whether the criticisms are fair or not. His lack of skill in this area is undermining his judgement, his ability to do his job and the company's reputation. You may wonder though why, if he is so good in other areas, he appears to have such a blind spot over PR. Is he really as good in other areas? Is there any basis for the criticism over labour relations, for example? Could he be under too much pressure? Is it a lack of confidence? Should he be chief executive of a public company if he can't handle the media part of the job?

As chairman you have ultimate responsibility for the company's reputation. You also have responsibility for the performance of the chief executive. So you need to do something, otherwise you are abdicating responsibility. Any further progress down the current path is bound to undermine the company. Your own ability to handle the press may be important. If you aren't strong in this area then the risk is even greater.

You have apparently been very supportive of him. Is the way you have been trying to influence him appropriate? Does he need firmer guidance? What exactly has been done to coach him before? How much training has he had? Was it at the appropriate level? Have you tried joint interviews so that you can actually observe what it is that goes wrong? Does the business have a clear set of messages, which it is trying to deliver to a defined group of target audiences, or does the public relations strategy need forming/developing? Are the current PR advisers appropriate?

A good relationship with the *Financial Times* is important for any UK listed company. It has an excellent reputation for even-handedness and the quality of its journalists. To have a poor relationship is clearly unhelpful to developing the company's reputation. What can be done to get the relationship back onto a healthy footing? What also should be done about the letter to the Pearson chairman? What is likely to be the response? Is the problem confined to one newspaper and one journalist in particular, or is it much broader? It would be surprising if it were confined.

What do the key institutional shareholders feel? Are investor relations good? Poor handling of the press is bound to be picked up by them, so they will need some background.

How to decide?

In order to decide anything, you need to understand exactly what it is that is going wrong. Having done so, you then need to determine whether the chief executive is capable of fixing it.

Some research conducted by Cranfield School of Management for 3i and Sanders and Sidney in 1999 showed that dealing with the press was one of the most stressful and least enjoyable aspects of a public company chief executive's role. Is there anything you as chairman could do to reduce the pressure for the chief executive to enable him to perform better? Would the chief executive be better moving to a less stressful environment?

A lot depends here on how well you know the chief executive, how much respect there is between you and therefore how easily you can influence him. This is a dilemma where your judgement as to whether the chief executive an deal with the situation is key.

What to decide?

It would appear that you definitely need to do something. If you don't, the share price and reputation of the company are in danger of being undermined. You have two problem areas: what to do about the Pearson letter, and what to do to sort out the chief executive.

You could ignore the Pearson issue on the assumption that there will be a polite letter back saying something to the effect that they are:

Sorry that the chief executive feels disappointed by the article. As I am sure you will appreciate, editorial freedom resides with the Financial Times *and is not influenced by Pearson in any way. I have passed on your letter to the editor of the paper and I am sure he will talk to the journalist and respond to you directly.*

There will then be another polite letter from the editor thanking you for your letter and saying that he has reviewed the article with the journalist and that while the language may have been a little harsh, the paper stands by its view.

With regard to the more important matter of the chief executive's general approach, the first thing you may decide to do is to make sure that this is the only problem he has and that it isn't a symptom of other deeper problems.

Could a *'low profile, no interviews for a period'* approach work? You can certainly try this, but if you are a public company you have to report your results every six months. If you are a consumer company, the general press as well as the financial press will be interested. Once they think they have a fertile source of critical articles, it is hard to avoid it.

Can you use someone else as the company's spokesman without undermining the company? For the results, many public companies use the finance director as a key spokesperson. NIMBO could do this if the finance director is good with the press. It can work in other situations as well, but often only if that spokesman is in the corporate affairs position. Occasionally other executive directors, particularly if they are heir apparent, can make it worse. What many businesses do is to have a number of different people in the company as spokesman for different issues. In this way dependence on one key figure is reduced, the load is shared and the company appears to have more breadth of senior talent.

Should you just give the chief executive the simple objectives of resolving the situation? You might do this as a threat: *'Sort it out, improve your relations with the press, or we'll have no alternative but to fire you.'* Before you issue a threat like this, you must be prepared to carry it out and have a contingency plan.

Alternatively, you could do it in other more supportive ways through much more active coaching, more rigorous rehearsing and so on. If the chief executive really has had all the training that it is possible to have, then training isn't an option. If it is only the one journalist at the *Financial Times* then you might decide it is a simple matter of letting things cool off and then getting the chief executive, perhaps with yourself, to launch a charm offensive. If this is the situation then you have to get the chief executive to remove the personal angle. The chief executive needs to build confidence in dealing with the issue. Maybe targeting other journalists who feel more positively to write some balancing pieces would help build confidence.

How to communicate it?

For the chief executive this is a highly personal and threatening situation. You therefore need to communicate in a way that is sensitive, firm and recognizes the threat to the company. Once you have decided which course of action to take, you will probably want to communicate it quickly to the chief executive.

Depending on what you have decided to do, you will want to speak to the PR agency and other key advisers as well as the rest of the board. This will need doing in a way that doesn't further undermine the chief executive.

What happened?

The Pearson response was pretty much along the lines described above. Hence it wasn't an issue for long, although clearly it didn't improve the relationship between the journalist and the chief executive.

As it turned out, dealing with the press wasn't the only part of the chief executive's game that wasn't going well. There were some tensions among the executive directors and a feeling that the business was starting to outgrow him. Paul had done an excellent job in focusing the company and squeezing as much profit out of it as he could, but he was struggling to come up with a growth strategy.

The chairman considered three main options:

1. Fire him.
2. Get someone else on the board who was more imaginative and more personable and who would be capable of being a successor in 12 months' time.
3. Try and coach him strategically and on the PR front.

It was true that the chief executive wasn't the most imaginative of people, but it was also true that he was good at implementing the ideas of others. He was a very proud man and was aware of where things might be heading. Nothing filled him with horror more than being fired, especially after the press he had had.

The chairman realized this and decided that the best thing to do was to be completely frank. After setting out what he saw as the situation, he painted pictures of the three alternatives above. He then asked the chief executive which one he would prefer. The chief executive went for getting someone else in who could be a successor in 12 months' time. Why? Because he certainly didn't want to be fired and he realized that he wasn't enjoying the job anymore. Even with coaching he felt he would end up in a job he didn't like. Essentially, he and his chairman did a deal that saved face, recognized his contribution and avoided damaging the reputation of the business. The successor has worked out reasonably well. The company has a far better reputation and has made a number of good acquisitions. It isn't as tightly managed as before and is currently looking for a chief operating officer.

SOFTFIN

Softfin is a highly successful software business, which has grown rapidly to sales of £40 million in the five years since it started out. It is owned by the three founders (90 per cent) and the staff. After losses in the first three years and a breakeven last year, Softfin is forecasting a £4 million profit before tax for the current year. The balance sheet is relatively highly geared, as net assets are minimal, but this year's strong cashflow has reduced debt to only £4 million. In summary, Softfin is in good shape financially.

Paul Hind, the driving force behind Softfin, is delighted with the changes he made to the management team two years ago. Paul is an extremely bright and friendly mathematician whose main strengths have been on the product development and technical side. His two co-founders, Jim Dance, originally software development director, and John Grimble, the original finance and operations director, ably support him. Jim is now Internet software director.

A new finance director, Dave Adler, was recruited two years ago when John was becoming stretched by the role. John made the suggestion that he focus solely on operations and that an outsider be recruited to fill the finance director's job. Two independent directors make up the balance of the board. Both are respected figures in the software industry. One of them, Hap Werner, an American based in New England, has proved critical to Softfin's successful US launch. Softfin is therefore well blessed with a highly committed and able top team who get on well. They are a bunch of down-to-earth guys whose success is beyond their wildest dreams and while they are not really driven by financial motivation, they have a very good sense of value.

Softfin's advisers have been chosen wisely. Armitage and Hinchcliff, the local accountancy firm, has been particularly useful and indeed suggested John as a candidate for the FD job.

So what on earth could Softfin have to worry about?

Over the last year, Softfin has been hounded by a London corporate finance house called Megacap. Megacap specializes in high technology companies and has a record of achieving high capitalizations on flotation or trade sale. Megacap's aggressive senior partner. Peter Smittenwith, has shown a particular interest in Softfin. He believes that the new Internet-based products will enable the company to *'get away at a capitalization of £150 million on IPO next year.'* Although the team have no natural empathy with Smittenwith, the numbers he has talked about have excited their interest and all have agreed to continue the process.

Smittenwith has proposed an IPO for a number of reasons: first, to secure the financial independence of the founder shareholders, secondly because it will give the company a wider international profile. He has also suggested that going through the IPO process will be good for the business and prepare it for significant growth. One additional recommendation is that the board should consider forgetting about the London market and go straight to the NASDAQ market in the USA.

While the founders know several former colleagues who have floated on AIM or on the main London market, they don't know much about the process. They wonder what being public is really like. For them the idea seems as daunting as it is exciting.

They appreciate the considerable publicity a NASDAQ quote would bring and the benefit for their US marketing. However, Paul has become a little edgy about it all and has asked you, as a friend and an experienced plc director, to give him some impartial advice.

You are not on the board. What do you say?

What are the issues?

There appear to be plenty. Is the company flotable? Do they really want to float? If so, why and are these valid reasons? What real benefits will it bring? What are the risks? Are the founders at one on the issue of floating? What do they need to consider and have in place if they are? What are the implications if they are not united on the issue? Will they feel comfortable as public company directors? If they do want to float, which market should they choose?

How are Armitage and Hinchcliff likely to react? A flotation may not be in their best interests; they'll probably lose their most exciting client as a consequence. Is Smittenwith the most appropriate adviser for the company? What are the costs if they embark upon the flotation route and then abort for some reason? How would a flotation affect the employees? There's £15 million of value if Smittenwith is right.

How to decide?

None of these issues above should really be addressed before finding out what real objectives Paul and his co-directors have for the company and for themselves. Then they can put the flotation issue into context and work out whether a float would help them in achieving their aspirations.

How flotable is Softfin? If a float is not feasible for whatever reason, then the issue of whether to float can be quickly dealt with. If this is the case, there may be other issues to resolve.

So what is Softfin's 'flotability quotient'? What needs to be considered? First and foremost there are several fundamentals such as the company's growth prospects. These need to be excellent and clearly explicable. The next thing to consider is one of scale. This is related to the market they pick, but right across the world smaller capitalized stocks have been out of favour. Even on the most hungry technology markets, the NASDAQ and the Neuer Market, size matters. Unless the business is above or will quickly become above £100 million in value, it is pretty hard to do it.

If Softfin has excellent growth prospects and is likely to get to the critical mass required quickly, then the next thing to consider is management. Are they capable of running a public company as well as the business? Even if they are, will they be happy doing so? No one should go near a float without having talked to several people who have been through the process. For many it is a great disappointment. They find the extra disclosures and criticism harder to live with than they think. Do they need to recruit at a senior level to increase the management capacity in the business? Running a public company consumes additional management resource.

Even if Softfin's 'flotability quotient' is high and a float is feasible, they need to ask themselves why they want to do it and whether a float is the best way to achieve these objectives. For many, a flotation is a significant achievement to strive for, especially if they started the business from scratch. Ego or personal ambition seldom appear on a prospectus as the reason for a new issue. One, or more likely all, of the following will appear.

- Raise capital for expansion.
- Enhance the profile of the business and increase awareness.
- Enable the company to use its shares for acquisitions.

Which of these apply to Softfin? All might. However, a trade sale may produce more cash for shareholders and cash to develop the business. Venture capital funding may also meet those needs more efficiently and at less cost. With regard to profile, a listing does enhance a company's credibility while it is performing well. Yet the benefit of the profile of a languishing, small-capitalized stock is a risk to consider.

The key consideration is the attitude of Softfin's directors. How will they deal with it? Unless they have a high level of enthusiasm for the float based on real knowledge of what they are letting themselves in for, it is not advisable to proceed down that route.

If they decide they are able to float and that they want to, then considering the appropriate choice of adviser matters enormously. There sounds like a poor fit in terms of style between Smittenwith and the company. He is clearly more interested in having another IPO to his name, the prestige of NASDAQ and a fat fee, than the longer-term interests of the company. Has he been picked following a proper selection of suitable advisers? What is his real record like? What references can they get on him? What is his reputation in the relevant markets? How will he work with the company's other advisers? These and many more questions will need to be answered satisfactorily before you would feel comfortable with the choice.

Armitage and Hinchcliff are likely to put their client's interests first and, albeit with some sadness, recognize that the business has outgrown them. If Softfin does decide a change is required, whether it determines a float is the right route or not, then it will need to take great care in getting the right accounting advice.

Apart from the directors, they will need to consider the other employees of the business. How would a flotation impact on them? If

Smittenwith is right, they will be worth £15 million between them at flotation. How many will look to cash in their chips? Will this provide a great incentive to attract other high quality people? There are a range of things to discuss relating not just to the employee share schemes and incentives post-float.

What to decide?

The options are reasonably clear. They could float on NASDAQ, if feasible, with Smittenwith as their adviser. They could float on another market, for example AIM, again with the help of Smittenwith. They could float with a different adviser, decide a float is a good idea but in the longer term, or not float at all. The values being put on the business may make them consider an outright sale of the company.

Exploring these options will inevitably prompt them to look at the strategy and the board of Softfin. Even if they don't decide to float or sell they may make some changes.

What did they do?

Their friend advised caution. She offered to hold a meeting with Softfin's directors to discuss the dilemma. She suggested bringing along another friend of hers who had recently floated successfully. Paul agreed.

She started the meeting by getting the team to restate Softfin's strategy, then got them to talk quite openly about what they wanted for themselves. Given the strength of the team, this worked. For less united teams it wouldn't. When they had all made their views known, it was obvious that the most important thing for them was for Softftin to become a significant player in its market segment and for them to continue to build it. They loved the business and wouldn't have sold it. At the same time, they all wanted to have financial independence guaranteed as soon as they could.

The friend who had recently floated successfully described with tremendous enthusiasm what quoted life was like. Meeting analysts, doing presentations and dealing with the press were highly stimulating for him. The more he spoke the more Paul realized this wasn't for him. However, he did want to, as he described it, *'put some money behind the clock'* and ensure his family was secure.

Then they discussed what the alternatives to a flotation might be. The friend asked if they had ever considered a private placing of some of the equity with an institution. While this obviously wouldn't be at a flotation or full sale capitalization, it would provide a significant sum and allow them to continue to control the company. Her idea seemed to have resonance with the directors. Armitage and Hinchcliffe were instructed to explore this option in more detail and this is what actually happened. Each of the directors raised £1 million post-tax.

Softfin went from strength to strength and remains a highly successful private company of considerable value. They have turned down many offers from potential acquirers over the last few years, but plan to sell the company next year.

QUESTIONS AT THE AGM

The Annual General Meeting is in itself a dilemma for many directors. There is a wide range of views on their usefulness. As the company secretary of one FTSE100 company put it:

> *I do not believe there is much, if any, upside for a company in the way it conducts its AGM, but there is unlimited downside if it is not handled properly.*

For bigger public companies the cost of staging the AGM can sometimes be larger than the combined value of the shares that those attending hold. Some chairmen feel that the AGM is a dreadful ritual that just has to be got through. Others, including Warren Buffet, who regularly pulls in 15,000, view it as a great marketing opportunity. Most, even those who find it an uncomfortable experience, will say that the rigour and discipline of having to prepare for it are healthy.

This dilemma is treated in a different way to the others. What follows is a look at some of the issues surrounding the AGM and then a collection of stories from FTSE100 company AGMs. I am extremely grateful to those company secretaries, chairmen and finance directors who provided them.

What is the point of the Annual General Meeting?

In their excellent *Guide to the Best Practice for Annual General Meetings*, the Institute of Chartered Secretaries puts this succinctly as:

> *Although all companies are required to hold an AGM of their shareholders, the event is not merely a matter of legal form. It provides the principal forum in which the directors account to the shareholders for their stewardship of the company. It also gives shareholders an opportunity to raise issues before voting on matters which require approval.*

What are the normal resolutions to be voted on?

Typically they are:

- Consideration of the Directors Report and Accounts.
- Approval of the final dividend, if any, recommended by the directors.

- Re-election of the directors.
- Appointment of the auditors.
- Authorizing the directors to set the auditors remuneration.
- Usually also some alternation to the company's share capital or amending the Articles of Association.

These matters usually take little time and receive minimal shareholder attention. Administrative errors or miscommunication prior to the meeting can cause problems. One such occurred at the AGM of a joint venture company where one of the joint venture partners voted against the reappointment of the auditors without warning because the previous day the group had changed its policy.

Several larger companies have taken to putting up a slide with the number of proxies cast for and against each resolution to make it even quicker. While improving the efficiency of the meeting, it does serve to ram home the impotence of the attendees. The reality for many public companies, especially those in consumer goods, retail or services, is that most of the time is taken up with:

- Consumer rather than shareholder-driven issues.
- Explaining policy on matters such as
  ethical investments;
  government in XYZ country;
  green issues;
  millennium computer alliance;
  the latest accounting standards.
- Director's remuneration, their equity and share option positions.

All of these are important, yet is this really an acceptable balance of items?

So what other issues are there?

Who to bring along apart from the directors can be an issue. Do you need a lot of support from within the company to answer questions before the meeting or help during the meeting? Some people prefer to populate the front rows with friendly faces.

How do you play the microphone game? Do you have roving microphones? Some have one or two microphone points that questioners have to walk down to the front to use – a natural inhibitor if ever there was one. How do you know the questioner is a shareholder? Views differ on the effectiveness of colour-coded cards for the various types of attendee. Do you insist that people stand up and state their names and, if appropriate, who they represent? If you are going to do this you need to avoid the situation one chairman found himself in. He started the Q&A session by saying:

> *Would you please wait for the microphone to arrive, stand up so everyone can see you and then state your name. If you are representing an organization, please inform the meeting.*

The questions proceeded smoothly until one person was handed the mike and didn't stand but started to ask his question. He got as far as 'Mr chairman …' when the chairman interrupted and said:

> *I'm terribly sorry, but could I ask you to stand up and state who you are representing?'*
> *'I'm afraid the first bit is a little difficult, but I'm happy to tell you I represent the disabled and can't stand.*

Most company secretaries are now very good at ensuring that AGM venues are friendly to the disabled.

Do you go for the glitzy presentation or for a more low-key approach? Should you try to anticipate all the questions you might get asked and work them into the presentations? Does it work asking shareholders to write in beforehand with questions and opening the Q&A session with these? How many questions do you want to allow for? Is there a time limit? Do you answer the questions asked or take the politician's route of answering the question you would have liked to have been asked? How do you deal with the person who tries to hog the meeting and uses his question as an opportunity to make a speech? Do you have a rules-of-engagement style introduction to the question time, such as:

> *I want to make it quite clear as chairman of the meeting that this part of the meeting is for shareholders to ask questions of the board about the company. It is not an opportunity for representative groups to make speeches.*

Even the calmest of chairmen become exasperated with the lobbyist who won't give up. But don't fall into the trap of one chairman who was absolutely livid with the questioner who had ignored all the guidance about making speeches and went on for 10 minutes. After several valiant attempts to interrupt, the chairman unfortunately lost his patience and said, *'Look either I'm stupid or you are ...'.* Before he could complete his statement the questioner joyfully interrupted him with, *'Perhaps we should put that to the vote.'*

Another chairman was able to deal with a very reasonable shareholder that in the chairman's eyes was getting a bit close to some sensitive issues. The disgruntled shareholder asked six questions, all of them good and fairly tricky for the chairman to deal with. Remarkably, the chairman responded by thanking him for his vote of thanks and closed the meeting.

Preparation is the key to dealing with AGM questions. Getting people from within the company as well as your advisers to pose all the difficult questions they can think of is good practice. One of the main reasons for having the AGM in my view is that it does force you to think through all of these issues. The rigour of preparation is healthy and there are questions that get right to the heart of the matter. If you are having problems with the repetitive questioner or keeping order, then the Institute of Chartered Secretaries guide provides some very useful tips.

For major international companies, broadcasting the AGM may become necessary. The form of a broadcast meeting may need to be quite different from when it is simply in one room.

The UK government, in its review of the Companies Act, has explored the idea of doing away with the current form of AGMs for public companies. A proposal, which they floated in the press, was to replace the current meeting with one with an independent chairman who is not the chairman of the company. The idea received a negative response from almost all quarters.

If you really don't believe in the concept and want to deter people from coming, then you could always try the trick that many use of having their AGMs at very inconvenient times and less than convenient locations. I've been invited to them on Boxing Day before now. When I was in Yorkshire I was invited to one on New Year's evening. It was held in a freezing works canteen.

Some tales from the real world

Here is a selection of tales and views from chairmen, finance directors and company secretaries, mostly UK and mostly public companies:

> *❛Unfortunately the food ran out within 10 minutes. Although the entire meeting had gone smoothly, the lack of food was the only point of discussion after the meeting. The staff who were present to help with the AGM had*

been scoffing for a full hour and a half before the shareholders! My instruction to cut the budget from the previous year was obviously a mistake.

'The chairman was asked a technical question, which he simply couldn't answer and referred it to the production director, who at the time was rocking slowly back on his chair. It came as such a surprise to him to be called upon to say anything, that he managed to tip his chair backwards off the platform, disappearing into the curtain behind.'

From the same company secretary:

‘ We have always tried to operate a system of closing the doors to the AGM at the time of commencement of the meeting. The meetings are relatively large, about 400–500 people, and it does disrupt proceedings to let latecomers enter. The instructions therefore are to let latecomers watch the proceedings on a video outside. These instructions had managed to translate themselves to the security guards as meaning a complete barring of anybody. After one such shareholder had been overzealously barred, she was eventually let into the meeting whereupon, by that time emotionally overwrought, she managed to address the chairman through her tears for at least 10 minutes.

'In recent years we have sometimes been troubled by an increasingly eccentric professional shareholder who has challenged the Mafia connections of the auditors and the personal integrity of the chairman. Generally he has been called to order by the other shareholders. Usually he chooses some obscure topic as his lead-in item. His best question so far was whether the company had the perfect number of trustees for its pension scheme. In the heat of the moment nobody gave the correct answer, which is "Yes, because as you will know, six is a perfect number".

'Sadly the wonderfully entertaining octogenarian who launches attacks on the board in Latin seems to have retired this year.

'For God's sake don't attempt to hold it before about 11 am. To do so invokes indignant questioning from those shareholders who are unable to use their bus passes.'

From a large service business:

‘A little problem we had for our first AGM was knowing how many to cater for. We had recently floated with 46,000 successful public applications. We knew 20 per cent of the postcodes were local, so we could have a large turnout. So we booked the town hall. We set out seats for 300 and got 60.

'Elderly shareholders are very good at letting a questioner know they've gone on too long. The coughing and rustling of sweetie papers is much more effective than slow hand clapping or booing which I gather happens elsewhere!

'Most of the interesting comments are to be found in proxy cards where shareholders with no intention of attending give vent to their spleen with uncensored comments.

'Our chairman and most of the non-executives get confused about the cards given to attendees. Shareholders get red cards and proxies get blue. But of course the blue cards never get used unless we have a motion defeated on a show of hands, which has never happened to date. On more than one occasion I've had non-execs asking me why they never got to use their blue cards, and I've had to correct the chairman when he got his colours mixed up and offended all the red card holders (who are of course the majority of those attending).

'The chairman's wife had been admitted to hospital to give birth to their fourth child. A mobile phone rang during the meeting the chairman's elderly mother answered and left the meeting. We made preparations to deputize for the chairman, but as it turns out it was simply another relative ringing for news!

'As one of the auditors of a company, I had a wager each year with the company secretary about the number of seconds the meeting would take. I lost more times than I won and I now suspect two of the directors were colluding with the company secretary. Two hundred seconds was fairly typical.'

From the AGM of one of the UK's largest financial institutions:

Questioner: 'Anyway, I will now tell you a little story about how bright they are in Yorkshire. It's wash day today and we have to prop the line up where there is a bit more stirring of air so you get your clothes dried and this woman nagged her husband to bring a new prop home and eventually he brought one and reared it up at the side of the house and she came out and noticed it hadn't a little v cut in the top so he went to borrow a saw. When he got back he couldn't reach so he went to borrow a ladder and she saw him struggling with this ladder and said, 'Well, you great silly beggar, you could have reached it out of the bedroom window!" Anyway, that's it then.'
Chairman: 'Thank you Mr X. I think from the applause you had everyone recognizes that these meetings would not be the same without you.'

Another one from the same company:

Questioner: 'If the Bank of England didn't agree with what was going on, they would soon let everyone know, wouldn't they?'
Chairman: 'The Bank of England would act in its normal labyrinthine and complex way, but you can rest assured that they would find a way of telling us. Yes, absolutely.'
Questioner: 'You can't do anything without they agree with it.'

Chairman: ‘ *Well, that's overstating the position.* ’
Questioner: ‘ *Well, I know but it's simplified for me.* ’
Chairman: ‘ *I can't simplify something which is complex.* ’
Questioner: ‘ *I can only deal with simple things, you see.* ’
Chairman: ‘ *The simple answer is no.* ’
Questioner: ‘ *No. No what?* ’
Chairman: ‘ *No, they don't.* ’
Questioner: ‘ *No what: they don't keep an eye on you?* ’
Chairman: ‘ *They keep an eye on us but they would not influence the board unless they felt that we had gone and got some sort of blaggard on the board, then they would certainly find a way of letting us know.* ’
Questioner: ‘ *They are really looking after us. If there were anything vitally wrong they would let you know.* ’
Chairman: ‘ *They are looking after you.* ’
Questioner: ‘ *We can trust them, thank you very much, sir.* ’

And another:

Questioner: ‘ *Now my questions are very simple, you only have to say yes or no. How many directors are Freemasons and if so who? Yes or no, and who are you – put your hands up.* ’
Chairman: ‘ *I have no idea. I do not get involved in the personal affairs of the members of the board. If it gives you any consolation, or indeed discomfort, I don't know which – I am not a Freemason.* ’

Following a six-minute speech by a questioner:

Chairman: ‘ *Mr X, can I ask you if you are going to come to your question? You've been on that podium quite a long time.* ’
Questioner: ‘ *Are you having a democratic debate? You took 19 minutes.* ’
Chairman: ‘ *I want a democratic debate.* ’
Questioner: ‘ *You took 19 minutes.* ’
Chairman: ‘ *The debate is democratic if a lot of people take part in it.* ’
Questioner: ‘ *You took 19 minutes at the start, sir.* ’
Chairman: ‘ *I'm just urging you to please cut your remarks short and ask us the questions.* ’
Questioner: ‘ *I have a few remarks to make. Chair, may I continue please? Thank you.* ’
Chairman: ‘ *I'm not prepared to give you very long. If you've got questions to ask …* ’
Questioner: ‘ *If the Hall wishes to hear me then I would ask them to applaud now (applause). Thank you very much, chair.* ’
Chairman: ‘ *That was what you call a thin ripple of applause and if people would like me to cut him off when he speaks for too long, please clap now*

(louder applause). Now that's your warning. Please address your questions and get on with it.'

From the somewhat chauvinistic chairman of another company:

Questioner: *' Why are there no women on the board?'*
Chairman: *' I've never enjoyed much success with the ladies but I have high hopes for my successor.'*

Happily, one of his successor's first actions was indeed to appoint a woman to the board.

MR INVINCIBLE

Ed runs a small public company with a market capitalization of £60 million. He became ACO's CEO at the time of a £10 million management buy-out. This was a brilliantly timed deal. ACO was bought in a difficult time in the industry on a price earnings multiple of five from a troubled conglomerate. Ed had been put in to turn the company around two years earlier. After stabilizing the situation very quickly he'd started to grow it. However, he needed capital and the group came under serious pressure from its bankers and were forced to sell.

Ed has become something of a local celebrity and is fêted by all and sundry. He has also started to enjoy his new-found wealth, though he has made some big purchases that he is feeling a bit uncomfortable about. The £500,000 cruiser moored at Cowes has proved difficult to get to from Middlesborough despite the helicopter, which seems to be parked at the airport most of the week.

Ever since the float he has felt people have been treating him differently and despite his outward display of increasing confidence, he is not completely sure who to trust any more. The truth is that he is feeling a bit lonely. As a consequence he is listening less and less to advice. However, the business, which has gone from strength to strength, still gives him a tremendous kick.

Moderate concerns you had about the cohesiveness of the board and its capacity to develop the company to a market capitalization of £150 million became heightened when you heard Ed pronounce in exasperation at a recent board meeting, *'It's hard to soar like an eagle when you are surrounded by turkeys.'* He feels that the other non-exec is a poodle.

You joined the board at the time of the buy-out and have a good rapport with Ed, but haven't been as involved the last year or so. Ed has continued to be chairman and chief executive, a position the institutions were comfortable with at the float. Indeed, the lead investor was on record as saying that the clarity of purpose that resulted from this structure was an excellent feature of the investment. Recently an analyst irritated Ed by raising the issue again.

As a non-executive on the board of ACO do you feel any responsibility to intervene and if so, how?

What are the issues?

Ed is the issue and Ed has lots of issues. Success and money seem to have combined to make him lose contact with reality in a classic way. Arrogance and isolation are the consequences, and the final result if he continues down this route is likely to be that serious errors of judgement will arise. How long will it be before this and the issues below affect performance?

He is also showing signs of boredom. Not a good thing in an entrepreneur, boredom can quickly lead to disruptive behaviour. What is Ed's end game? Does he know? Maybe he is just one of those people who lives for the moment. Although it doesn't look like it, it could well be the case that he is also finding the growth difficult to cope with. You might also wonder whether Ed enjoys life in the spotlight as much as he indicates.

With regard to the turkeys, are they really turkeys? If so, who picked them? Almost certainly Ed. Perhaps the cause of their underperformance is the way they are being managed. If they really are turkeys, then how can Ed be relied upon to replace them with more appropriate people? Would changing the other members of the team really alter the situation, or would things end up the same after a honeymoon period? Whatever the real situation, Ed's attitude towards them is untenable.

You are an issue as well. You have obviously taken your eye off the ball and are out of touch. Why and what does this mean for your ability to influence Ed? The other non-executive director has been described as a poodle; are you? Has he just done what you have done and not got involved? Can you and he together act to help Ed?

The final issue, and one that has already been raised, is whether the roles of chairman and chief executive should be split. This is a source of obvious tension for Ed. Yet maybe if he had split the roles before and had a decent chairman, some of his current problems might have been avoided.

How to decide?

The urgency of the issue is an important matter to determine first. How serious is the problem at ACO? There is evident potential for significant erosion of shareholder value, but it doesn't look as if the company is at any real risk of failing. How long will it take any action to have effect? It may be that you do need to act now, even if it doesn't look like there will be a problem in the short term.

You probably need to talk to Ed and re-establish your relationship with him before deciding anything. You will also need to form your own view on the capability and suitability of the rest of the top team. This could take some time to do properly.

Should you share your concerns with the other non-executive? Turning him into an ally could prove extremely helpful later. Do you trust his judgement? If you do then you could calibrate each other's views.

Another decision that will need taking is whether now is the time to split Ed's role as chairman and chief executive. If you end up deciding it is, then which role should Ed take? If he becomes chairman, is there an internal candidate for CEO? Internal or external, how will they cope with Ed as chairman? If an external candidate is required, how attractive would ACO be to them? Can you get Ed busy elsewhere to give the new CEO space? Doing so may make it much more attractive. If Ed stays in the CEO role then you may need to think about whether you would be an appropriate chairman of ACO. If you're not and the other non-executive isn't either, then it might be worth sounding out a head-hunter for ideas.

What to decide?

You could just decide to do nothing. Few responsible and high calibre non-executive directors would ignore such a serious breakdown in the relationships between the executive directors. There doesn't seem to be anyone else involved who will change the current course.

If you do decide to intervene then it looks pretty hard to get anywhere without increasing your influence with Ed. How might you do this? Probably just through spending more time with him and not rushing it. Given the description it sounds as if there are a lot of issues in the business, particularly with the people. More likely than not, Ed has made mistakes in the way he has managed the team. Coaching leaders is sometimes easier to do by talking about their team, and finding a way for him to recognize the consequences of his current behaviour is bound to help.

Developing a stronger relationship with Ed will probably provide the insight required to decide if Ed can adapt, should change roles or whether he needs removing. If Ed needs removing, you need to decide how this can be done and how he will be replaced. Even if Ed adapts, is it tenable for him to continue in the dual role of chairman and chief executive?

Deciding that Ed's role needs to change and that it isn't tenable for him to remain as both chairman and chief executive means you have to decide which role he will take and how the job he is giving up will be filled.

How to communicate it?

Persuading Ed to adapt or change his role will be the key communication. There would be a greater loss of status for Ed in relinquishing the chairmanship than the CEO position. Whatever you decide, you have to get him to really buy in to the idea and then make it work. Painting Ed the pictures of a successful future where he is seen to have made the smart move, or the public embarrassment of outstaying his term, is probably the only way to achieve it.

Moving Ed's role to chairman is probably the easier solution from an external communications point of view. However, you will need to make it clear that he has to give the new CEO space to do the job and that both of them will have to agree their respective roles. Having a full-time executive chairman and a chief executive usually results in friction. So you will need to get Ed busy elsewhere as soon as possible.

Getting the other non-executive to become more involved and less of a poodle may prove hard. Perhaps the best way to achieve this is through admitting that you both need to become more involved for Ed's sake.

What did the independent director do?

The first thing he did was to kick himself for not spending as much time on ACO as he felt he should have done. The second thing was to decide that he was the only one on the board who could avoid the situation deteriorating into something much more serious. Fortunately, he was a high calibre non-executive who had just been too busy elsewhere.

Ed was partly right in that he did need a stronger team, but he had tended to pick poodles rather than turkeys. They were an average rather than sparkling bunch. The independent director's solution was very straightforward. He got Ed to agree to get in some stronger people and for himself to become chairman. He achieved this through painting Ed some pictures of the alternatives and giving him some very direct feedback on what other people were saying about him. One decision he had taken before he spoke to Ed was that he would resign if Ed didn't go along with the proposed changes. Fortunately, he didn't have to use this as a threat, but he believed the fact that he was absolutely determined to resign if necessary helped to increase the conviction with which he spoke.

Why did Ed go along with this without putting up a fight? The reason was that he was desperately unhappy with his life and hated the isolation. He thought the independent director had lost interest. For some reason he felt anxious about discussing it with him. Consequently he was delighted at the revitalized interest that was shown. While one independent director had delivered when required, the other that was remained a poodle until he was replaced about six months later.

Ed and his new chairman agreed that they would rebuild the management team together. In the process Ed's eventual successor was recruited. The City took the division of roles well and the independent director resigned from one of his other roles to free up the time to do the job properly. ACO's already strong performance improved and all was set after a couple of years for Ed to retire and take up a chairmanship elsewhere. However, an overseas competitor made a very attractive bid which, after an honourable but not very convincing defence, was agreed.

THE RADIO-CONTROLLED ACCOUNTANT

It is now three years since Danny was appointed as finance director. He's done a good job. The board have found him far more compliant and reliable than his predecessor, who seemed to embody all the worst characteristics of the species and none of the good.

Danny enjoys his job and can always be relied upon to have that spreadsheet ready, that scenario analysed and that deferred tax explanation to hand. However, you and the rest of the board are a little worried that while healthy profits have been reported the last few years and all members including Danny have had good bonuses as a result, the company's cash position has deteriorated. For a while this was put down to growth in working capital to support expansion. Sadly, a recently appointed non-executive has been asking some tricky questions at the board. He has suggested that the stock and tax positions of the company need independently reviewing.

The result of this review has shocked the board. Profits have been overstated and the current stock value is unrealistic. There is considerable concern over the real tax position. Worse, there is significantly more off balance sheet financing than was thought. The company has been in breach of banking convenants, though the bank seems unaware. The MD has challenged Danny but his reaction has been as helpful as ever: *'If you'd like me to tell the bank, I'll do so right away.'* All of the directors are embarrassed. All agree they should have recognized the situation earlier.

You are a recently appointed non-executive director and the only one. The chairman, who is a man of high integrity, wants to fire Dan today. The managing director is extremely nervous about doing this. They both appear to be looking at you for leadership on what to do and to come up with a solution. Danny, ironically, is the one that suggested there be a non-exec in the first place and was a key factor in your selection in preference to someone else.

How should they recover?

What are the issues?

There are a range of issues involved. First, is Danny's overstatement deliberate, incompetent, or both? What about the rest of the management information? How good is that? Is there collusion? Who else is involved if there is? Why is the managing director so nervous of firing Danny? Confidence will be rocked among the top team. The judgement of all of the directors will be questioned. What will be the effect on morale throughout the company?

If there is an audit committee, how did it miss it? What was it doing? What about the auditors? What did their last management letter say? Is there an issue with the auditors?

This is a defining moment. How the company recovers will determine its future.

You may be wondering about your own position and questioning some of your own judgements. Thoughts may turn to the impact on your other appointments, the additional time you are likely to have to spend, and your own credibility.

How to decide?

Those who have experienced these situations will know that letting an incompetent and potentially fraudulent finance director continue in the role for a moment longer is foolish. At least not having a finance director isn't adding to the damage, and getting the facts out of Danny appears a dubious place to start.

What you need is to find some way of creating space with the bank to enable a confirmation of the true position of the company to take place. In this particular situation you may also be trading while insolvent, which has serious implications for all of the directors.

For this situation you will need excellent legal and accounting advice, yet there may be an issue relating to how it might be paid for. The accountants should feel compelled to help if there is any question that the last set of audited accounts was inaccurate. The bank and others may have supplied additional credit on the basis that they represented a true and fair view.

If you cannot persuade advisers to help, then the horror of having to appoint an administrator may become in reality the only option.

The key to deciding what to do is the severity of the company's financial position.

What to decide?

There are a number of decisions to make. Dealing with these in turn, the first concerns whether to fire Danny or not. It is difficult to see any argument for keeping him in place. To knowingly carry on with an incompetent or fraudulent finance director, particularly given the risk of insolvency, would be most unwise. Consequently, he should be suspended immediately pending a thorough investigation and fired the moment the evidence is gathered. The protests that it will undermine credibility at the bank because you'll need to come clean, or that you will lose his knowledge of what has actually happened, are weak. You will have to be honest with the bank immediately anyway and his knowledge is clearly suspect.

Will you report the matter to the police? Many don't in the belief that not doing so will enable the matter to be kept quieter. The damage that such a disclosure might have through undermining confidence in the company would loom large in the mind of any director. However, the forensic skills and experience of commercial fraud detectives may enable them to get there quicker than anyone else. You also have a duty to report a crime if you are aware one has been committed. But what is Danny's crime? It may not be clear whether he has stolen money for himself or whether he has used the money to secure banking facilities under false pretences. Some directors fear being drawn into criminal proceedings. The decision is obviously a personal one for the directors involved. The company's lawyer should be able to provide a view on this subject and would generally advise notifying the police in almost all circumstances.

You need confirmation of the financial position as soon as possible. How do you get it? In this case you will probably need to borrow someone from the auditors. However, as we have already discussed, they don't appear blameless either. The bank may insist on an independent firm. This will be all very well if there are the funds to pay for it.

This brings us on to what to do about the bank. You must come clean, but it is better to do so with a plan. The bank will be looking to see that the situation is under control and that there is a better prospect of recovering their debt with this plan than appointing an administrator at the outset. Coming up with a plan without the facts is tough, so the key part of it is to buy enough time to establish what they are. This might even include loans to the company by the directors, an injection of funds by shareholders, a freeze on payments to suppliers and other crisis measures.

How to communicate it:

Who needs communicating with and in what order?

- your fellow directors;
- the company's lawyers;
- the accountants;
- Danny;
- relevant staff;
- other key advisers (insurers etc);
- shareholders;
- the bank;
- the police.

Depending upon the exact circumstances, there may also be a need to inform customers. In this case there was no requirement to inform the stock exchange or the media. When there is, this adds considerably to the communication exercise and expert advice is required from the company's chief financial and public relations advisers.

A brief and accurate statement will need to be prepared for external purposes along the lines of:

The board has discovered several accounting irregularities and has suspended the finance director pending a further investigation. We have appointed X to confirm the current financial position and will provide an update as soon as we can.

Clearly this won't suffice for shareholders, the bank or others close to the company, so a more detailed explanation of what has occurred, what the implications are, and what the board is proposing to do about it will be necessary.

With regard to how to communicate the news to Danny, the chairman should be the one to deliver it. In this case it would be wise to have this conversation in the presence of the company's lawyer and to have prepared a written notice of suspension and the justification for doing so. The meeting should be kept brief. He should be given the opportunity to rebut the allegations and advised to consult a lawyer. It will be very important to do this as calmly as possible – difficult when you may feel you have in front of you the person who might have destroyed your life's work. Definitely a situation in which to remember Kennedy's *'Don't get mad, get even'* advice.

Your lawyer should make a careful record of the conversation and, if at all possible, get Danny to sign it as being an accurate reflection.

What did the independent director do?

In this specific case he resigned immediately and the company failed shortly afterwards. He was a director of a plc and very concerned about the collateral damage to the plc's reputation, even though he had only just joined. It would be a long haul to sort the problem out and in his view there was a low probability of survival. He knew the bank concerned well and also that neither directors nor shareholders would have or would be prepared to provide any additional cash. He had to decide one way or the other. He was extremely upset about his own due diligence on the company:

> *I didn't meet the finance director before taking the appointment. Something I will never repeat. I knew the managing director as a former colleague. The business had a good reputation and although it looked a little stretched, appeared to have potential.*

In another similar case where the independent director formed the view that a rescue was more feasible, she seized the moment and got a mandate through the insecurity of others. The reason why she did that was that the company's market position was much better and, more importantly, it had a stronger balance sheet. In her assessment it was therefore much more likely to withstand the shock. The shareholders put up sufficient funds for the company to trade, a new finance director was recruited, and the company overcame the problem.

I'VE BEEN ROBBED

Your recent appointment to the group board has crowned a tremendous year. The division you run is now the highest performer in the group by a long way. Sam, the group chief executive, who has been your mentor for the eight years since you joined, obviously sees you as his successor. With only three years to go before his retirement, there is more than enough time to prove to the rest of the board that you are capable of succeeding him. The only competition is from the recently recruited finance director, Jonathan. Jonathan in your view is an excellent numbers man and has a fearsome intellect, but is somewhat aloof and lacking in the charisma department. Superficially you seem to be getting along well, but the relationship is somewhat formal.

A lot of your own success has been put down to the ability to manage and motivate aggressive sales-led managers in all departments. Several of these, including Harry, the highest performer, were taken on against the advice of the human resources department.

Today has been a day like no other. It began ordinarily with some routine review meetings and a lengthy call to one of the biggest customers. The thunderbolt came just before lunch. Sarah, your secretary, interrupted an appraisal meeting with the systems director to inform you that Jonathan would like to see you urgently in his office.

Your sense of foreboding increased when you saw Alec, the internal audit manager, in Jonathan's office.

Please sit down, Jim. I'm afraid I've got some rather bad news for you. We've discovered a serious fraud in your division involving the theft of £50,000. Harry Ramforth is the perpetrator, but unfortunately it also involves employees of BINCO (a supplier) and BILCO (a customer). This is a dreadful time for this to occur with the share price where it is. All that work I've done getting the analysts to take us more seriously was just starting to pay off. A 15 per cent increase isn't won easily, you know.

You make a weak effort to say something, but the news has hit you hard. All that emerges is a meaningless mumble.

While it is technically a corporate theft, to you it feels deeply personal. You recruited Harry. It was you who singled him out for promotion, you who covered up for some of his slight excesses, like the fact that his car only ever seems to do five miles per gallon. How could he be so stupid? He earns a fortune as it is and had the potential to earn a lot more.

Jonathan discovered the fraud – a simple theft involving collusion with a supplier and a customer. He believes the facts are easy to prove and is furious about the situation. Adverse publicity or any questioning of the company's control systems would be inconvenient, given the current depressed share price. He makes it clear that the whole thing is your responsibility and you are the one who needs to sort it out.

What do you do? Fire Harry on the spot? Suspend him? Kill him? Call the police? Talk to the company lawyer? Get him to put money back and tighten controls? Talk to the lawyers and human resource advisers? What will you say to the rest of the staff? How can you face other board members? Who's going to trust your judgement now? All sorts of thoughts race through your mind.

You tell him that you will fire Harry and that you will do it in as silent a way as possible. Your resolve stiffens but your anxiety increases when you confront Harry with the situation and he says, *'Look, I'll make it easier for you. Give me £10,000 and a good reference, and I won't say a word to anyone, promise.'*

What are you going to do now?

What are the issues?

Why did you confront Harry so quickly? How did you do it? Did you have a witness? What's the outcome? It sounds like the conversation has happened sooner than it should.

Determining what needs to be done in fraud situations is far easier if the facts are clear. Yet gaining the evidence is not always straightforward. For example, in this case is the collusion confined solely to BINCO and BILCO? Is Harry really the only employee of the group involved? If Harry's known transgressions are tolerated, then others may assume consent to do the same. It is important to find out exactly what evidence the finance director has to back up what he has said. A forensic accountant from the police or from an accountancy firm can be of considerable help in establishing what has actually happened and providing objective advice.

In business, the embarrassment factor means that occasionally people really do get away with daylight robbery. Firing someone quietly can avoid the damage to the company's reputation, the calling into question of control in the business and the considerable time taken up in going through a proper legal process. It can also make the wound less open. So the attitude of the board to fraud will be an issue. Many boards discuss this before there is ever a situation to deal with. Making sure there is a clear understanding about what will happen is helpful. Letting it be known that the company's policy is to press charges and involve the police may also act as a deterrent.

Who needs to be informed is another important issue. Who should communicate with BILCO and BINCO? Should the police be involved? Do you need to inform the Stock Exchange? Should all directors of the company be informed, and what about the people in Harry's team? Harry hardly sounds like a quiet chap tucked away in the corner. The rumour mill will be working overtime. What do you want to say within the company?

Any good non-executive, on hearing about a fraud in a subsidiary, will want to be sure that the financial systems and controls elsewhere in the group, are appropriate and that there is a process for reviewing and updating them where required. For the chairman of the audit committee there may well be some additional soul searching.

In this case there doesn't appear to be any question of the fraud causing the company to fail. In some companies there might be, and this is bound to affect the thinking of the board. Telling a bank that the security they are relying upon for an extended facility isn't really there, is a tough thing to have to do. However, not to do so is to join in the fraud.

What would be the impact of Harry going? Will any others leave? What will happen to his key customer relationships and so on?

News like this is bound to knock your confidence. The situation could obviously ruin your chances of becoming the group chief executive and take you a long time to recover from. An ambitious finance director who covets the top job is likely to use this incident for some time to come.

The final issue is to pause for a moment and think of Harry. What are his rights? What is he likely to do if he is fired? Do you need to suspend him before you fire him? What should the process be? What sort of reference will you give him?

How to decide?

Harry's attempt at blackmail may quite naturally result in anger. Anger, despite its power to strengthen conviction, is not always a healthy state of mind to be in when making important decisions. So the sooner you can move from a state of anger the better able you will be to make the right decisions. But how? You've already rushed it.

Establishing a couple of clear objectives might help. If your objectives are to minimize the damage to the company and your own reputation, then you will need to enlist the support of others and make sure that everyone involved will end up praising the way you handled it. A strong sense of responsibility for sorting things out doesn't mean you have to do it all on your own.

Making sure you get the right professional input and gathering the evidence is then the next step. Relevant professional input will come from the human resources director, the internal auditor, the company's lawyer and possibly the police.

Armed with the evidence and appropriate advice, it's decision time. Unquestionable evidence of Harry's guilt will reduce the number of decisions. Claims for unfair dismissal, for example, will be unlikely. There is always the danger when the evidence is clear that the despatch of the guilty is done in haste and the potential for a wrongful dismissal claim emerges. Sometimes the difference between unfair dismissal and wrongful dismissal is confused. The easiest way to avoid confusion is to remember that unfair dismissal is about whether someone should be dismissed and wrongful dismissal is about how it was done.

Questionable evidence will mean more judgement calls and a less smooth process. One potential area for muddying the clarity of the evidence relates to the involvement of BILCO and BINCO employees.

It also can muddy the removal process if those companies have different approaches to dealing with these situations and if the communications between the three companies are not clear.

One final thing to consider is where Harry is. In terms of the process, if he is off-site, on holiday, or away for some other reason, this can mess the process up.

What to decide?

This depends very much on the evidence. With clear evidence, firing Harry in the most effective way is the obvious action. Deciding to do this alone is inadvisable, so the decision is who to involve as a witness or whether to ask the HR director to do it with the company lawyer as a witness.

You may need to suspend Harry pending an investigation if the facts aren't clear or evidence needs collecting.

To involve the police or not is the next thing to decide. Involving them in the process early on is advisable if you have a policy to bring proceedings. Obtaining evidence that can be used in court is key if you want them to bring charges.

Making sure he has access to a lawyer is the next thing to consider. It may help considerably for him to be advised by someone sensible.

How to communicate it?

Who needs communicating with? Harry, BILCO, BINCO and then the staff of the company.

Firing Harry yourself with a witness present should be done briefly, clearly and with a prepared written statement. Suspending him is straightforward in terms of communications, though care is needed over what is said as to the reasons for the suspension.

In either the firing or suspension situation you will probably want Harry escorted off the premises as quickly as possible. To do this involves making preparations. Many want to take all the company possessions of the guilty party straight away. This may make you feel better, but it can cause unnecessary hassle for little benefit. For example, is suspending him pending an investigation and then asking him for the keys to his company car a smart move?

BILCO and BINCO's chief executives are the most appropriate people to speak to. If you already have a relationship with them then this will be easier. Whether you do or whether you don't, you will need to be very factual and clear about the process you propose for dealing with the situation.

For your staff, much depends on Harry's relationships. Morale is bound to be affected. What's needed is a feeling that you have things under control, it is very serious and the matter is being dealt with as fairly and as effectively as possible.

What did the divisional MD do?

The situation came as such a shock to him that he wasn't thinking clearly when he stormed straight from the finance director's office to Harry's. He slammed the door shut and told Harry in a highly emotional way that he had found out what he was up to and wanted him out of the building 'before I kill you'.

Harry pretended that he didn't know what he was talking about and a loud and violent argument ensued until Harry said:

> ‘ Look alright, you're right, I did it, but XXXX at BILCO put me up to it. Sacking me and making a big deal of it will ruin your reputation. Look, I'll make it easier for you. Give me £10,000 and a good reference, and I won't say a word to anyone, promise.'
>
> 'No way you *******' was your response. ’

At this point the internal auditor arrived. Jonathan had been concerned about the divisional MD's manner when he left his office and sent Alec down to make sure he did nothing silly. Too late!

Alec suggested that the divisional MD leave Harry's office. He then called the human resources director and asked him to join them immediately. Together they did a tremendous job of restoring some order to the situation. They explained to Harry very calmly that they had reason to believe that he was involved in a serious fraud and that he would be suspended on full pay immediately pending an investigation. This investigation was likely to take two weeks and would involve the police. Harry was asked to make himself available for interview during the two weeks and told to remain in his office until a letter was prepared confirming the situation. Alec and the HR director then went off to prepare this and their respective deputies arrived to look after Harry until they returned.

The investigation revealed that Harry was indeed the perpetrator. The scale of the fraud turned out to be much larger, at just under £85,000, and one of Harry's staff was also involved. The police were able to gain sufficient evidence to convict Harry and three of the four others.

The divisional MD never recovered. His confidence and faith in his own judgement were destroyed. His emotional reaction allowed

Jonathan the excuse to propose to the board that he should be fired. The group chief executive persuaded the board that the divisional MD's reaction was completely out of character and that given his length of service and track record, firing him would be inappropriate. The board reluctantly agreed but only on condition he was moved to a different job. Another suitable job was hard to find and the divisional CEO's confidence suffered further. In the end he retired early on health grounds.

A sad tale, and one in which a moment's calm collection would have produced a very different outcome.

CONVO

Convo is a south coast food manufacturing business, founded ten years ago by its chairman and chief executive, Archie Cresswell. Archie is an infectiously enthusiastic and effervescent process engineer who has grown Convo from nothing into a £40 million turnover business. In the process he has been awarded a CBE and developed a profile for the business far in excess of its size. Convo has also won a Queen's Technology Award, together with a string of industry prizes for innovation.

The business manufactures a mix of own-label and branded products for the major UK multiple supermarkets. It wins customers on the strength of its highly innovative way of processing, preparing and presenting its products.

Three customers account for 70 per cent of sales, the balance being smaller retailers and an exciting but somewhat volatile French agent.

Archie's former employer, BigFood Company, supplies most of the processing plant. They also own 40 per cent of Convo through their initial support of Archie. Archie, his finance director, Paul Tate and the other two executive directors own 15 per cent. Five per cent has been granted in employee shares. The balance is held by an institutional syndicate which invested five years ago to fund the building of a new plant. It did so in anticipation of a float three years ago.

The business has a public aura of success but the institutions are clearly becoming concerned, hence your recent appointment to the board. You can understand some of their increased anxiety and have decided to jot down the following analysis.

The company's strategic direction is making it increasingly reliant on its few key customers. It also seems to be moving it closer to competing head on with global players such as Unilever and Nestlé.

The cash generative growth years fuelled by a high margin environment are over. Surplus cash has been invested in developing new brands and building plant capacity. The recent construction of a new head office/warehouse complex has exacerbated the problem through cost overruns and disruption to deliveries. The retailers have been unsympathetic, so have the institutions with regard to deferring dividend payments. Convo is up to its overdraft limit of £8 million.

You feel that the business has outgrown its management, which is largely inbred. Financial controls are poor, management information is over-elaborate and tends to cloud rather than highlight key issues. You are not convinced about the profitability of two of the eight key product groups. Management is demoralized by constant changes in strategic direction by the mercurial but much loved Archie. His board, as you can see from the profiles below, is an interesting mix.

The relationship with BigFood has become strained and less productive for Convo. Convo had to become far too involved in the detailed design of the latest machines and in fixing the considerable number of teething problems on installation. BigFood's new chief executive has allegedly been questioning the strategic sense in holding minority investments. Having said that, you are suspicious that they might be interested in acquiring control on the cheap. The Convo board is divided into two (if not three) camps and there is much gathering of interest groups before board meetings. BigFood's board representative has become ever more vocal and disparaging in his remarks.

This and next year will probably be loss-making, given the margin squeeze from the retailers and the fact that the latest equipment is still producing at costs much higher than budgeted. There is no possibility of a claim on BigFood.

Despite all of the above, this fundamentally remains a business with enormous potential in its market and it has a deeply committed and talented workforce.

As the only independent board member, all partners (other than BigFood) seem to be looking to you to take the lead and catalyse the situation.

So what are the issues? How could the current situation have been avoided? What are the options? What should you, the independent director, do?

Note. The Articles of Association for the company give BigFood two board votes, the institutions two board votes and the management one vote. There is no casting vote for the chair. There are no compulsory purchase provisions for departing directors who are shareholders, except in the case of termination for cause as stipulated in the service agreement of the individual director concerned. In this instance an executive shareholding may be compulsorily purchased at valuation.

Board profiles

Archie Cresswell (45) chairman and chief executive

An extreme workaholic. He loves the company – it's his baby and he knows every single employee on a first-name basis. Over the years, despite his ego, he has never paid himself adequately and 18 months ago the board insisted on awarding him a 100 per cent salary increase and forced a three-year rolling contract on him. He seems a straightforward, open chap who can see that all is not well. He dominated the company, is strongly defensive of his own position and feels let down by his team. Beneath a seemingly naïve and homespun exterior he can prove wonderfully adept at playing off the two-shareholding factions (BigFood and the institutions). Domestically, he is supported by a strong family who think the world of him and his achievements, even though he neglects them.

Paul Tate, FCA (42) finance director

A local man who qualified with a minor firm in the next town but got bored with auditing. Two years after qualifying he moved into broader commercial management, mostly in trading and commodity businesses. When Archie set up Convo and asked him to be finance director, he was flattered and thrilled, considering the prospect hugely exciting. He did, however, have to gear up and borrow from his father-in-law to invest at the start and in subsequent rounds. A natural over-complicator who will often miss the central point, Paul is, like Archie, a workaholic and is having severe problems at home. He and his wife enjoy the reflected glory of being part of the Convo success story and, despite a relatively low income, are big spenders.

Terence Foster, PhD (38) technical director

A brilliant food technologist who pioneered the first, and still most successful, Convo product. He has always worked with Archie and has an undying loyalty to him despite growing frustrated at the difficulty in finding cash to enhance the plant. Financially and commercially unaware, he is very much the brains of the team. He hates formal presentations to investors but is always thrilled at the prospect of showing visiting buyers and the local university round the plant. He dislikes any general management activity.

Heather Brigland, MBA (41) commercial director

Joined only two years ago from Unilever after an earlier spell at Bain and a career break. Brought in to bring more rigour to strategic thinking and planning, she has never been able to break into the core team of Archie, Paul and Terence. Heather is considered and treated very much as an outsider with no influence at the board. This is a real shame as intellectually she makes excellent points and if she were listened to would add a great deal. However, she often tends to blow it by missing trivial practical points. She also seems to be perpetually trying to alienate René (see below) by scoring points.

René Faux (45) BigFood Co representative

Joined BigFood as a graduate in France the same year as Archie. They didn't meet until they both got their first general manager's jobs. Initially they got on well, but they once sat on the same project group and fell out violently over a redundancy programme. René's career faltered and he has been deeply envious of Archie's independence and very visible success. However, recently he feels he has been gaining ground and, with two highly successful acquisitions behind him, has risen to prominence within BigFood. He only got the board representation job at Convo when his predecessor, a former mentor of Archie's, retired. There is nothing more he would like than to put Archie in the position of having to report to him or give up his business. Archie dislikes René with a surprising intensity.

Angelique Beaulieu (32) BigFood's second representative

René's associate. She tends to be quiet but has remarkable insight and presence when she does join in the conversation. René is slightly irritated by her ability to say what needs saying in a few well-chosen and charming words.

Clive Maxwell (37)

The board representative from the lead venture capital investor. Convo is his star investment and he's done much trumpeting of it inside the institution. He's becoming increasingly uncomfortable as he is out fundraising himself and it isn't going that well. His boss has made it clear to him that if the fundraising falls through because of problems at Convo, he won't have a job.

You – the independent director

A seasoned campaigner with experience of five appointments in young food companies, all of which have experienced growing pains. You love a problem. That's handy!

What are the issues?

There are a whole series of issues relating to Convo's financial position, strategy, people, board structure and ownership. Your own position sounds pivotal. Convo's institutional investors are relying on you. Yet what real authority do you have? You're the newcomer; you have no equity; what is your motivation? If you need external help where will it come from? Who will pay for it? The company?

On the financial front, Convo has run out of cash. There is a mismatch between the financial structure and the requirements of the business. Capital investment appears to be funded from cash flow. Financial control is lax and there are questions over the accuracy of the financial position.

With regard to the strategy, have they got one? It looks mighty confused if they have. They seem to be competing in world markets but operating as a little local company. Dependency on BigFood is an obvious issue.

Convo has a clearly dysfunctional board and management team. Archie looks to be the main problem. His style and capabilities are a poor fit for Convo's current stage of development. He has not built a strong or cohesive team around him. There are also many individual issues apart from Archie. The finance director looks out of his depth and under considerable stress, Heather is demotivated and not able to do her job, René's antipathy for Archie is getting in the way and so on.

There are diverse objectives among Convo's shareholders. Some don't appear to have objectives for their shareholding and there seems little communication between them. The link with BigFood is a major issue and one that threatens the survival of the business. Any change will be difficult to achieve given the current voting structure.

It looks as if the board hasn't been well advised. Convo's advisers may have gone to sleep in the warmth of Convo's earlier success. On the other hand they may have been frustrated in their efforts and given up. It will be important to understand who they are and what they think.

How might the current situation have been avoided?

The board needed changing as the business developed. A key point was the institutional investment. This provided an excellent opportunity to appoint an independent chairman, almost essential in co-owned situations like these. Retaining the chairman and chief executive roles and doing them both well through such a period of growth is extremely difficult, even for the most talented of people. To try to do so without cohesive ownership is to attempt the impossible.

Should the finance director have been replaced earlier? This looks like a no-brainer. Are the independent directors appropriate? With the exception of you, they all have vested interests. Should René have been put in such a role, given the personal animosity between him and Archie? Have the institutions been diligent or negligent? Looks like they are suddenly awakening. The financial structure needed changing to reflect the company's need for cash as it grew. Did the institutions and BigFood recognize this?

A major capital project, ie the new building project, has been poorly managed. Does Convo manage other projects well? Is this just an isolated incident? Is it now sorted out or are there still problems?

The voting arrangements were almost set up to allow Archie to divide and rule. It is difficult at any time, but the voting position could have been more easily addressed when times were good.

How to decide?

Who do you turn to for advice? How do you maintain your honest broker status? What extra information do you require in order to decide what to do? What do shareholders want? Do you think it really does need more money? Do you think you have persuasive powers over Archie? Can you get BigFood and the institutions to act together? These thoughts will be going through your mind before you can decide on a strategy for resolving Convo's problems.

So the first step must be to gather as much knowledge on the priority issues as possible. Consultation with the shareholders will probably be the key to developing a solution. Before taking responsibility for sorting it out, you will need direction, a mandate and possibly some money from the shareholders. Asking the bank for views on what to do may result in panic.

This may be a situation where you need to come to a speedy decision over how much time you can allocate. To sort this one out will require a major time commitment. Determining the exact financial position is essential. External verification of this an imperative.

The next step will be to build alliances to enlist as much support for whatever solution you come up with, particularly if this involves you becoming chairman of Convo.

What to decide?

Let's look at the options. You could do nothing and let them sort themselves out. After all, what's the upside, you have no equity? But what about your reputation with the institutions? To turn and run, even if sensible, is unlikely to enhance it. Presumably when you took the appointment it was clear that it might be a situation requiring increasing commitment. Some people like to wait until the situation reaches crisis point before they act. This one has.

Forcing an immediate sale to BigFood, a trade buyer or a management buy-in is another option. All look difficult to achieve given the current shareholding split. Moreover, Convo is not in an easily buyable state. Any purchaser would need to be very confident in their knowledge of what they were buying and their own management capability. This would presumably be reflected in the price.

Firing Archie is a possibility. There is no obvious successor so his replacement would have to come from outside. The impact on employees, suppliers and customers, given his charisma, needs to be taken into account and managed. Will shareholders support you or consider it too risky? How would you compensate him for loss of office? Does his service contract contain anything to make this course of action difficult in practice? What about his shareholding? Who would tell him? Would you replace him as chairman and recruit a chief executive?

You could redirect and restructure management and raise cash for a limited period. Removing the finance director, re-establishing financial control and giving Archie greater direction may be all that is needed. As a part of this you may be able to persuade BigFood to swap René for someone who doesn't have any personal issues with Archie. To do any of this you would need a strong chairman. Could it be you? Even if you regroup, has Convo a viable future as an independent entity? You may just be stablizing the business before a sale.

Whatever route you choose to adopt, the voting structure means that you will need the support of two of the key constituencies. The most powerful combination is BigFood and the institutions.

How to communicate it?

Considerable diplomatic skill will be required to resolve this situation. In trying to bring BigFood and the institutions together, René mustn't be alienated. However, getting closer to René might have an adverse impact upon your relationship with Archie. Another thing you need to do is to ensure that there is greater communication between the different parties and set a new standard. Do you need additional contacts at BigFood and at the institutions to achieve this? Again, you need to be careful you don't alienate René and Clive by appearing to go over their heads.

Getting Archie to look to you for support and guidance would also be helpful, so you need to strike up a good friendly rapport with him and not appear to be a threat. To get anywhere you will need to be confident and assertive but not aggressive in your communication style. Asking good questions rather than making assertions will probably win the day.

With Archie, painting pictures of the likely outcomes once you have established a good rapport may work.

What did you, the independent director, do?

You decided fairly quickly that the business had outgrown the management, especially Archie and the finance director. To you a sale was the only real solution. However, you also thought that to attempt to achieve this in the short term would be madness. Convo had a tremendous reputation in the market. Its competitors and customers seemed unaware of the difficulties within. Trying to sell Convo in distress would destroy this illusion. So you decided that the best route forward was to stabilize the situation in order to buy time to make the best judgement.

You asked the lead institution to make an introduction to René's boss, which they did along the following lines:

> ‘As you know, the independent director has been in place a short while now. He has formed the view that some urgent action is required at Convo. I think you would find his detailed analysis of the situation very interesting. He is one of the most impressive turnaround chairmen we know. The reason I am calling you directly is because one of the things he is most concerned about is the relationship between René and Archie Cresswell. They seem to have developed an intense dislike for each other, which could potentially undermine Convo. He has asked me if I could talk to you to arrange a meeting for you and him so that he can share his views with you and also get a feel for your objectives for your shareholding in Convo. I think this is an excellent suggestion. For the moment it might be helpful not to raise this with René until after you have heard what the independent director has to say.’

The BigFood co-divisional chairman was intrigued and agreed. René was due for a promotion, so he thought it might be interesting to find out how he was doing at Convo. He then picked up the phone immediately to René and asked him for a report on the current position at Convo, without disclosing why. René was a little put out and not quite sure what to write.

You got on very well with BigFood's divisional chairman. Between you, you agreed a strategy involving appointing you as chairman. You decided to fire the finance director and appoint an interim director from the auditors to establish what the exact financial position was and to restore financial control. As you sensed that the business might be able to find cash from within, you ignored the issue of the cash shortage, believing that until you knew the exact position this was a premature discussion. An operations director would be appointed beneath Archie, allowing Archie to focus on selling the company once it was in a stable position. You both also agreed that you would obtain the institutions' agreement and then break the news to Archie.

You rehearsed your conversation with Archie several times with Clive. You decided that you needed to get Archie to face reality and then paint him some pictures of the possible outcomes. In the short time you had known Archie, you realized that the two most important things to him were his reputation in the industry and the wellbeing of his staff. He was not motivated by money at all.

You told Archie that the business was out of control and likely to fail. You also told him that until recently the institutions and BigFood Co had not been communicating effectively, but now they were. The pictures you then painted were obvious. One involved Archie's reputation in tatters, the other in which control was restored and the company achieved a high-profile sale. Initially Archie brushed off the problems and tried to persuade you that it would be all right. You then went through the analysis you had given to BigFood and the institutions and what they proposed to do. Archie quickly realized that with 80 per cent he had little choice:

'Why don't you just fire me then, if you think I'm so awful?' asked Archie.

'Because the company is you, Archie, and you are the best possible seller of it. The best person to ensure as many of the jobs are saved as possible. We really need you.'

Archie was persuaded, but only if he could remain as chairman in title. You then took a gamble that many wouldn't. You agreed, but warned Archie that if he didn't keep up his end of the deal, you would have him removed. Archie then relaxed and was about as committed and loyal to the agreement as you could possibly imagine. The institutions and BigFood reluctantly agreed, but only on the basis of your reputation. Financial control was quickly restored by appointing an interim director from the auditors. Costs were reduced and working capital management improved to the extent that although it was tight, no extra cash was required.

You managed the board meetings and set the agendas. You also ensured René and Archie had few opportunities to disagree. Eighteen months later the company appointed an investment bank to market it. Six months later it was sold to an American competitor who had no presence in Europe. Archie is now their president of worldwide marketing. He's a little regretful but in no way broken.

If you want to take this dilemma further, you might like to try out these subsequent challenges:

1. Having stabilized the position, you decide that management has to be regrouped and that Archie has to go. You have obtained the attached summary of his service contract. The institutions are behind you but you haven't discussed it with BigFood yet. *What board process do you need to go through and what difficulties do you foresee in implementation?*

2. Instead of removing Archie, you decide to adopt a gradual approach and persuade Archie to bring in a new managing director beneath him, together with a new finance director to replace Paul Tate. After 18 months Archie falls out with both of them. You remain impressed with the changes they have made. *What would you do now and what board process do you need to go through to implement your decisions?*

3. The financial position deteriorates significantly and the business needs an injection of £5 million. The institutional investors have been asked and they have resolved that they will only put this money up if there are management changes. BigFood is prepared to provide the money without changing the management, but insists on acquiring control at a depressed rights issue price. Archie refuses to open up the bidding to outside parties. *What would you do now?*

SERVICE AGREEMENT
ARCHIBALD CRESSWELL (the 'Executive')
AND
CONVO LTD (the 'Company')
Summary Points

Position:	Managing director or in such other capacity as the Board of Directors of the Company ('the Board') may determine.
Period:	For three years from 31 March 2000 until 31 March 2003 and thereafter unless and until determined by either party giving to the other not less than 12 months prior written notice.
Remuneration:	Salary £150,000 per annum inclusive of all director's fees subject to an annual review on 31 March in each year. The executive and his family are to be entitled to private medical insurance. In addition 10 per cent of salary will be paid annually into a private pension fund. The company will also pay for life assurance cover equal to four times salary.
Expenses:	All reasonable expenses incurred by the executive in the discharge of his duties will be reimbursed.
Motor car:	BMW 730i fully expensed.
Restrictions:	For so long as the executive owns shares or is employed by the company he will not compete with any food businesses of the company or its subsidiaries, solicit customers or entice away employees. If his employment is terminated the above restrictions apply for 12 months following the date of termination.
Termination:	The company can terminate, without notice, if guilty of material or persistent dishonesty, misconduct or serious breach of obligation, if incapacitated by illness or mental disorder or subject to bankruptcy. In such an event the executive can make no claim for compensation.
Suspension:	If allegations arise out of serious breach of obligations, the board can decide to suspend the executive.
Board appointments:	Upon termination of this agreement, the executive resigns his directorships.

A CHEMICAL REACTION

For the chairman of Chemco, a north-west based chemicals company, the last 15 hours have been a nightmare. An explosion yesterday at one of the company's plants resulted in the deaths of three people. A cloud of toxic gas was released, causing evacuation of local buildings within a one-mile radius.

Chemco has had an excellent record for safety since it was founded 50 years ago. Like many similar companies, there have been minor leakages over the years, but this is the first serious incident. As a large private company in a small town it has built up strong links with the local community and is widely regarded as a good employer.

Today Chemco has sales of around £30 million, of which approximately one-third are in Holland. Most of the sales are of products that are manufactured in small batches and are tailored to specific customer requirements. They are therefore uneconomic for the major producers, which has enabled Chemco to develop high margins in most of its business.

Rather than call an emergency board meeting last night, the chairman chose to focus on ensuring the plant was made safe, dealing with the media and personally visiting the families of those killed. Fortunately, he managed to speak to all of the executive directors face-to-face and the two independent directors by telephone.

The experience has been traumatic for him, Chemco's management team and the employees. As yet no obvious cause for the explosion has been identified.

A regular monthly board meeting was scheduled for 10 am with the agenda set out below. The chief executive, technical director and sales director have all prepared initial reports on the incident. These, together with profiles of Chemco's board, are provided below.

How should the chairman of Chemco handle the meeting and deal with the issues raised by the situation?

Should the board meeting go ahead? If so, what should the agenda be now?

ORIGINAL AGENDA

**Chemco Board Meeting
at 10.00 am on today's date
Chemco offices**

1. Previous Minutes
2. Managing director's report
3. Finance director's report
4. Pricing strategy for next quarter
5. Potential acquisition for £4 million of Small Chemco
6. Company car policy
7. Annual insurance review
8. Presentation by our Dutch MD
9. Any other business

12.30 pm, Lunch
Guests: Rudi Van den Dam (Dutch MD), Mike Smith (Small Chemco MD)

The Chemco board

Chairman

A 53-year-old experienced chemical manufacturing man who spent his early career with ICI. He joined Chemco 10 years ago when the turnover was £5 million and profits were £300,000. He led a management buy-out eight years ago and became chairman. A consensus style of leader with strong communication and marketing skills.

Managing director

Another ex-ICI man. Joined 10 years ago as production director, became MD two years later at the time of the buy-out. A traditional, highly professional attender to detail who is well regarded in the industry and a leading light on safety issues. Proud of Chemco's strong performance and in particular last year's record £1.5 million pre-tax profit. Slightly autocratic and somewhat intolerant, but commands considerable respect within the business.

Finance director

The audit partner before the MBO. He joined shortly afterwards. Known as 'Mr Scenario' in the company. Always presents the options available and is a perfect judge of their outcome, but he is not a natural decision taker. A highly professional and likeable 39-year-old.

Technical director

Known as 'Brains' within the company. An exceptionally bright chemist. Has in-depth knowledge of the company's plants and processes. Less commercially adept, though wonderful with customers when explaining the company's technical merits. Not generally confident when dealing with the outside world. Recently nominated as technical advisor to the Industry Safety Council.

Sales director (not on the main board, but usually attends)
Home grown, natural salesman. Strong on motivating the sales force. Slightly difficult relationship with production, but wins their respect through performance rather than attitude. Particularly sensitive to the company's image and reputation.

Independent director 1
Nominee of the institutional investor. Seasoned campaigner from the chemical industry who has been successful in an earlier MBO and subsequent sale.

Independent director 2
Previously European MD of a multinational engineering company. He is highly numerate and marketing led, and is on the board for his international management experience.

Managing Director's Initial Report of the Accident

- At approximately 10 am a pipe in section 16 of the main plant burst, showering high temperature toxic gas on a team of 10 who were performing maintenance in the area. Debris from this explosion also burst a nearby storage tank causing leakage of product X producing an orange, pungent cloud which, although not life-threatening, caused major eye and skin irritation.
- Buildings were evacuated (as per the regular safety training) and staff assembled in the car park.
- The injured were attended by first-aiders, again in accordance with procedure and training.
- Side effects of the leaking gas (eg severe eye and skin irritation and coughing) exaggerated the fear of a further explosion.
- Emergency services were on the scene in minutes.
- All mains power and services were isolated.
- Of the 10 in the area, the initial report was that the three nearest were dead, three others unconscious and the rest suffering severe shock and blast injuries.
- Gas and power officials arrived within 15 minutes to assist the fire service and make safe the plant.
- The company's lawyers provided a solicitor on site within an hour to help with employees' statements and to advise the company generally.
- The media arrived in force with some fairly intrusive camera crews and aggressive questioning of employees: 'Whose fault is it?', 'Was this an accident waiting to happen?', etc. Distressed employees became angry at the intrusion.
- Two hours after the blast, the first factory inspector arrived.
- The chairman and the executive directors present took the decision to close the plant and send everyone home at 10.45 am.
- It was not clear who was working on the section immediately prior to the explosion, though two of the three dead were maintenance contractors, one an employee on training.
- The police and the insurance company representative arrived at 15 minutes past 10 and 12 noon respectively.
- By 9 pm the factory inspector was satisfied that the plant was safe and could be re-opened following six days of repairs/modifications and tests.

Sales Director's Report

You asked me for a clear and concise assessment and some suggested actions.

This is a major blow to our credibility because safety/quality has been a major selling point of ours and we have been able to command a higher price because of our record:

- Our competitors will have a field day. We will need to cut prices to respond.
- Hopefully, the cause will be due to the maintenance contractor and we can rightly say it was their responsibility. We should change contracts immediately to reinforce this message.
- We will need the chairman to visit our top 10 customers ASAP (ie this week) to reassure them.
- The more active PR campaign discussed at our May board meeting should be activated immediately.
- We must do something immediately to restore the morale of the sales force. I suggest that the increased delegated authority proposals we discussed at the last board meeting are implemented immediately.

Technical Director's Report

You asked me for a clear and concise assessment and some suggested actions:

- We have followed the emergency procedures to the letter and I am convinced we could not be faulted on compliance grounds.
- There must always be the possibility that the maintenance was not carried out in accordance with the procedures manual, although given the incapacity of those actually present, we just can't say at this point.
- The contractor has been used by us for the last four years. All of the contractor's staff performing maintenance yesterday were trained on this type of plant and accredited as per the contract. However, all were new to our plant. Our own trainee who was joining them as a formal part of his key programme is still in his six-month probationary period and the supervisor who was scheduled to join him was absent with flu. The stand-in supervisor decided to continue as the maintenance was classified as essential and was a routine item. I was not notified of the supervisor's absence.
- In order to help the company I feel I should resign with immediate effect. I must accept responsibility.

Before addressing the three questions posed, we should consider the issues arising from Chemco's tragic accident.

What are the issues?

Safety is bound to be uppermost in people's minds. Has the plant been made safe? Are the reported medical incidents likely to be the only ones or will there be others? What actions does Chemco need to take with the Health and Safety Executive and the local health officers? Is Chemco doing what it should for the families of the bereaved and injured?

Considerable reliance will be placed on Chemco's disaster plan. Chemical companies are required to have highly detailed contingency plans for eventualities such as this. Having an excellent plan won't change the situation but it will reduce stress and help reduce the risk of consequential problems.

During a major disaster the quality of communications is of paramount importance. Chemco will need to communicate with a broad range of people through a variety of channels and ways – employees, families of the dead, customers, suppliers, local press, possibly national press, investigators and so on. A draft communications plan is usually an important part of the contingency plan. One detail often overlooked is where the communications hub will be. Chemco will probably have contingency arrangements, but are these now in a safe place?

Ensuring that investigations into the accident are properly handled and the company is seen to have behaved well is also key. Any investigation is a threatening experience for those who take part. Giving them the support required to do a good job sometimes goes amiss. Delegation of some or all of their current day jobs is often what is required. Establishing the facts will be critical to Chemco.

Chemco has a strong management team and is a high performer. The morale and capability of Chemco's board and senior team are key to Chemco overcoming the disaster. It is important that this isn't lost sight of. The damage to morale will be quite considerable. Tiny cracks in the team's relationships with each other could become far more serious. The sales director's style and approach are clearly going to be a problem. His report hardly signals the mindset of a team player.

Is the team up to the task? Does help need to be drafted in from outside? Should roles change to reflect the company's new situation? There will be a whole range of management issues arising. Chemco's external advisers should be able to provide considerable assistance at a moment like this. Which ones should be involved? The public relations agency, the lawyers and insurance advisers are obvious, but who else?

What do you think of the managing director's report? Do you believe what has been said about the plant restart in six days? It sounds implausible that a factory inspector who hasn't established the cause and has only visited once would have said this. Nevertheless, the issue of when to restart the plant is a key one. The report isn't a model of clarity in the matter of how many fatalities there potentially could be.

Is there anything else in the MD's report that looks odd? Remember the circumstances in which he is likely to have written it.

The technical director's suggestion that he should resign will need responding to. What are the implications for him and Chemco of his resigning now? Is it tantamount to admitting it was his fault and Chemco was to blame for the accident? Would his departure hinder the investigations? How would the press report it? A sudden departure before the facts are known seems wrong. He may be completely shell-shocked and suffer a loss of confidence. Does he need some professional counselling? Think clinically for a moment. If you persuade him to stay, how useful will he be?

Chemco's relationship with the maintenance contractor is another obvious issue. Establishing the precise nature of the contract and where liability rests will be high on the list of priorities.

How will Chemco's customers be supplied? Are there already arrangements in place with competitors to cover such an eventuality? Again, the contingency plan should have the basics covered. However, businesses and customer requirements change. Some of Chemco's customers' contracts may include penalty payments for non-delivery. This is another area to review.

What is the overall commercial and financial impact of the accident? What will the insurance position be? Is Chemco getting appropriate advice on how to deal with claims it will want to make and claims made against the company?

A look at the original agenda shows that two guests were coming. Is this still appropriate? What does it mean for Chemco's plans to acquire Small Chemco? What should the chairman say to Mike Smith?

Should the board meeting go ahead?

Not to hold a board meeting would be negligent in these circumstances. It is important for the chairman to ensure that all directors are appraised of the situation and approve Chemco's plan for dealing with it. The executive is likely to have been up all night and will inevitably have a long list of tasks ahead of it. This is an occasion when the non-executives can bring real value through their objectivity. The executive may require additional support from them. They look like useful people.

Time is of the essence and there is a need to focus on the priorities. Assuming Chemco's offices are at the plant, it may not be possible to hold the meeting there, so an alternative venue may be required. The chairman may also feel that it would be helpful to have the company's lawyer and public relations adviser available.

If so, what should be the agenda?

One approach would be to abandon the original agenda, tell the guests not to come, and focus on the accident. However, there may be some things on the original agenda that are still relevant even if they are dealt with in a different way. Taking each in turn:

- The nature of the directors' reports will be different and unless there is something of appropriate significance, be either taken as read or dealt with another time.
- Pricing strategy seems somewhat academic if there isn't anything to sell.
- The acquisition needs a brief discussion. Who knows, Small Chemco may be able to help. A decision to press on, defer, or terminate acquisition discussions may be needed. Much will depend on the stage Chemco is at in the process. Communication needs to be clear either way.
- Car policy shouldn't be on a board agenda in the first place.
- The annual insurance review looks eerily timed and may well be useful to keep.
- Rudi's presentation is likely to be irrelevant, but he might still be asked to attend. He may have something to offer and he may already be on his way.

The chairman decided that the meeting should go ahead and that the following agenda was appropriate.

REVISED AGENDA

Chemco Board Meeting

1. Communications
   - employees
   - customers
   - suppliers
   - media
2. Accident investigations
3. Likely financial impact
4. Plant re-start
   - when
5. Stock shortages/customer reaction
6. Small Chemco acquisition
   - press ahead or call a halt?
7. Rudi Van den Dam's presentation
8. Any Other Business

How the chairman handled the meeting and dealt with the issues

Chemco's chairman had a few clear objectives for the meeting. These were to:

- unify the team;
- make absolutely sure they all knew what had happened;
- ensure clarity and unity of purpose;
- establish clear responsibilities.

He opened the meeting by thanking everyone for their '*Tremendous commitment overnight*' and suggested a minute's silence. He then told everyone that:

This is a tragic event in the company's life but one I am sure we will recover from. There is an enormous amount of hard work to do and we will be in the spotlight. Our professionalism and ability to work as a team will be tested as never before. I am sure we will rise to the challenge.

This set a well-balanced tone for the rest of the meeting, which covered the topics on his revised agenda. Instead of the presentation he had planned, Rudi spoke for 10 minutes about what he felt the impact on the Dutch business was likely to be and how his part of the business might be able to help.

The chairman dealt with the technical director before the meeting. In a highly sensitive way he told him that although his feelings were understandable, he couldn't accept his resignation:

> *You're bound to feel like this, I know I would. But once you are past the emotion of the moment you'll realize that now is the time we need you most. Who else will be able to figure out what happened? Who else will make sure we deal with the investigations properly? Who else will be able to figure out how to get us back in production as quickly as possible?*

He didn't tell him about the other reason resigning would be bad for Chemco, namely that a resignation at this stage could be perceived as an admission of blame. The chairman had also told the managing director to make certain that the technical director's morale was boosted.

Chemco's sales director was dealt with in a slightly different way. The chairman was appalled by his report and the lack of sensitivity it showed. However, he decided that loose cannons are best kept busy and aimed towards empty spaces. Consequently, he asked the sales director to see him before the meeting. He told him that rather than attend the board meeting and anything else he had planned, he was to prepare two urgent reports for the board. The first was a pricing review following the accident. The second was a quick competitive review to establish competitor reactions. The chairman did this in such a way that the sales director felt he had been listened to and was due for his board seat at last. In fact the chairman was terrified that the sales director would get near the press. He also felt he would be damaging to morale. He resolved to attend to him later!

As it turned out, the cause of the accident was never really identified and five people ended up dying. Investigators were critical of Chemco on some minor procedural matters but overall Chemco, unlike the maintenance contractor, came through the investigation well. The maintenance contractor proved very difficult to deal with as it tried to apportion blame to Chemco. The incident eventually caused the failure of the maintenance contractor's business.

Because the cause wasn't identified, the chairman decided that it would be right to replace the equipment with something completely different. He also felt that they should clear a small area where the accident happened so that a plaque could be put up. He was very concerned about the morale of the workforce and wrote a personal letter to them all. The letter was a fine balance of sympathy, openness and confidence that Chemco would overcome the tragedy. It also contained a strong 'we need your help' passage at the end. Given the chairman's natural style and genuine respect for his staff, it came over very well. A cynical chairman and a cynical workforce might need another way of communicating.

Chemco was fortunate that it had had such a good year financially; this meant it was able to survive through the month it took to get back into production at the plant. It was also fortunate in having an excellent lawyer who managed to deal with the many issues emerging in a sensitive and highly professional way. Chemco's public relations adviser, however, turned out to be useless. He was fine for everyday commercial issues but had only limited experience of dealing with the national press or a situation like this. This became apparent very quickly and Chemco switched to another adviser recommended by its lawyer.

The technical director never really regained his confidence and after a couple of years moved to a more advisory role. The sales director also suffered a blow to his confidence five months later when the chairman fired him. Rudi turned out to be a real star and proved superb at arranging alternative supply during the month-long shut-down.

Chemco had to deal with the item of the Small Chemco acquisition, largely because completion of the deal was only a week away. The board had intended approving the acquisition at the board meeting after a review of the due diligence. Smith was invited to lunch to meet the rest of the board. This was a tough call for the chairman to make. He decided that the deal made sense as long as the bank funding remained in place and Smith could be persuaded not to walk away. He called Smith before the board and told him that although he could quite understand why Smith might want to walk away, Chemco didn't. He suggested two alternatives. First, they could proceed as planned but with a month's delay. Secondly, they could call the deal off for now and talk again in a few month's time. Smith chose the latter. They ended up not doing the deal.

In summary, the Chemco chairman handled this terrible situation extremely well. The accident would have easily wiped out many lesser companies. Chemco had a very tough time. There was a difficult and protracted battle with their own and the maintenance company's insurers which eventually they won. However, the team's confidence was never quite the same again. They were decent people who felt responsibility for the deaths, even though they were not at fault.

THE REVOLUTION

Wilnet has had a spectacular year as one of the few UK Internet site development companies of critical mass. It has taken full advantage of explosive market demand and its reputation for highly creative projects delivered on time to a premium price.

When you joined as finance director, six months before the float, you knew nothing about the Internet market. You were bored stiff by your previous job in one of the big five accountancy practices. Wilnet's charismatic chief executive, Bill Fortis, and the effervescent culture he propagated were therefore of considerable appeal. The cut in salary was well worth the 10 per cent of the equity in options that you were offered. Problems with basic financial controls and pricing policy were things you felt well equipped to sort out. Hence Wilnet looked like the opportunity you had always dreamed of and well worth the risk.

Any high expectations you may have had when you joined have been surpassed. Getting on top of the control and other issues didn't take long. Wilnet's listing went extremely well and it has been tremendous fun to work with a winning team in such a high growth area. Today, just two years since the float, your equity and options are worth £8 million.

At the time of the listing there was a lot of heated debate. This was not just over whether to float, but also which market to go onto. The chairman still goads the rest of the board that if Wilnet had gone to NASDAQ, as he had advocated, the business would be 10 times the value. Although he is right, you sense that Bill, and for that matter yourself, would not have been that comfortable with life as a NASDAQ company.

Wilnet's board consists of six quite different personalities. Jeff Hupe, a lively New Yorker, is chairman. Jeff had previously floated a company on NASDAQ and has added an enormous amount in terms of experience, credibility and contacts. He was superb at the time of the float. His only weaknesses are a low boredom threshold and a desire to get an instant response to everything. As a former mentor of Bill's he was involved right from the outset. Jeff has 10 per cent of the equity.

Another founding director was Alan Tosper. He owns 20 per cent and runs the media and publishing sector. Alan is a bit of a loner. He runs the most successful part of the business, yet is probably the least comfortable member of the team. Nobody would be surprised if he just up and left one day, cashing in his chips and starting all over again.

Dave Sorpet couldn't be more different, a real team player with a tremendous sense of humour. He covers the fast moving consumer goods sector, which although not as profitable, has developed some of the most leading edge products. Dave is more modest than Alan and has also put more time into developing the company's overall positioning.

Apart from being chief executive, Bill is the technical brains behind Wilnet. In addition he runs the business that supplies the technology sector itself. Bill is highly rated by analysts and he and Wilnet have been getting some tremendous publicity. His only regret is that he only had enough money to buy 5 per cent of Wilnet's equity.

Wilnet's final board member is John Forbes. John is a highly polished corporate financier by background. He joined Wilnet just before he retired in the run up to the float. Jeff and he get on especially well but he enjoys a good relationship with all of the board. Wilnet's smooth rise has meant he hasn't had to do a great deal recently.

The major contribution you have made to Wilnet's success has been well recognized. Not being one of the founders meant that for a while you felt you were treated very much like an outsider. However, you now feel that the others are, at last, slowly accepting you into the fold.

This morning, just before a board meeting, the chairman and Alan asked if you would join them for a quick meeting. You are aware that there are tensions between the chairman and the chief executive, but feel that Bill and Alan got along well. Indeed Bill has often defended Alan's somewhat selfish behaviour. So what they have to tell you is something of a shock.

Jeff opens the meeting by telling you that he and Alan believe the time has come to replace Bill. They believe that this is necessary on the grounds that the business has outgrown him, he's too inward looking and not strategic enough. In their view the best course of action is to replace Bill while the company is strong. They have decided to confront the issue and to appoint Alan as chief executive. Jeff and Alan want your support for this idea so that they can move forward and appoint lawyers. In that way they can present it as a *fait accompli* to Bill and avoid a messy or protracted boardroom bust up. They believe their views will come as a shock to Bill. *'Too right,'* you think. They've come as a big shock to you. *'How long have they been plotting this?'* you wonder.

Despite the fact that they do have a bit of a point about the business outgrowing Bill, you feel a deep loyalty to him. Instinct tells you Alan would wreck the business as chief executive. Wilnet is a people business after all. Shareholder confidence, once knocked, is probably unrecoverable. All sorts of thoughts are racing through your mind. You decide to play for time and say:

> ‹ While I've been aware of tensions, I had no idea you two felt as strongly as this. I think it is important that we consider all the issues involved here. I'm a bit disappointed that you have sprung it on me like this today just before a board meeting. Consequently, I'd like to reflect on what you have said and I'd like to meet with you tomorrow to discuss it further.›

They reluctantly agree. The plan was to tell Bill today. They insist you don't speak to him to alert him. You agree not to discuss it with him until tomorrow. The board meeting was an odd affair and somewhat tense. Bill sensed something wasn't quite right and asks you after the board meeting what's up with the other guys.

How do you respond and how do you deal with the various conversations that will ensue?

What are the issues?

Not a particularly pleasant situation to be faced with, especially if you are convinced that if Alan and Jeff get their way, the business will suffer serious damage. If they don't, then they'll probably have to go. Either way a boardroom battle will ensue and undermine the company with investors. The damage to your own wealth will also be significant.

Assuming the voting rights are equal, that Dave will vote with Bill and John with Jeff, then the reason they approached you is obvious: your vote will swing it. They don't seem dumb enough to seek a vote and lose.

Could they be right? Has the business really outgrown Bill? What's the evidence for this view? Even if it has, is this the way to deal with it? Why have they chosen to do things this way? What will be the effect on the share price of Bill going? How would Bill react? Are they right about Bill but wrong about Alan? If you support Bill's removal, can you avoid Alan being appointed his successor? What does this mean for Dave? Will he be next? Depending on your confidence and ambition, it might also cross your mind that you could be a compromise candidate for chief executive.

Is there a solution available which doesn't involve such a dramatic split? What should John's role be? Has he already been consulted? What would he think? Could he be the one to sort things out? What do the company's brokers and other key advisers think of the chairman and Alan? How damaged would the business be if they went?

Should you speak to Bill before responding to the chairman? You have agreed not to. However, you may consider the way in which they have treated you means you are free to do whatever you consider right. Does deciding to talk to Bill mean implicit support for him? Jeff and Alan will probably see it that way. Should John be consulted first? Perhaps the combination of you and him might persuade Jeff to drop the idea.

Whatever happens, life on the Wilnet board will never be the same again.

How to decide?

Unless you take the decision to involve Bill, Dave or John, it looks difficult to make any progress. More information is likely to have little bearing. However, this is new territory for you, so maybe chatting it through with someone you think might have experienced something similar before may help. Jeff sounds as if he is someone used to winning fights. If you decide to join forces with Bill, you may need some support. Should you enlist that support before you speak to him, or involve him in gaining it?

What is best for the company? Working this out may not be straightforward, but helpful nevertheless. Does supporting Bill mean that Jeff and Alan would end up going? If so, what would be the impact and how could you do it with minimum damage? What's the legal position? Do Jeff and Alan have the power to do this? Is there anything in Bill's service contract to stop them?

This is definitely a situation where instincts matter a great deal. A lot has to do with the trust between the various board members. So what are your instincts telling you?

No doubt the impact of the different alternatives on your own position and wealth will be taken into account. Would jotting down the different possibilities help?

What will the key institutional shareholders think? Asking them at this point may not be a great idea. Confidence evaporates surprisingly quickly in technology stocks. What about the company's professional advisers? Do you have a confidant at one of them whose counsel you could seek?

What to decide?

Balancing what is in the best commercial interests of the company with a concern for proper corporate governance and a desire to do what is fair to Bill could be difficult. The decision turns on how strong you think Bill is and whether supporting him will do less damage to the business. Whether or not you should talk to Bill depends upon this. Clearly, if you come down on the side of the chairman and Alan it would probably be best not to.

Deciding who to talk to first is therefore important. Much will depend on your relationship with John. He looks like a possible honest broker and calming influence. Yet if the bond between him and Jeff is the strongest, and he thinks Jeff is right, this could be a big mistake.

How to communicate it?

'Carefully' is the word that springs to mind. Bill is bound to be highly charged. Jeff is impulsive and could leap to the wrong conclusion. Alan will clearly be tense. You are in a state of shock and high anxiety.

In a situation like this there is a high probability that what you say is not what gets heard. Using as few calm words as possible and concentrating on the facts will reduce the likelihood of confusion. Having said this, conveying how you feel may well help turn the situation, particularly with John and Jeff.

If you decide to speak to Bill, be brief and if you have decided to support him, make sure that he is in no doubt. He's no idiot, so he will realize the seriousness of the situation immediately. He is bound to be angry, so making sure he doesn't do anything rash is important.

At this stage it is wise not to tell anybody else within the company and try and ensure that no one gets the impression that there's a bust up on the board.

What did the finance director do?

This was a very tricky situation. Alan and Jeff had a point about the business outgrowing Bill. However, their approach incensed the finance director (FD). He also felt that Alan would be a disastrous choice as chief executive. He thought that he would do a better job himself, but he didn't feel he was ready to be a chief executive yet and certainly not in this situation.

Alan and Jeff's behaviour made him even more convinced that their proposal would be bad for Wilnet. Talking to Bill seemed the only way to block them. The option of enlisting Dave's support and trying to head them off without Bill knowing was quickly discounted. The FD and Dave would be no match for a committed Jeff and Alan.

When he spoke to Bill, he told him that the chairman had asked him to support the appointment of Alan as the new chief executive because *'Jeff thinks that while you have been great for the phase we have been through, Alan is the right man for the next phase'*. He continued:

> ❛I have to say I was shocked, Bill. I don't think it's a good idea at all. While you are bound to have to hand on at some point, it isn't now. Alan would be the wrong successor, anyway. I'm very concerned at the way they are going about it. You have to take this threat seriously, Bill. We need to try and stop this idea.❜

Bill was outraged and was determined not to let them take what he sees as his company away from him. He couldn't understand how the chairman could have betrayed him: *'Alan must have put him up to it. Wonder what he's told Jeff. Thought he'd been a bit sheepish last week'.*

To his credit Bill calmed down very quickly and suggested that he and the FD both meet later with Dave and come up with a plan of action. Dave was as shocked as the FD was and added some helpful insight. He had overheard Alan and Jeff a few weeks ago and was surprised to hear Alan taking credit for some of Bill's ideas and rubbishing Bill's new plan for expansion in Germany. At the time he put it down to one of Alan's grumpy moods and thought nothing more of it.

The plan was based on the premise that Alan had been feeding Jeff misleading information and that once Jeff was aware of this, it would be Alan who would be leaving. But how could they make Jeff realize this? He was bound to be suspicious of the FD's motives if the latter told him on his own. Could the FD see Alan and get him to yield? It took him a while to decide how to go about achieving his aim.

He decided that they should discuss the situation with John and be open with him. If he wouldn't offer support then they would speak to Jeff and, as a final resort, threaten to resign en mass.

John had had a glittering career and been involved in many difficult situations. Somehow he had always emerged calm, smooth and with honour. When the FD saw John he was very much in listening mode and was non-committal. He told the FD that he thought the best course of action was for him to speak to Jeff and establish exactly what had happened. Although he didn't say much, he did give the FD the feeling that he could be trusted.

The FD never really found out what John said to Jeff. The next morning Jeff asked Bill, Dave and him to join him in his office. He said:

‹ Guys, I'm afraid I've made one hell of an error of judgement but I'm happy to report that it has now been rectified. Alan has decided to leave the company at the end of the month. He's made a great contribution to the business over the last few years and we will be kind to him in the PR. Although he should go, I still think there are some issues we need to address together. Now is not the time. ›

Alan's successor was recruited as someone who had the potential to take over as CEO when Bill retires, aged 40, in two years' time. He is well on track to do that. Wilnet has gone from strength to strength and is as highly rated as ever. Alan now runs his own small business and has benefited from keeping his Wilnet shareholding.

I WISH WE'D TOLD THEM EARLIER

Azco, a small public company, has issued profits warning this morning – the first since it became a quoted company four years ago. The statement was brief but honest:

> ‘ We regret to announce that the directors of Azco have reviewed the latest information available to them and come to the conclusion that results for the year to 31 March will be some 30 per cent below those indicated at the interim stage and those being forecast by most analysts.
>
> ‘The directors remain confident of the long-term outlook for Azco. The shortfall is entirely due to the launch of the company's new MZ product range. While sales of MZ, launched four months ago, have fallen below anticipated levels, the directors remain convinced of the range's long-term success and are encouraged by the highly positive reaction MZ has had among early customers and in the trade press.’

Azco's chief executive and finance director have been on the phone all morning with analysts, key institutional shareholders and journalists. The share price has fallen over 30 per cent. Both are upset and feel that the City has over reacted. Azco has been a strong performer since flotation, always met forecasts and enjoyed good relations with investors. Indeed the finance director is speaking at an investor relations conference next week. They have never been in a situation like this before and the shock is considerable.

As well as being chairman of Azco, you are also chairman of GLOBCO, a FTSE100 company. The only reason you weren't at Azco this morning was that you were chairing GLOBCO's Annual General Meeting. It has to be said you also underestimated the reaction to the profits warning. You had expected Azco's CEO and FD would handle communications well and the City would put the hiccup in results into context. As soon as the AGM is over you call Azco's CEO to see how things have gone. You can't get through to him or the finance director. GLOBCO's finance director picks up the Azco story when checking the financial news to see how the AGM was reported. He alerts you to the fall in Azco's share price. You decide, as Azco's offices are not too far away, to get your chauffeur to take you there. On the way you call your secretary to reschedule this afternoon's meetings at GLOBCO. Finally, you get through to the CEO; he sounds very stressed. You tell him you'll be arriving in 10 minutes and that you will do everything you can to help.

The reason you are prepared to be so supportive is that you genuinely feel that Azco is well managed and that the MZ range has enormous potential. Financial control and information systems have never been a problem at Azco. You trust the management.

What will you do when you get there?

What are the issues?

The key dilemma is how to rebuild the confidence of Azco's CEO and finance director and then restore the company's reputation in the City. However, there are some other issues to address.

How important is the MZ range to the future of the company? It must be put in perspective. Is the MZ range as good as hoped? If it is, is the market as promising as suggested? A weakness in either of these, if Azco is heavily dependent on MZ, has the potential to turn what looks like a setback along the way into a major disaster. As a part-time chairman, how much do you really know about the MZ range and its true potential?

A profit warning is often the result of inadequate financial control and reporting. Sometimes it arises because the board doesn't pick up the signals. Neither sound to be the case here. It is well worth checking nevertheless. You will have to have absolute confidence that the revised profit projection is delivered. You will also have to ensure that any other statements Azco makes, particularly with regard to MZ, are realistic. This can be tough to achieve when you are trying to establish confidence and get others to believe in the future.

Investor relations are clearly now a priority. Has Azco been as good at managing communications with the City as has been said? Whether it has or it hasn't, it's likely to need a different approach from here on.

How vulnerable is Azco to a bid as a result of the profits warning? This could be a perfect time for a competitor to strike. Azco's low share price, long-term potential, shell-shocked management and low support in the City may make it an ideal target for someone who has faith in MZ.

Does the shortfall in MZ revenue impact on the cash flow adversely? If so, how significantly and is this a stock timing issue or something more serious? How strong is Azco's balance sheet? MZ needs to be put into context again.

Morale across the company following a shock like this is inevitably low. You will want to ensure that the spinning bottle of blame is left in the cupboard. The impact on the wealth of staff could be quite considerable if Azco has any share-based incentive schemes. Many of the staff in a company like Azco will hold shares.

Azco will inevitably consume more of your own time for the next few months. Have you got it? If not, can you clear sufficient space to make time? How can you use the other non-executive directors to help? They can do more than be aware. Whether you plan to use them or not, they are bound to be interested and may have some useful input.

For Azco's CEO and finance director the next few months will be very pressured. Does Azco have any spare resource to allow greater delegation of things that are now a lower priority for the top team? The more you can reduce pressure on them, the better things will be.

One very familiar technique in situations like this is the offering up of a sacrificial lamb. In this case, maybe the MZ director, if there is one, or perhaps the finance director could be the likely victims. Sometimes this is well deserved, but frequently it isn't. Moreover, it is often the wrong lamb that gets slaughtered.

Do small public companies ever really recover from situations like these? My own brief research suggests that very few do. An analyst I know says that, *'Once you've disappointed the market you are always disappointing to the market.'*

The market is unforgiving and it can only take one slip to obliterate a long track record of success.

How to decide?

'What's to decide?' you might think. Why don't they just keep their heads down and deliver the results? If they have absolute faith in what they are doing, then it should just be a matter of time before they get the results they hope for.

Of course they should focus their efforts on delivering the results. Obviously they shouldn't be panicked into doing anything silly. However, a share price of over 30 per cent is significant. The issues above need to be addressed.

Hopefully the existing bid defence plan will have been well prepared. If so, it may be a straightforward matter of updating it, refreshing the memory of the board as to its contents. Part of the update will include identification and assessment of the likely bidders.

Deciding what to do about MZ may be more difficult. Step one is to ensure that the board has an accurate picture of the real status of the product. They may also decide to prepare a contingency plan in the event that MZ completely fails.

The right time to develop a communications plan to restore confidence is when you have made a judgement on the likely progress with MZ and the rest of the business. A temporary setback plan will be quite different to a batten-down-the-hatches major disaster plan.

There may be some decisions required in relation to management at board level and below. How well do you really know the team? There must have been a meeting of the board prior to the issue of the profit warning. You will no doubt reflect on that meeting and what you were told.

What to decide?

They could, as has been mentioned, just keep quiet and focus on ensuring that they surpass the revised expectations.

Shock may result in a defensive and oversensitive response. This would only make it worse. Clamming up and arguing with the press or analysts is never a sensible thing to do, no matter how hurt you feel. Clam up and you risk people assuming the situation is worse than reported. Before you argue, remember that journalists and analysts get to have the last word.

In every situation, the optimist will look for a way to turn such a difficulty into an opportunity. You'd have to be a raving optimist to do that here. However, if the Wilnet team can recover, they will emerge all the stronger.

How to communicate it?

As Wilnet's chairman, you need to inject calm confidence while still recognizing the seriousness of the situation. The main groups to communicate with are the key institutional shareholders, the analysts and journalists who follow Azco, the staff, customers and suppliers. This assumes of course that key advisers are fully appraised already.

There is always the danger of over-promising to make up for the current disappointment. The wise manage somehow to avoid this temptation or impulse. Another danger, especially for the over-stressed, is that of manic patterns of behaviour emerging.

In these situations it can be powerful to use others to communicate on your behalf. When you are under pressure you don't always remember your fans. Azco may well be able to use those who regard it or MZ most highly to say so.

What happened?

You are a big, engaging man who exudes warmth and confidence. Your presence that afternoon soon cheered up the chief executive considerably. You told him two things very quickly. The first was that you would be as supportive as you possibly could. The second was that you were concerned that Azco would be a take-over target. You felt that the bid defence plan initially drawn up just after the flotation four years ago would be out of date and require urgent review.

You made no attempt to probe any further on MZ or question the way the communications had been managed in the morning. This had the effect of the chief executive feeling obliged to say that he hadn't handled things well. After a good start, he let one of Azco's more pompous institutional shareholders rattle him and became a little over-defensive. This made him nervous about the next conversation and that didn't go well either. Fortunately, he recovered well for the remaining conversations and regained his normal style.

You suggested that they hold a board meeting as soon as possible to make sure all the directors had a good understanding of the MZ situation and to approve new bid defence and investor relations plans. You suggested they do this in about a week to give time for sufficient preparation.

When the directors met the mood was supportive. The atmosphere grew a little more tense when the finance director explained that it was really very difficult to be certain about the revised projection. The MZ situation was difficult to call. Overheads had been significantly increased in anticipation of strong sales. People just didn't seem to be buying. No one knew why. All aspects of the launch had been reviewed, including pricing. The decision, given MZ's favourable customer response, was to premium price. Early adopters had been delighted and sales in prospect were more than enough to meet the revised projection. It wasn't clear cut that MZ was a disaster, but there was some concern over the timing of sales. The 30 per cent cut in forecast profits was a conservative guess.

You were right to worry about the bid. Three weeks later a major US competitor made a bid for Azco. Their offer was at a price only 5 per cent below the pre-profits warning price. The effect of a bid at this price was to cause analysts to question whether they had over reacted and suspect the competitor knew something they didn't. As this was the competitor's first bid and it was seen as opportunistic, the analysts also believed they would pay substantially more. So Azco's price rose a further 20 per cent in the week following the bid.

Through some brilliant presentations and some good press, Azco managed to fend off the US bid. The price fell back briefly but it was still above the pre-profits warning price. Six months later, when MZ was starting to produce some real results but was still below the revised projections, a German competitor made a bid at a 30 per cent premium. This was increased a little. The offer was recommended by the Azco Board on the basis that it offered very good value for shareholders.

The Azco team became a lot wiser and lot more streetwise as a result of this experience. They are, however, not terribly happy with their new owners and are looking for a challenge elsewhere. As a result of the sale they have sufficient capital to buy into another company.

JOINED AT THE HIP, NO MORE

Janet and John joined the group board of Raceco about a year ago. Raceco is a highly successful industrial service company with 200 branches across the UK. It also has a small but flourishing international business. Janet and John were seen as highly able contenders to run the UK business when the previous incumbent retired two years ago. Both had been with the company in excess of 15 years and were respected throughout the business. They had also got on extremely well together; indeed they were frequently described as *'being joined at the hip'*. Moreover, John had been something of a coach to Janet right from the time he recruited her as a graduate trainee. She had always shown great respect for him.

The reason they were joint managing directors was that the board had genuinely found it difficult to decide between them. At the time, Janet was viewed as the up and coming, highly polished and aggressive candidate; an obvious potential group chief executive. John was considered the wiser and stronger operationally of the two, ie the safer bet. For fear of losing the loser, they decided to split the role.

At the outset neither considered the other a threat. There were wider group responsibilities for each of them to take and more than enough to do, given the strong growth of the business. Each viewed the compromise positively. Although she would have preferred the complete freedom of the role of sole UK MD, Janet felt it was a step forward and very much a transitional move. John saw things pretty much the same way in that he planned to retire in three or four years' time, welcomed Janet's energy to share the operational workload and felt that he could coach her into the sole role.

Raceco's group chief executive, Howard Grapple, although highly rated by the City, faced some tricky questions from analysts over the compromise appointment. He was able to head these off by playing the *'Trust me guys I haven't let you down yet'* card. Howard found this particularly uncomfortable, as he probably would have taken the risk to appoint Janet. It was unfortunate that one or two of the three non-executive directors felt she was a bit young. Howard thought the fact that Janet was female was also an issue for them. He sees her as his successor; this is the message he keeps giving her and the main reason she accepted the compromise.

The pair quickly clarified the boundaries of their respective roles and did an excellent job of communicating these to the rest of the group. Desperately keen to avoid any misunderstandings, they decided to talk to each other every day to ensure each knew what the other was doing and what they had said to others. They also resolved that no key appointment would be made unilaterally. Both would be involved in the selection process and if they had a difference of view, the third compromise candidate would get the job.

For the first three months things worked well. However, after such a promising start the events of the last few months have been terribly disappointing for Howard. In summary the situation is as follows.

Sometimes, quite naturally, Janet and John have different views. They frequently differ over senior appointments, pricing strategy and the style of external communications. The result has been that they no longer communicate as frequently as they did, nor as well when they do. A number of these differences have been misinterpreted by others. A few mischief-makers beneath take great delight in telling tales. The formal clarity about the definition of their respective roles has become blurred in practice.

The lack of a clear figurehead has proven to be as difficult to manage externally as it has internally. The assumption has been made that neither Janet nor John was strong enough for the job, so the board fudged the decision.

Janet's assumption that Howard would appoint her tomorrow if the non-execs would agree has made her a little aggressive towards them. She has taken great delight in making a fool of two of them in recent board meetings. John, reinvigorated by his new role, has built a much healthier relationship with them. The word on the street is that Janet and John no longer get on.

Things seem to be coming to a head. Janet was furious at John's performance at the sales conference today. John had been a bit dull in his closing speech. He had also given the impression that growth would be harder to achieve than Jane had indicated earlier in the day. She has called Howard and told him she wants a meeting tomorrow to discuss her future.

John's speech is the final straw for Janet. A head-hunter who has been in touch with Janet for a number of years has suggested to her that she push Howard to give her the whole job or move. Conveniently, he has a highly attractive position available which, on the face of it, she seems well suited to. Discussions have progressed to the stage where they have made her a very attractive offer.

Janet has decided against threatening Howard. She has a low opinion of those who use this as a tactic to get a better job or money. She also assumed Howard is well aware of her frustration and that he must be powerless to do anything about it because of other views on the board. Her intention is to tell him that she is resigning no matter what he offers her to stay.

Imagine you are Howard. You sense she might be about to hand in her resignation. How will you respond if she does? Imagine you are Janet. What will you do if Howard offers you the job you have coveted so much?

What are the issues?

In a situation like this there are some big issues for Janet, for John, for Howard and for the company. There is then the general question: *'Does having joint MDs ever work?'*

Howard and Janet's issues are covered below. So let's start with the general question. It's hard to find examples of joint MDs working. Why is that?

One of the main reasons people give is that role clarification can be difficult in a changing business. Show me a business that isn't changing! Often, what is a clear and well understood division between the two is a muddle to others. They then become overwhelmed by the challenge of communications.

If there is a chairman or chief executive above, they will inevitably have their own preferences. These are bound to be displayed at some point, resulting in additional insecurity. Another reason is that the toughest decisions MDs make are the judgement calls. Unless the joint MDs are clones, differences of view over major decisions are inevitable. But most of all, as anyone who has tried to share a joystick in a high action computer game knows, coordination takes a lot of practice, neither of you has control, but both of you get to crash.

Raceco has some other issues. There is a sense that cohesion on the board may be one of them. The chief executive doesn't seem to have the full support of his board. The chairman doesn't seem to be in the loop. Why? Is he ineffective? Is the chief executive up to the job? Are the non-executives appropriate? At some point Raceco's board disharmony and lack of cohesive leadership in its core business will come home to roost in performance. A geographic organizational structure sounds like it fits the nature of the current business, but is it appropriate for the next phase of development?

A final issue relates to Howard's succession. If Janet goes for some reason, is there another suitable internal candidate, or will Raceco be looking outside?

What would you do if you were Howard?

Howard has a major judgement to make. How is he going to decide what to do? Any solution will involve a casualty. Whatever he decides to do he will need to sell it to his chairman and the board.

So, imagine you are Howard for a moment. Janet has told you she's going to resign. Your choices look limited:

- You express disappointment but accept. You then give John the job and the hunt is on for your successor again.
- You give Janet the UK MD's job and find another role for John.
- You make the ultimate sacrifice for the good of the company and propose Janet as group chief executive.

Whatever you decide, you need to get board support. How?

The decision ultimately turns on how good you think Janet is and whether you have the conviction and power to follow through your choice. If you can't persuade the chairman to agree, can you force him?

What about your own position? It sounds an unhappy one. Why do you continue? Have you got financial independence? If you have, does this affect your resolve?

Could you organize the business differently and solve the issue in the process?

The final thing you would probably do if you were Howard is to promise to yourself that you would never, ever again say *'Trust me guys'* to a bunch of analysts.

What would you do if you were Janet and Howard offered you the UK MD job?

Janet must have considered Howard might react this way. So it is quite straightforward as long as the emotion of the moment doesn't influence here. Frequently it does turn on the emotion of the moment. A dewy-eyed boss who is worried about his own position is not likely to make any difference to someone whose loyalty elastic has snapped. On the other hand, a highly charismatic one who is good at painting pictures just might.

Janet has to decide between the alternative tracks. Is the potential of the new job greater than the one at Raceco? The final thing she needs to consider if Howard does persuade her to stay, is how to deal with John and the chairman. If Howard hasn't had the support to make her his clear successor, what are her real chances of succeeding him?

So what actually happened?

Janet really was determined to leave when she entered Howard's office. She was therefore stunned when, before she could say anything, Howard told her that he had some difficult news to tell her. She let him continue. He said:

❝ *I'm afraid you're not going to like this. As you know I have been pressing the chairman for months now to persuade the other non-executives that you should be given the sole job of running the UK. It's been obvious to me that things are not working out between you and John. Sadly, the chairman refused to support me, even though he agreed that you were the right person to succeed me when I retire.*

'Unfortunately, I was so frustrated I decided to try and force him into it. I told him unless he agreed I would resign myself. He told me not to be so silly and carry on for a few more months and things might change.

'To be honest Janet, I've had enough, so I handed in my resignation this morning. It was accepted. John will be taking over as chief executive. ❞

Janet told him her news and he was absolutely delighted. His own position wasn't that bad: he was highly regarded in the industry, had had more than enough money and had plenty of outside interests. Raceco lost its way until a chief executive from outside was recruited two years later.

THE AFTER LIFE

Jessica, a successful bond trader in the City, was inviting her mother Jane to lunch to celebrate the £200,000 bonus she had just been paid. Not daring to tell her mother exactly how much the bonus was, she said:

‘Mum, seems like we haven't had one of our chats since you retired. Why don't we celebrate you're freedom? I've just had a really nice bonus. Come down next week and I'll treat you to lunch at Langham's. I'll take the afternoon off and we can do some serious shopping.’

Jane was delighted by the idea. She hadn't seen nearly enough of Jessica recently. Getting the early train from Leeds meant time to visit her favourite bookshops before lunch. Taking the last train back meant that she could see the new Judi Dench play with a friend. As the day came close she became increasingly happy.

Jane had brought Jessica up on her own while working her way up to become finance director of one of Yorkshire's biggest private companies. She had separated from Jessica's father when Jessica was just a baby. He had emigrated to New York with an American journalist he met at a conference in London. Jane had never remarried, despite numerous offers. Her life was focused on Jessica and her job. She is extremely proud of Jessica and thrilled at how happy she was. Her job also had given her tremendous satisfaction even though she knew she was poorly paid and taken advantage of. The people were pleasant, the business was interesting, they were very flexible about things when Jessica was young and she got to live in her favourite place, Harrogate.

Coming to terms with retirement hasn't been easy for Jane. She'd not really given enough thought to it beforehand. Jane was a control freak's control freak; she'd been working flat out right until the end to make sure her successor knew as much as he possibly could about the company. The shock of being home alone without a report to write or papers to read had hit her hard. The opportunity for a bit of a break in London was too good to miss. Maybe opening up a little to Jessica might help her find a new direction. Jessica was so enthusiastic, so carefree and full of ideas.

Jane's mood changed the moment she entered the lobby of the investment bank. Such excessive waste of space and money when she had spent her life being so careful was hard for her to handle. For some reason it also made her feel seriously underdressed. Meeting in the lobby often made Jessica feel a little uncomfortable as well. Jane's traditional quip about the opulence and waste was as irritating as it was predictable. Jessica had always looked up to her mum, but felt that she had put in ridiculous commitment to the company for little reward.

Lunch was superb, but it was obvious to Jessica that Jane had something on her mind. Jane didn't want to ruin Jessica's obviously good mood by talking about herself too quickly, so she waited until the dessert. Just as she was about to mention it, Jessica beat her to it:

> *So mum, what are you going to do with all this time? I'm really envious. I never seem to get a minute. Must be fantastic to have the freedom to decide what you want to do.'*
>
> *'Well, to be honest Jessica, I'm not finding it that great so far. I miss the buzz of the office, sorting people's problems out, tidying up all those little messes. Two months ago I was someone who mattered. Now I'm just another retired old biddie. It's a bit lonely at home. Everything in the house is sorted out.*

At this point an almost tearful Jane stops. She has always been the one who has supported and guided Jessica. This is the first time in her life she has been so open about a problem of her own. She said:

> *I'm sorry, we're supposed to be celebrating. I'm sure I'll sort myself out. Now let's get stuck into this wonderful strawberry tart.*

Jessica is not sure what to say. She had assumed that Jane had planned it all out and would have been as busy as ever by now. She feels guilty that she didn't ask before. The first thing that enters her head to say is:

> *Mum, I'm amazed. I thought you'd have had it all planned out. Look, today's the day for fun. Let's have a great time and then I'll come up at the weekend and we'll see what we can work out together. With your talent and energy it should be easy to find something interesting.*

Jane decides to leave it at that and doesn't pursue the subject again. They have a marvellous day together and Jane is much cheered up at the end of it.

Unfortunately, Jessica's new boyfriend has booked a secret weekend away. He tells her very excitedly on the next Thursday that he has spoken to her boss and arranged for her to have Friday and Monday off. *'Pack a bag of smart casual, some beach gear and your passport. I'll pick you up from your flat at 6 am.'*

Jessica tries to tell him that she'd promised to see her mum this weekend and although it sounds great she's not sure she can come. She's also a bit irritated by the fact that he's spoken to her boss. *'Of course you can, your mum will be there next weekend, the tickets won't. I've been planning this for ages. It's cost a fortune. Tell her you'll make it next weekend.'*

Jessica agrees. However, she feels terrible about doing so. She discusses the situation with you, her best friend.

What do you say?

What are the issues?

Issue number one is, who should Jessica spend the weekend with? Will she lose her boyfriend if she doesn't go with him? How will Jane feel being let down so close to the weekend? How would Jessica explain it to her?

Setting aside the timing issue, what advice should Jessica give her mother? Jane's situation is very typical. Many people who have a busy and a very successful career find coming off the corporate wheel at the end of it disorienting. Many of life's planners fail to plan for themselves. So concerned sorting everyone else out, they somewhat surprisingly forget about themselves.

Until the boom in outplacement consultancies and the rise in delayering, there was little discussion on this subject. Today there are numerous books, from Charles Handy's superb *The Empty Raincoat* to Rosemary Brown's wonderfully practical *Good Retirement Guide*. Although many leading companies have some excellent pre-retirement support, most companies still leave it to individuals to sort things out for themselves.

Jane's confidence is clearly an issue. She really does need to do something. Yet she is not 'opportunity aware'. Jane also sounds lonely. If she has worked long hours most of her career and Jessica has been away from home for 10 years or so, most of her time awake has been spent with people at work. She's bound to miss them.

How to decide?

These situations are much easier for best friends. A best friend can be much more direct. Dealing with whom to spend the weekend with is probably easier than giving Jessica some advice on how to help her mum.

With regard to the weekend, you need to help Jessica make her mind up. Of course her mum will still be there next week; her boyfriend may not be if she lets him down. Jessica needs to make a judgement based on who is most important to her. If you know Jessica really well, the situation is easier.

When it comes to her mum, Jessica needs to find a way of helping her decide what to do. Jane is the one that has to make the decisions. All Jessica can do is support and encourage her. Retirement is not something Jessica is likely to be an expert on. Could she get some ideas from someone else she knows? Are there any good books? What possibilities are open to Jane? How does she put herself in a position to get them? Maybe all Jessica has to do is to provide some motivation.

What happened?

One advantage Jessica's friend had was that she was a young version of Jane: fiercely independent and very down to earth. She told Jessica that the first decision about whether to spend the weekend with her mum or her boyfriend was easy:

> *Who is more important? Your mum or some bloke you met a few months ago? If he really cares about you, he'll be ok as long as you make it up to him. Do you think he'd take me instead? Just kidding!*

Jessica decided that she'd go to Harrogate, but she really didn't want to lose her boyfriend. She remembered her big bonus and called him:

> *Luke, I know this is tough, but I've decided mum really needs me, so I'm going to Harrogate tomorrow instead. Your idea was so sweet. I think we should do it. Try and see if you can change the dates. If you can't, I'll pay for us to go wherever it was next weekend. I swear I'll make it up to you.*

After a bit of a limp attempt to persuade her otherwise, he reluctantly agreed.

On the train on the way to Harrogate she skimmed all the books she could find on retirement and tried to search for some pearls of wisdom. Most of it she found depressing and unrelated to her mum. Her mind wandered back to when she was trying to figure out what to do after graduating. She remembered Jane's advice very clearly:

> *Don't be like me. Go and explore. Find out what's possible. Decide what you really want to do. Go for it and don't let anyone get in your way.*

She decided that her mother simply needed to follow her own advice.

Jessica and Jane had a great weekend together. Jessica reminded Jane of her own advice and asked her if she had really found out what the part-time possibilities were. Jessica thought she meant part-time finance director jobs, something she had no interest in at all.

> *No'*, said Jessica. *'What about being a non-exec or running a charity? Knowing you, you could do both.'*
> *'Well, I've obviously thought about that, but I really don't know how to go about it. I haven't applied for a job for 20 years.*

Jane quickly realized how silly she had been and applied her usual rigour and determination to the problem. While she gave a fair bit to charity, she didn't really want to run one. The idea of non-executive directorships wasn't new; her chairman had suggested it. That was something she really did want to do. Another thought was sparked off by a friend of hers who was an administrator at the local business school. Why not teach?

To start with, the networking proved very difficult for Jane. It was amazing to her how people who had once been so keen to see her seemed awkward to get meetings with. Jessica had to give her targets to get her to keep up with it. Fortunately, Jane stuck at it and within six months she had three non-executive directorships. Two of them were down in the south-east, one close by in Bradford. She also became a part-time lecturer at the local business school. Of all the things she is now doing, it is this that gives her the most satisfaction. Jane is a great coach.

The other thing that Jessica advised her mother to do was a course in using computers. Jane hadn't been very strong in this area. Jessica believed that she was perfectly capable of it, it would give her something to throw herself into, and it would be very helpful if she did decide to go down the route of part-time appointments.

Jessica sadly had a less happy time. Her boyfriend dumped her shortly after the weekend away incident, and a year later she lost her job when the bank she worked for was taken over. Jane was then able to remind her of that simple advice again!

References

Bartlett, C and Ghoshal, S (1998) *Managing Across Borders*, Century Arrow, London

Berne, E (1968) *The Games People Play*, Penguin, Harmondsworth

Brown, R (1998) *Good Retirement Guide*, Kogan Page, London

Christensen, C (1997) *The Innovator's Dilemma*, Harvard Business School Press, Harvard, MA

Cohen, W and Cohen, N (1993) *The Paranoid Corporation*, The American Management Association, New York

Dunne, P (1999) *Running Board Meetings*, Kogan Page, London

Gates, B (1999) *Business @ The Speed of Thought*, Penguin, Harmondsworth

Goleman, D (1996) *Emotional Intelligence*, Bloomsbury, London

Handy, C (1995) *The Empty Raincoat*, Arrow, London

Institute of Chartered Secretaries, *A Guide to Best Practice for Annual General Meetings*, Institute of Chartered Secretaries, Administrators, 16 Park Crescent, London W1N 4AH

Landsberg, M (1997) *The Tao of Coaching*, HarperCollins, London

Landsberg, M (1999) *The Tao of Motivation*, HarperCollins, London

Lorsch, J W (1990) *Pawns or Potentates*, Harvard Business School, Harvard, MA

Marx, E (1999) *Breaking Through the Culture Shock*, Nicholas Brealey, London

Mauborgne, R and Kim, W C (1997) Fair process: managing in the knowledge economy, *Harvard Business Review*

Mole, J (1995) *Mind your Manners*, Nicholas Brealey, London

Oudes, B (1989) *From the President: Richard Nixon's Secret Files*, Andre Deutsch, London

Strouse, J (1999) *Morgan: American financier*, Harvill Press, London

Townsend, S (1992) *The Secret Diary of Adrian Mole aged 13¾*, Mandarin, London

Tricker, B (1998) *The Pocket Director*, Economist Books, London

Index